- Do schools teach the type of skills measured by standardized tests of ability?
- Do all students share equally in the resources of the school?
- Can schools work independently of their students' home backgrounds?
- Are physical resources such as class size or per-pupil expenditure important determinants?

In answering these questions, the authors compare the conceptual framework of effectiveness with the reality of the school setting. Intended primarily for school personnel, sociologists, legislators, and students of education, the book nevertheless is written in a way that laypersons can understand. More important, it gives all professional readers an excellent insight into the entire problem so that they can explain it to concerned citizens, make informed decisions on government expenditures, and help in the creation of improved public policy in all areas of educational research, design, and measurement.

Soundly researched and lucidly presented, the book draws on data gathered throughout the entire country and abroad—particularly from Britain where school effectiveness is also being debated. The authors' optimistic conclusions that our schools *can and do* make a difference will cause considerable discussion in a controversy that now threatens not only educators but the facilities and resources many people have traditionally regarded as important to the school environment.

About the Authors

George F. Madaus and Peter W. Airasian are professors in the School of Education at Boston College. Thomas Kellaghan is the director of the Educational Research Centre, St. Patrick's College, in Dublin. The three authors have just completed a five-year study of the effects of introducing standardized tests in a random sample of Irish schools.

School
Effectiveness

School
Effectiveness
A Reassessment
of the Evidence

George F. Madaus
Peter W. Airasian
Thomas Kellaghan

McGraw-Hill Book Company
New York   St. Louis   San Francisco   Auckland
Bogotá   Hamburg   Johannesburg   London
Madrid   Mexico   Montreal   New Delhi
Panama   São Paulo   Singapore
Sydney   Tokyo   Toronto

Thomas Quinn and Michael Hennelly were the editors of this book. Mark E. Safran was the designer. Thomas G. Kowalczyk supervised the production. It was set in Times Roman by Rocappi, Inc. Printed and bound by R. R. Donnelley and Sons.

Library of Congress Cataloging in Publication Data
Madaus, George F
  School effectiveness.

  Bibliography: p.
  Includes index.
    1. Educational surveys—United States.   2. Educational tests and measurements—United States.
I. Airasian, Peter W., joint author.   II. Kellaghan,
Thomas, joint author. III. Title.
LB2823.M26   379'.15   79-20329
ISBN   0-07-039378-8

1 2 3 4 5 6 7 8 9 RRDRRD 8 0 6 5 4 3 2 1 0

Contents

Foreword

The evaluation of student learning in a particular classroom is fairly straightforward. If the students are roughly equal at the beginning of the year or term, then all that is needed is a clear statement of the objectives and the content to be learned, a valid test of the extent to which these objectives and content have been learned by the end of the term, and some way of summarizing the students' responses to the test to determine how well they have learned, what they have learned well, and what they have learned less well.

But, even this highly simplified picture rapidly gets more complex. Only rarely are the students "roughly equal" at the beginning of the term. It is difficult to develop a clear statement of the objectives and content to be learned. It is even more difficult to provide instruction that is effective for the different objectives and content. Testers and teachers have much to do before they can create testing procedures which have high validity for the objectives and content to be evaluated. Finally, how the student responses are to be evaluated and summarized is rarely as simple a problem as we have suggested in the previous paragraph. Even so, with patience, time, skill, and good communication between the teaching process and the testing process (frequently it is the teacher who does both) it is possible to get a reasonable solution to these problems and steps in the evaluation process.

But, how much more complex is this evaluation process when we attempt to determine the effectiveness of a single school, a national school system, or to compare the school systems of a number of nations. During the past two decades, we have mounted major evaluation studies to do each of these tasks. We do them crudely at first, but if we listen to our critics carefully, we can improve our evaluative efforts and, at least, finally understand what we have accomplished and what problems we still must solve.

Madaus, Airasian, and Kellaghan are the principal investigators in the Irish Project which has been concerned with the effects of new evaluation methods on the curriculum, instruction, teachers, and students in the Irish schools. They are thoroughly aware of the many problems involved in massive evaluation studies from the viewpoint of the evaluator as well as the educational researcher.

They come to this book on *school effectiveness* as sympathetic critics. Rather than dismissing the problem as an insoluble one, they point to the specific problems that must be solved if such studies are to be sound and to yield important findings. The problem of school effectiveness has been with us for centuries and is likely to be around for centuries to come. Hopefully, we can develop increasingly valid and useful approaches to this perennial problem.

The authors point up the major problem of determining what about the schools really makes a difference in the learning of the students. Is it the homes from which the students came? The teachers or the teaching? The curriculum? The time devoted to the learning? The resources available to the school? Or is it a complex combination of these different characteristics about the students, the instruction, the nature of what is taught to the children, the way in which time is used, and the resources of the school?

They also point up the problem of developing evaluative instruments which are sensitive to the schooling effects. Some instruments are so crude and irrelevant to the specific changes being produced by the schools that they give a false and misleading picture. The task of the evaluator, working closely with teachers and other school personnel, is to select or construct instruments which can clearly reveal what the schools have accomplished and what they have not accomplished as yet.

They further point up the sampling and research design problems. Should the evaluation study be a cross-sectional survey taken at a particular time, a longitudinal study showing the effects of several years of effort by the school, or even an experimental study attempting to determine the causal effects of the different approaches to education? It is likely that the evaluation studies of the future must incorporate some features of each of these approaches.

Finally, there are the problems of the ways in which the evidence is to be summarized and the statistical methods to be used. Each statistical approach has its advantages and its weaknesses. The reporters of the evaluation results need to be very sensitive to the underlying assumptions of each method of summarizing the evidence and the conclusions that are warranted. Frequently, it is at this step in the evaluation process where the evaluator is tempted to make a "good story" and arrive at conclusions that will startle his readers.

Having devoted most of my career to the problems of evaluation, I am still optimistic that evaluation studies can be improved as a result of improvements on each of these features of the studies. While the evaluators are likely to make new errors, at least they shouldn't repeat the old errors—after they have been made aware of them. It is my hope that this large and growing body of evaluators and educational policy and decision makers will learn both how schools can become more effective and how this increasing effectiveness can be studied and evaluated. All teachers, administrators, researchers, and students of education need to understand our present approaches to determining school effectiveness and the means by which each of us can become more sensitive to what the schools can accomplish, do accomplish, and should accomplish.

BENJAMIN S. BLOOM
University of Chicago

Preface

Over the past fifteen years, concern with schooling and its consequences has reached major proportions. In the rush towards social reform of the early sixties, the belief was widespread that schooling could make a major contribution to the attainment of equality of educational opportunity for all citizens and, though this was not so explicitly stated, to the prevention of social deviance, particularly in inner-city areas.

Through the sixties and into the seventies, however, traditional faith in schooling has been subjected to severe assault. A major source of evidence for this assault has been the federally sponsored *Equality of Educational Opportunity Survey* which on its publication in 1966 raised serious doubts about the contribution of school facilities to student achievement. Evaluations of compensatory education later led to a questioning of the ability of the school to teach basic cognitive and social skills to pupils living in disadvantaged backgrounds. At a higher educational level, a chorus of employers, college teachers, and commentators voiced anguish at the inability of high school graduates to perform basic reading, writing, and computation tasks, while reported decline in Scholastic Aptitude Test scores has been interpreted as meaning that not even the more able students in our schools are preforming as satisfactorily as once they did.

In the light of these phenomena, the conclusion of many commentators has been that schools have little impact on the development of their students. If this view is accepted, it is difficult to make a case for increasing educational expenditure to provide more teachers or any of the facilities or resources which many people have traditionally regarded as forming an important part of the school environment. As the funds which are available for social services decrease in the face of increasing taxpayer resistances, as school enrollments decline, as the voter rolls are swelled by older Americans, we may expect mounting pressures to cut back on educational expenditure. The pressures are likely to be all the greater if social scientists are unable to demonstrate that the educational resources purchased by expenditure are not significantly related to student development.

For the past four years, the authors of the present volume have been engaged in an examination of issues pertaining to the assessment of school effectiveness. This book is an outcome of this examination. In considering studies of school effectiveness, we have been especially concerned with assumptions underlying the studies—assumptions about the way schools function and about the nature of the achievement which they attempt to foster. In a number of empirical studies which we carried out we have employed alternative models of schooling to test hypotheses which arose from our examination of earlier studies. Our overall assessment of the evidence relating to school effectiveness led us to conclusions which are considerably less pessimistic than those drawn in the wake of the *Equality of Educational Opportunity Survey*. A consideration of the problems, conceptual and methodological, associated with large-scale studies of school effectiveness, in combination with the findings of our own investigations leads us to the conclusion that when schools are assessed in terms of their own objectives, between-school differences in achievement are larger than earlier findings have indicated. Furthermore, such differences are related to school-based factors, particularly climate and press ones.

We wish to express our appreciation to the Carnegie Corporation of New York, which has long been interested in the issue of school effectiveness and, by supporting our work over the past four years, has made this book possible. The excellent advice and moral support of Fritz Mosher of the Corporation has been particularly helpful. For assistance at various stages of our work, we are also indebted to Ernest Rakow, Alan Brimer, Bernard Chapman, Denis King, Robert Wood, David Cohen, and Joseph Pedulla.

For clerical and secretarial assistance in the production of the manuscript, we are indebted to Mary Rohan, Patricia Kingston, Mairead Byrne, Glen Schneiders, Virginia Cahill, Ruth McLoughlin, and Mary Louise Burckhart. Tom Quinn's interest and editorial assistance was also greatly appreciated. To all of the above, we wish to express our gratitude.

chapter 1

Concepts and Issues

INTRODUCTION

In recent years, the effectiveness of schools has been a matter of controversy, both in the technical literature and in the popular media. Controversy about schools and school practices is probably as old as formal education; however, in the last ten years, it reached a level of intensity and seriousness which at times seemed to undermine the very raison d'être of schools.

Part of the reason for the recent growth in concern about schooling arose from the fact that by the mid-1960s, the United States Congress had made a substantial commitment to education as a policy area in which significant efforts were to be made to rectify perceived inequalities in American society. The commitment was both financial and moral: financial in terms of the vast sums of money allocated to interventions such as Head Start and Title I, and moral in the sense that the aim of legislation was to eliminate educational—and through education, ultimately social and economic—imbalances due to race, color, and national origin.

The main foci for the controversy in the United States have been a national survey of public schools carried out in the mid-1960s (Coleman et al., 1966) and the problems of low-achieving students, particularly those in inner-city disadvantaged areas. Other issues have also been brought into the argument, such as purported declining scholastic standards in schools and lack of student social responsibility. But the main empirical data on which the controversy rests have been the findings of the national survey and the reports of evaluations of compensatory programs for disadvantaged children.

It was in 1966 that the results of large-scale studies of the effectiveness of schooling and of compensatory education programs first became

1

available. Instead of documenting gross inequalities in educational opportunity between black and white schools, relatively small differences in school resources and facilities were found. Instead of demonstrating the efficacy of compensatory education programs in narrowing the achievement gap between disadvantaged and advantaged pupils, few lasting effects on achievement were reported. The long-nurtured and much-cherished belief in the power of schooling appeared to be under siege, just at a time when schooling was being relied upon to shoulder the major burden in attaining equality of opportunity.

Does the research evidence justify pessimism about the role of schools in society? To many people it does; for them, the evidence is interpreted as indicating that schools are largely "ineffective," not just in terms of achieving equality of opportunity but also in terms of doing what most people believed they did best, that is, provide children with basic scholastic skills. On the other hand, there are those who regard the empirical research findings as counter-intuitive. After all, it would hardly have been possible to build and maintain the educational systems of the Western world over the last 150 years if there had not been a strong belief that formal education contributes substantially to the development of individuals. Why should this belief be suddenly abandoned?

In the light of long-standing beliefs about the effectiveness of schooling, it seems reasonable to attempt to assess carefully the evidence on which contrary conclusions are based. The matter is more than academic. Questions regarding school effectiveness are also in the political arena. While a variety of beliefs and values play a role in political decision making, empirical data also have a distinctive contribution to make. The decisions that might be made can have far-reaching consequences. Such decisions can result in expanded educational programs or in retrenched ones, in good school buildings or in poor ones, in extensive provision for in-service education for teachers or in poor provision. It seems important that we move toward a position in which the contribution of research to such decisions can be offered with greater confidence than at present.

In this book, we shall examine the evidence on which statements about school effectiveness have been based. Our primary, though not exclusive, focus will be on the Coleman study and evaluations of compensatory education. We believe that our examination, which will be supported by empirical research on schooling carried out since the Coleman study, leads to conclusions about school effectiveness which are considerably less pessimistic than those which have been in vogue over the past ten years.

Before proceeding in later chapters to consider major methodological issues associated with the interpretation of evidence relating to school effectiveness, we shall outline in this chapter some background issues and concepts. First, we shall consider traditions in assessing schools over the past 150 years, noting the interest of various publics in school assessment and the variety of criteria which have been applied. We shall then describe the context—one of growth in policy-oriented studies in education—in which recent studies were carried out, since it is from this, to a large extent, that the studies derive their significance.

Since problems in research on schooling and research interpretation arise to a considerable degree because of the complexity of the phenomenon which is being studied, the complexity of schooling, with its variety of foci, objectives, processes, and results will also be considered. One thing that will become clear from this discussion is the variety of goals which schools may have. For this reason, and because one goal in particular, equality of educational opportunity, has figured prominently in recent debates about schools, a separate section will be devoted to the goals of schooling. Finally, since the debate on schooling centers on the effectiveness of schools, the concept of effectiveness and the related one of efficiency will be considered.

ASSESSMENT OF SCHOOLS

Before considering recent studies of school effectiveness, we should take a brief look at earlier traditions of assessing schools. In doing this, we will see that the functioning of schools has been assessed by different publics using different techniques and criteria. The change in techniques and criteria which we shall observe in formal evaluations is of particular interest since it may help explain why earlier views of the effectiveness of schooling were more optimistic than recent ones.

Parents, who have an obvious immediate interest in the functioning of schools, must ask themselves countless times: how are our schools doing? Most often they will ask the question in the context of a particular school or of a particular child. They will make judgments about the effectiveness of schools when they choose a school for their child (where a choice exists), and they may make such judgments repeatedly throughout the child's school-life as they observe his or her progress through the school system. Parents will, on occasion, also make more general judgments, as when they come together to consider the overall effectiveness of a school rather than just its impact on a particular child.

No doubt parents use a variety of criteria in their assessments of schools. That they do make such assessments is shown by the fact that they do not always choose a school which is most convenient in terms of travelling distance. Some parents even choose a place to live because it allows them to send their children to a particular school or school system, and as is well known, some parents have strenuously resisted efforts to change neighborhood schools by busing. While the criteria they employ may vary, parents are, at least implicitly, acting on the belief that some schools are "better" than others. Religious affiliation is an obvious criterion for some parents in choosing a school. Probably the parents' primary interest in this case is the school's likely influence on the religious and moral behavior of the child, in addition to his or her scholastic development. Choice of a school in terms of academic, vocational, and comprehensive distinction, on the other hand, is more likely to be in terms of the school's curriculum offerings and the level and type of educational qualification which parents would like their child to achieve. Such a choice may also be influenced by considerations of the social status of the school and the socioeconomic level of students attending it. Where schools have no obvious religious or curricular distinctions, factors frequently cited by parents as indicators of a "good" school are the "quality" of teachers (rather vaguely expressed and understood), the "discipline" of the school, and its physical facilities (Gallup, 1969). In passing, we may note that when formally asked, parents express a general satisfaction with the school system (Acland, 1975; Gallup, 1969, 1976), though recent data indicate slightly less positive attitudes (Gallup, 1977).

Evaluations of the effectiveness of schools which have been carried out by administrative and political bodies during much of the history of mass state-sponsored education have very often been as informal as parents' evaluations. The continuous monitoring of schools through inspectoral systems in Western European countries, while formal in procedure, has been rather informal and intuitive in terms of criteria. The ad hoc commissions formed from time to time to carry out overall reviews or to deal with pressing problems have also tended to be informal and intuitive. For example, until the 1950s, it was the exception rather than the rule for such a group to obtain empirical data as a basis for decision making. For the most part, it was the opinions of "experts" or "informed" people and interested parties that formed the basis of evaluations and recommendations for change.

In such evaluations, much of the attention was focused on the inputs to schools: quality of teachers, curricular offerings, physical plant, teacher-pupil ratio, library facilities, and the like. The assumption seems to have been that inputs are causally related to school outcomes, such as attainment. While the input-output relation may not have been stated explicitly, its recognition seems implicit in many statements and decisions about schools. Over the years, common wisdom seems rarely to have doubted that improvement in school conditions would lead to improvement in student performance.

There is also a history of more formal attempts at school evaluation which focused on school output. During the nineteenth century in Britain, tests were developed to monitor standards of achievement in universities and, later in the century, to overcome the patronage in certification of competence for the civil service and for the trades. Oral and later written essay-type examinations were used to test achievement in very specific areas, such as history, language, arithmetic, handwriting, spelling, grammar—all areas closely associated with the working of schools. In the United States, as early as 1845, similar tests were used in an annual examination of the pupils in Boston grammar schools. The purpose of the examination was to obtain data for comparisons among schools that could be used in making decisions about the annual appointment of headmasters. Differences in achievement among schools were noted, prompting Horace Mann (1845) to infer that "children could learn if the teachers had taught."

The use of examinations grew in the second half of the nineteenth century. The kinds of tests which had been developed for use at higher levels were adapted for use at the lower levels. Tests in basic school subjects were used in primary schools and over a range of subjects in secondary schools—at the individual level to certify competence at a given level of education and to select for employment, and, at the institutional level to assess the effectiveness of schools at a time when large amounts of money were being expended on education. In the United Kingdom, for example, a payment-by-results system was introduced in 1862 to help increase reading and mathematical skills, improve teacher efficiency, and save money. In this system, the allocation of funds to schools was linked to pupils' attainment as measured by a series of written and oral examinations in reading, writing, and arithmetic. It is interesting to note that under this regime, as under Mann's, the responsibility for the failure of pupils was placed squarely on the shoulders of teachers.

The tradition of identifying school and teacher efficiency through pupil examinations continued into this century in the United States. It was a process that found support in the emphasis on "scientific management," or systematization, standardization, and efficiency, which had become a powerful force in administrative theory in educational as well as in industrial circles (Biddle & Ellena, 1964; Bobbit, 1913; Callahan, 1962; Cremin, 1962). Interest in educational measurement in education and school surveys followed. By 1915, thirty to forty large city school systems had completed or were working on comprehensive surveys that provided data on a wide range of aspects of school life (Kendall, 1915; Smith & Judd, 1914). The findings of such surveys were used for a variety of purposes: to diagnose specific system weaknesses, to standardize curricular practice, to evaluate experiments, and to assess the overall performance of a system as well as to make decisions about individuals (May, 1971). These studies, for the most part, were carried out at the local, rather than the state or national, level.

From around the turn of the century, educational researchers, with backgrounds in education, psychology, and sociology, have also examined empirically, in countless studies, questions relating to the effectiveness of schools, in particular the effectiveness of specific school practices. Rice (1897), one of the leaders of the scientific movement in education, investigated the value of drilling in spelling instruction. On the basis of pupils' performance on spelling and arithmetic tests in schools across a number of districts, he pointed out the need for raising standards in weak schools and providing a greater degree of equality in output than he had found. About the same time, Thorndike and Woodworth (1901) challenged current beliefs about transfer of training. Since these early investigations, numerous studies have been carried out by educational researchers. Various aspects of schooling—cost, school size, class size, school organization, teaching methods, instructional time, and attendance—have been related to various measures of school achievement (see Stephens, 1933, 1967). Typically, such studies were carried out on a relatively small scale, involved few pupils and schools, and were concerned with a single grade level, subject area, or school practice.

The type of test used in the United States during the nineteenth century did not vary much, at least from the time of Horace Mann (1840) onward. Tests were concerned with basic school achievement, usually measured in short essays. While there was a similarity between the type of test used in England and America, there was an important difference in the way the tests were used. In England, curricula and examinations were standardized nationwide, while in the United States, local school districts determined their own. This had obvious implications for measurement. Tests suitable in one locality might not fairly assess achievement in another. Partly for this reason, test results were not used in determining policy at the national level in the United States as they were in England. Specific achievement tests continued to be used at the local level in the United States. It was tests such as these which were used by Rice, Courtis, and Thorndike in their investigations of instructional time and practices, while tests geared to local objectives in specific school subjects were also used in the "scientific management" school surveys. These kinds of studies continued up to World War I.

New problems in education arose around the turn of the century which affected methods of assessment in schools. In particular, the expansion of education to an ever-growing school population meant that the problems of evaluation extended beyond those of job selection. Binet's seminal work on the problems of the slow learner, for example, resulted in the development of a test to identify children who could not benefit from the normal school curriculum. The problem was no longer one of certification or selection for a higher level of education, but rather of making decisions about the placement of pupils in the normal school system.

Binet's tests for the measurement of intelligence became popular in the United States and Britain. This popularity had implications for the measurement of attainment, which had traditionally focused on school-specific content and skills. Increasing awareness about the concept of intelligence and assumptions about its determination and distribution led to a reinterpretation of student performance on traditional achievement tests. The results on intelligence tests were used to interpret the increase in the number of students with poor achievement. Assumptions that everybody could learn were questioned: not all students could be expected to attain mastery. The result of this thinking was a shift in achievement testing from criterion-referencing, in which a student's performance was compared to some absolute standard of mastery, to norm-referencing, in which a student's performance was compared to that of other pupils. This general view also had implications for the concepts of accountability. Rather than blaming schools and teachers for pupil failure, the "fault" was more readily seen to lie in the student.

This trend received a boost at the time of World War I with the development of the Otis test. Although a group test, it owed much to the Binet tradition. The army needed a test, primarily to select officers, which could be given to large groups of people and could be quickly and objectively scored. The easily scored multiple-choice format, so successful in the Otis, was extended to measure school achievement. To be commercially viable, the tests could not be geared to any specific syllabus. Thus, the new achievement tests became very general in the nature of the constructs they measured. Furthermore, they were based on an individual differences model; that is, the tests were deliberately constructed to maximize variation between people on the traits being measured.

Commercial standardized norm-referenced tests continued to be used for a variety of purposes during the 1920s and 1930s. They were widely used in school surveys, as well as for individual decision making in schools (e.g., grouping). For example, the Philadelphia School District used standardized test results to make intradistrict and interschool comparisons as well as to diagnose individual learning needs (Philadelphia Board of Education, 1926). A notable exception to the use of such tests for evaluation during this period was Tyler's Eight Year Study (Smith & Tyler, 1942), the last large-scale study of the differential effectiveness of various types of schools until well after World War II. During World War II and the years immediately following, little development in school-related testing took place; the emphasis in testing during this period seems to have been primarily one of individual decision making.

Through the 1950s and into the 1960s, a new series of concerns emerged which called for new approaches to testing. The Soviet launching of Sputnik, and concern about civil rights, equality of opportunity, and the disadvantaged in the United States, gave rise to concern about curriculum development and school effectiveness. Most importantly, federal government policy agencies became actively involved in questions of school effectiveness and of educational reform. This active involvement by the government marked the advent of large-scale studies which had as their aim the resolution of educational policy issues (Caro, 1971; Cohen, 1970). The purpose was to use empirical evidence gathered about schools and schooling as the basis for setting national educational priorities and policies. Furthermore, federal government agencies became involved in educational provision for certain groups of students, most notably the disadvantaged, and tied to this provision was a requirement for evaluation.

Such concern shifted the testing focus from assessing individual performance to assessing institutional and program adequacy. However, the development of new approaches to testing, necessitated by this change in emphasis, received little attention. Without much reflection, it seems, policymakers and researchers decided to use the techniques which were readily available to them in their evaluations of schools and programs, without considering the implications of using tests which had been designed primarily to assess individuals rather than institutions or programs.

A number of points emerge from this overview. While there is a long tradition of assessing various aspects of schooling, the criteria used in such assessments have been vague, or at best, not clearly specified. This is particularly true of assessments made by parents and by the numerous official commissions which have examined the workings of educational systems. Often, the criteria seemed to relate more to school inputs (facilities, curricula, etc.) than to outputs, such as achievement. This may have been because of the difficulty of measuring outputs. However, it also seems to have been assumed too readily that inputs are directly related to outputs. In fact, while the public continues to assume that there are sufficient differences between schools to warrant decisions to send a child to one school rather than to another, empirical researchers have not clearly identified any school variable related to instruction, policy, or resources which consistently affects output and so might form a basis for the kind of decisions parents make.

A second point that arises from our overview is that earlier assessments which employed measures of school output used more curriculum-sensitive measures than later ones. The switch from tests which assessed basic school achievement in such specific areas as arithmetic, spelling, and history seems to have come as a result of the development of norm-referenced standardized tests following World War I. The appropriateness of standardized tests to measure institutional effects will be considered in detail in Chapters 5 and 6.

A final point that emerges from a consideration of the history of assessment procedures is that the efficacy of the school as an institution was not seriously challenged until the 1960s. Parents may have doubted the effectiveness of particular schools, types of school, and school practices, but there is little evidence that they doubted the value of schooling itself. From time to time, the effectiveness of some school practices has been challenged publicly. But when Leonard Ayres (1909) wrote about the need to measure children's progress through the grades, he was challenging the efficiency rather than the effectiveness of schools. Some or all schools may be inefficient, curricula may be out of date, teachers may be inadequately prepared; but essentially, there was nothing that the school, given new curricula, better facilities, or an improved teacher-pupil ratio, could not set right. The challenge was not to the institution and its goals, but rather to specific practices. The basic challenge to schooling is a phenomenon of the 1960s and 70s.

THE GROWTH OF POLICY-ORIENTED STUDIES IN EDUCATION

The thrusting of schools into the public arena in the 1960s as important agents of social change has no doubt contributed to the questioning of their effectiveness. At this point, we may consider briefly the recent growth in policy-oriented social science activity, which includes studies of the effectiveness of schools and school programs, and search for some of its causes.

In a general way, such activity may be attributed to what Boulding (1966) has called the "movement of the social system into self-consciousness" during the mid-twentieth century. This movement, he points out, is "perhaps one of the most significant phenomena of our time" as "it represents a very fundamental break with the past, as did the development of personal self-consciousness many millennia earlier" (Boulding, 1966, p. 4). Its effect has been to increase dramatically empirical efforts to examine, reform, and restructure the society in which we live (Mostellar & Moynihan, 1972). Just as we might perceive ourselves as being ill or our bodies as malfunctioning and seek diagnosis and therapy, so too we now seek to diagnose the malfunctioning of the society in which we live and search for ways to change and restructure it. The most persuasive arguments regarding the role of the social sciences in the reform of society have been developed by Campbell (1969), who has urged the need for experimentation at the societal level in the traditional scientific mold.

Another reason for the growing interest in the effectiveness of school systems is to be found in studies of the economics of education. Education has become a very expensive commodity. In most countries, the proportion of national income spent on education has increased steadily since World War II, averaging between 3 and 5 percent (Sheehan, 1973). In the United States, the figure is much higher; in 1973, expenditure on education amounted to 7.6 percent of the gross national product (United

States: National Center for Education Statistics, 1975). Given the expenditure of such large amounts of money, the demand for cost-benefit analysis does not seem surprising; and some evaluation of the effectiveness of programs and practices in relation to outcomes, usually measured in terms of student achievement, became an important aspect of federal guidelines calling for educational expenditure. It is interesting to note that in the United States, interest in large-scale, policy-oriented studies of school effectiveness developed during the expensive war in Vietnam, the upkeep of which put unusual pressure upon domestic fiscal expenditure. This was just a century after Robert Lowe had introduced in England the idea of payment by results—an early and severe form of performance contracting—in the wake of the financial strain placed on the Exchequer by the Crimean War.

Also in the economic context, human-capital economists had been arguing that education increases a person's productivity and hence his income (Levine & Bane, 1975). Thus there is a tension between the growing cost and the presumed benefits associated with greater amounts of education. This tension has, in large measure, been reflected in recent demands for educational accountability.

While these factors have all contributed to the development of policy-oriented studies of school effectiveness, the most immediate impetus was ideological rather than economic. In the 1950s and early 1960s, the struggle against poverty, racial injustice, and unequal educational opportunity became more intense. Starting just after 1960, the effort to deal with these problems dominated domestic legislative action. Although the focus has changed somewhat, primarily to include women as an additional group which historically has been denied equal opportunity, efforts to define, monitor, and rectify perceived inequalities in society have continued to be a prime legislative and judicial focus. Attempts to document and remedy the problems of unequal educational opportunity, particularly as they related to minority-group children, provided the major impetus for school-effectiveness studies. In fact, major societal efforts to address the problems of inequality were centered in the educational sphere. It is not clear whether the choice of education as the principal domain in which to combat inequality was based upon political or educational considerations. On the one hand, schooling had traditionally been perceived to be the vehicle through which the cultural and linguistic barriers had been broken down: witness the belief in the leveling effect of schooling upon the various ethnic groups who arrived on America's shores after 1860. On the other hand, the idea of social and economic reform through educational intervention held a certain political appeal, since it represented an indirect strategy for change in other areas; change could be accomplished without a frontal assault on more politically sensitive areas such as housing and employment. The prevailing belief was that through educational programs, life for the "have-nots" could be improved without directly threatening the "haves" or requiring an immediate major redistribution of economic or social prerogatives (Hodgson, 1975).

It was in this climate of thinking that the Civil Rights Act of 1964 (Section 402), a cornerstone of President Johnson's "war on poverty," made provision for the Commissoner of Education to conduct a nationwide survey of the equality of educational opportunity available to American schoolchildren.

> SECTION 402. The Commissioner shall conduct a survey and make a report to the President and the Congress, within two years of the enactment of this title, concerning the lack of availability of equal educational opportunities for individuals by reason of race, color, religion, or national origin in public educational institutions at all levels in the United States, its territories and possessions, and the District of Columbia.

It is not clear why Congress ordered the commissioner to conduct the survey, although the phrase "concerning the lack of availability of educational opportunities" implies that Congress believed that inequalities in opportunities did exist, and that documenting these differences could provide a useful legal and political tool to overcome future opposition to school reform. Certainly James Coleman, who was selected to head the team of researchers conducting the survey, indicated in an interview in 1965 that he believed that his efforts would identify large disparities in the equality of the schools attended by black and white children (quoted in Mosteller & Moynihan, 1972).

Coleman's survey commenced in 1965 and was completed on schedule in 1966. Characteristically, Congress did not await its results before taking further action. Perhaps legislators were convinced that the survey would document large differences in school quality between racial and ethnic groups. It may also be recalled that the Great Society programs of the mid-1960s quickly attained a momentum of their own, and Congress, by not waiting for the findings of the Coleman survey, may have reasoned that affirmative action was required in the educational sphere. This action came in the form of two new programs, Project Head Start and the Elementary and Secondary School Education Act of 1965. Each was designed to intervene actively in the instructional process at the community level in the hope of remediating individual pupils' learning difficulties. These interventions were a far cry from the more passive survey commissioned in 1964.

When it became apparent early on that the Great Society would have to be achieved without politically alienating the power structures, educational reform became an even more crucial avenue through which to attain more general social reform.

> As other approaches to reducing poverty and racial inequality, notably "community action," ran into political opposition, they fell apart, and so the proportional emphasis on educational programs in the Great Society scheme grew. In the end, the Johnson Administration, heavily committed to reducing inequality, was almost equally committed to education as one of the principal ways to do it. (Hodgson, 1975, p. 25)

Congress turned to compensatory education as a means of attaining equality, and Project Head Start was funded under Title II of the Economic Opportunity Act of 1964. Head Start was predicated upon the belief that since intelligence was more malleable in the preschool and early elementary school years (Bloom, 1964; Hunt, 1961), education could have a large impact if disadvantaged children were "treated" early in their educational careers. Head Start endeavored to overcome the educational deficiencies which minority and poor pupils manifested when beginning school by providing preschool experiences for these children. The program was overwhelmingly popular. In the summer of 1965, its first year of existence, Head Start enrolled over 500,000 preschoolers in 2,400 communities. By 1967, over two million children had participated. Although initially conceived as a limited experimental program, Head Start was too attractive and too promising for educational leaders to be kept from virtually all who wanted it (Timpane, 1970).

The Elementary and Secondary Education Act of 1965 was intended to stimulate educational innovation in local schools, link research with the schools, and make the problems of the poor America's foremost educational priority. Title I, which provided for school aid to the disadvantaged, was the heart of the act, and consumed the bulk of the appropriated funds. The act's fundamental conceptions—and Title I's in particular—agreed with long-cherished American beliefs regarding the utility of schooling: that poor and minority students, given the resources and opportunity necessary to succeed in school, would then succeed as adults. Title I provided funds for local school districts to institute innovative and remedial programs aimed at poor and minority students. Funds were allocated to localities which met federal criteria, defined in terms of the percentage of "disadvantaged" children in the locality.

Thus by the late 1960s, the federal government had involved itself in education to an unprecedented degree. The involvement, which was both political and financial, resulted in a scrutiny of the working of schools on a scale and with an intensity which was also unprecedented.

THE COMPLEXITY OF SCHOOLING AND RESEARCH

A major problem for the researcher in studying school effectiveness is that the phenomenon is extremely complex. The point hardly needs making. At the very least, schools are institutions made up of people who, while they may share common roles and expectations, may implement those roles in highly individualistic ways (Getzels, 1969).

The complexity of the schooling process becomes immediately apparent when one tries to list the many interactions which can take place in a single school. Teachers differ from one another over a wide range of intellectual, attitudinal, personality, and experiential variables, and such differences can affect the manner in which a particular teacher will interact with a given group of learners. Some teachers will lecture, some will discuss, some will "mother" pupils, some will keep pupils at arm's length, and some will encourage diversity while others insist upon conformity. Students vary also, and the interactions between teachers and students are conditioned by the particular characteristics of both. There are also interactions among pupils, and the social composition of classrooms may influence peer interactions. The availability of certain resources and instructional aids may also play a part in the interactions which occur. A particular teacher with a particular class and a particular resource (for example, a movie on the social studies unit currently being taught) may use it, whereas another teacher with the same class and resource may not. One teacher may use the resource if it is a film but not if it is a workbook.

But even this level of complexity does not adequately represent the schooling process. During the school day, interactions occur in a wide variety of contexts. Schooling involves more than teaching particular subjects or using particular resources. It also involves providing students with at least a modicum of physical comfort, discipline, moral leadership, and social mores. Thus, a teacher is at once an instructor, disciplinarian, and social model. Students, too, assume many roles: learner, athlete, and peer-group member. Interactions between people playing different roles can vary greatly. A teacher acting as disciplinarian may deal with a pupil differently than when he or she is acting as motivator. The same student may be treated differently by teachers and peers depending on whether he or she is perceived as a member of the lowest reading group or the school's star athlete.

It is impossible to fully understand the schooling process without considering interactions between the school and the community. Communities consist of people whose values, attitudes, and practices have differing impacts on pupils. The characteristics of pupils from different home backgrounds also condition interactions within the school. Some pupils enter kindergarten able to read, while others enter totally devoid of letter-recognition skills. Parents in some settings are exceptionally "school conscious" and spend a great deal of time in the school setting, acting as volunteer librarians, cafeteria monitors, or classroom aides. Parents in other communities have little contact with their schools. Even the community at large influences the nature of the schooling process by setting a tone or mood regarding interest in, and support, of schools.

This catalog of interactions barely scratches the surface of the true complexity of the schooling process. For example, it fails to take into account differences between levels of schooling (elementary, junior high, senior high); roles and expectations in a college-preparatory school will differ from those in a vocational school (Getzels, 1969). It also fails to take into account the effects of school-related organizations (parent-teacher organizations, teacher unions), the impact of state or federal educational policies, and a host of other such factors. Clearly, it is difficult to represent the complexity of schooling in terms of input variables, particularly if such variables are conceived in static terms.

We would expect that what goes on during the schooling process will influence what pupils carry away from their school experience—that is, the outcomes of schooling. Some of the potential outcomes are readily apparent: pupils can or cannot read, can or cannot write legibly, can or cannot compute, name the capitals of the states, recite poetry, solve equations, repair a car. But the diversity of in-school interactions may have innumerable outcomes apart from subject competence. Teachers, peer groups, resources, and contexts, and the interactions among these, may affect pupils' attitudes, values, aspirations, motivations, self-concepts, socialization, and respect for minority groups. It is nearly impossible to enumerate all the possible outcomes which schools can produce.

If all the important schooling interactions or outcomes cannot be listed, how can a researcher hope to obtain a complete representation of such an exceedingly varied and complex phenomenon? In short, he or she cannot. When a researcher sets out to study a process as complicated as schooling, he or she is faced immediately with constraints which necessitate simplifying the process in order to make research possible. In practice, these constraints usually dictate the investigation of a limited number of important characteristics and the omission of others which may also be relevant. Research studies can never represent the richness and complexity of reality, but instead must abstract or simplify it by selecting a small number of variables for study. Thus, when a researcher indicates that he or she has studied the schooling process, it is important to ask, "What aspects of it?"

The constraints which demand simplification are of two types: practical and conceptual. Practical questions involve the funds available for carrying out the research, time limits, number of personnel, and other factors which may be subsumed under "manageability." Practical constraints such as time and money tend to impose limitations upon the number of variables which can be studied, the number of units which can be sampled, and the amount of data which can reasonably be analyzed and summarized. These factors bring the researcher relatively closer or farther away from the reality being studied.

While practical constraints in research are inevitable, their importance is secondary relative to conceptual ones. Thus, funding and personnel limitations may dictate that only a small number of variables be selected to represent a complex phenomenon. However *which* variables are selected will depend ultimately upon how the phenomenon to be studied is conceptualized. Partial, incomplete, or incorrect conceptualization will lead to the selection of variables which partially, incompletely, or incorrectly represent the phenomenon. Researchers are limited by the prevalent models and theories regarding the phenomena they study, for it is these which define or suggest the important variables.

Unfortunately, there are no well-developed theories or models of schooling to which the contemporary researcher can turn. This does not mean that he or she has no conceptual guidelines in designing a study. Obviously, some guidelines must exist or the selection of variables and analytic procedures would be little more than random. However, the conceptual framework underlying a study may not be clearly explicated or the assumptions on which it is based adequately recognized.

A large number of recent major studies of school effectiveness have made use of a relatively simple input-output model. In these studies, information was obtained on school inputs (such as facilities) which was related to information on school outputs, usually scholastic achievement, with little reference to the processes in the school which intervened between the two sets of variables. While appealing in its simplicity, the approach may also be extremely limited as a means of portraying the complexity of schooling. Even if one accepts the model as a reasonable one to represent at least some aspects of schooling, questions still remain about the choice of input and output variables and the manner in which the two sets of variables are related.

A number of questions arise when an investigator attempts to represent in a research design the functions of schools. He or she has to ask, what is it that schools try to achieve? Do they set out to teach verbal ability or achievement as measured by standardized tests, as most studies of school effectiveness seem to assume? Or are schools more concerned with teaching content and skills which are more specific than those measured by such tests? Again, is the objective of the school to provide all students with the same set of skills and knowledge or provide a variety of sets?

The researcher also has to ask how schools set about attaining their objectives. For example, what do schools perceive the role of the home and the community to be in the education of a student—as something independent of the role of the school or as something that interacts with it? And how are the school's own resources allocated within the institution? Do all students or all classes have access to all resources?

The researcher may not answer, or even ask, these questions explicitly. But his or her choice of variables and methods of analysis will imply some answers. It is only to the extent that the researcher, in the selection of variables and analytic procedures, reflects the objectives, processes, and organizational features of the school that his or her findings can be said to inform us about the actual functioning of schools.

We shall develop this issue in later chapters. Specifically, we shall consider problems in interpreting school effectiveness studies which arise from the measurement of school characteristics and outputs, and procedures to relate these two sets of variables. While our main concern will be to analyze problems relating to the measurement of school effectiveness, we shall also attempt to interpret what previous research, despite its inadequacies, tells us about the functioning of schools.

THE GOALS OF SCHOOLING

One of the major problems in considering judgements about the effectiveness of schooling is that the criteria of effectiveness used in judging schools are not always clearly stated. One might expect such criteria to be based on recognized goals or objectives of schooling. Unfortunately, there is no general agreement on what the purposes of schooling should be; indeed such agreement may not be possible in a pluralist democratic society. Objectives are matters of choice and, in the case of education, must be based on the value judgments of those responsible for the school (cf. R. Tyler, 1949).

We cannot consider here all the objectives and the associated value positions which have been posited for education. However, we can note that the numerous goals which have been posited may be categorized as either personal or institutional and as either short-term or long-term. Of all the goals of schooling, short-term personal ones which relate to the cognitive, personal, and social competencies which the student is expected to acquire in school are perhaps the ones that come most readily to mind. Of particular importance are literacy and numeracy skills which are normally acquired during the elementary school years. Even within an agreed-upon goal such as literacy, however, different emphases are possible, as an editorial in the London *Observer* (July 18, 1976) on the right to read and write illustrates:

> Reading is not a mere utilitarian skill, but the door to a world of enjoyment. To be able to cope with the delivery note of a [National Health Service] form is important, but what ought to catch the imagination of a child learning to read, or to read better, is the sheer pleasure that the skill opens up to him. So fiction is a better eventual goal for teachers than the income tax return (which even the well educated may find an inaccessible genre).

There is probably even greater divergence in views relating to the development of personal and social skills, values, attitudes, and motivations.

The range of long-term objectives that has been posited for the school is at least as diverse as the range of short-term ones. In a general way, it covers the competencies that are required to function "satisfactorily" in our society. These include occupational competencies necessary for the achievement of economic independence, personal factors relating to physical and emotional development, and social ones relating to living with other people as responsible citizens in democratic institutions.

Institutional goals overlap with the long-term personal goals of schooling. However, in the institutional context, the school is seen primarily as a social institution interacting with other institutions. Institutional goals take as their starting point the need to preserve the satisfactory functioning of society. Historically, the school served society by providing the basic skills required to cope with industrial development. More generally, the school may be seen as the institution which provides skilled manpower needed for society's functioning. At present, this means particularly the provision of scientific and technical personnel and the proper balance between different skills. These are rather practical objectives. Institutional goals may also have a more ideological basis; for example, the principle of equality of opportunity, which is concerned with the distribution of resources within society.

The mere positing of goals does not ensure their achievement. On the other hand, it may be that schools have effects which were not intended and thus were not formally identified goals, but which nonetheless should be taken into account in considering the effects of schooling. An example of such an effect is the development of feelings of failure, frustration, and alienation on the part of some students.

The objectives of schooling may not be the same for all participating individuals. A highly differentiated society demands a range of skills and competencies; it would not make sense to expect all students to leave school with precisely the same set of skills. Furthermore, the objectives of schooling will obviously vary with educational level. The objectives posited for education may be mutually antagonistic. For example, it may not be possible to provide the skills needed by a society at a particular time and simultaneously satisfy everyone's personal needs or wishes to acquire certain skills. And what if all schools achieved equality of output? Would the objective of equality of opportunity be achieved? Is it sufficient that variance between schools or social classes be eliminated? And were that successful, what would be the implications for another institutional goal—that schools should help provide the range of manpower skills required by society?

Of all institutional goals posited for schools, equality of educational opportunity is the one that has received greatest prominence in recent years. The concept, however, is not a new one, though interpretations of it have changed over the years. Traditionally, it was felt that equality of educational opportunity existed if free schools and exposure to a uniform curriculum were provided; in other words, if all children, regardless of creed, color, class, or gender had equal access to educational facilities and resources. Sometimes, attendance by children from diverse backgrounds at the same school and equality of expenditure within a school district were included in the concept (Coleman, 1968). Reflection on this concept of equality, together with a number of social and legal developments, has given rise in recent years to several new and more radical definitions of the term.

In essence, early conceptions of equality focused upon pupils' *access* to the facilities and curricula of the schools. The school's obligation was to provide an opportunity for pupils to learn by being available and free. The obligation to use or profit from the opportunity afforded by the school was placed squarely upon the pupil's shoulders. Under this definition of equal opportunity, the school's role was relatively passive, confined to providing free and equal access to education regardless of a pupil's background or social class.

A different conception of equality arose as a result of the Supreme Court's *Brown* decision of 1954. Faced with settling the issue of the constitutionality of "separate but equal" schools, which satisfied a definition of equal educational opportunity in terms of free access and a common curriculum, the Court decided that the *effects* of racially separated schools were potentially different. In essence, the Court shifted the interpretation of equal educational opportunity from simple access to an emphasis on racial composition and the effects of schooling. Under this new conception, equality necessarily involved consideration of the results of schooling. The role of the school was envisioned as more active, and schools were expected to produce or facilitate equality of *results* among pupils of different racial, ethnic, and class backgrounds. However, as Coleman (1968) observed,

> Because the decision did not use the effects of schooling as a criterion of inequality but only as a justification for the criterion of racial integration, integration itself emerged as the basis for still a newer concept of equal educational opportunity. Thus, the idea of effects of schooling as an element in the concept was introduced but immediately over-shadowed by another, the criterion of racial integration.

From defining educational equality in terms of results, two contrasting definitions flow. The first involves equal results given similar individual input to schooling; the second, more prevalent, definition concerns equal results deriving from different individual inputs. The notion of compensatory-education programs aimed at particular racial or economic groups is an example of providing extra inputs in order to attain equality of outcomes. In this sense, the aim is to attain equal opportunity by making school achievement independent of pupils' backgrounds. This approach turns the initial concept of equal opportunity completely around. Rather than equal access with an implicit expectation of unequal results, this concept calls for unequal or different access to attain equal results. Thus *equal opportunity*, defined as equal outcomes, is distinguished from *maximum opportunity*, defined as different pupil outcomes. With the emphasis shifted from access to results, the role of the school has shifted from a passive to an exceptionally active one.

In the last few years, five primary definitions of equal educational opportunity have been advanced. They refer primarily to what must be equalized in order to attain equality; the five are not mutually exclusive. In seeking to attain equal educational opportunity one may strive to equalize (1) a community's inputs to schools (e.g., per-pupil expenditure, school plants, science facilities); (2) the racial composition of the community's schools; (3) the intangible characteristics of the schools (e.g., teacher morale, expectations, and attitudes); (4) the results of schooling (e.g., student achievement, interest, and satisfaction), given the same pupil inputs in terms of class or race; and (5) the results of schooling given different inputs of pupils (Coleman, 1968). These varying definitions suggest lack of agreement on the meaning of equality of educational opportunity; indeed recently, Coleman (1975b) has cast doubt on the meaningfulness of the term at all.

In the context of the current debate on school effectiveness, it is interesting to note that the Coleman survey—the results of which form a key element in the debate—although conceived in the context of policies regarding equality of educational opportunity, in practice accepted short-term personal goals, the achievements of students, as its criteria of school effectiveness. The relation between the achievement of such short-term objectives and more long-term institutional objectives was not explored. Further, the study was not carried out in the context of any comprehensive theory of public expenditure, nor did it attend to a possible divergence between private and social valuation of schooling outputs. At best, despite its mandate and extrapolations from its findings, the study can tell us little more than how schools are achieving short-term objectives.

SCHOOL EFFECTIVENESS AND EFFICIENCY

Since the concept of "school effectiveness" is key to understanding the debate over the Coleman Report, a brief consideration of what is meant by the term is in order. A school may be said to be effective to the extent that there is congruence between its objectives and its achievements. In other words, it is effective to the extent that it accomplishes what it sets out to do. Effectiveness is not an all-or-nothing proposition; a school might only be partially effective. In correlational terms, a school would be regarded as effective if there were a high correlation between what it set out to do and what it actually accomplished; it would not be effective if the correlation were low (Getzels, 1969).

It will be clear from this definition that a knowledge of the school's objectives is crucial to any attempt to assess its effectiveness. Given the large range of school objectives, a comprehensive study of school effectiveness would be a very vast effort indeed. However, one might legitimately select one or more objectives and examine the extent to which a school or school system attained them. One could then say whether or not the school was successful in attaining at least some of its objectives. One should be quite sure that the objective one selects for examination is, in fact, an objective of the school, and that one has adopted appropriate procedures to assess it. As we shall see, this precaution is not so obvious that it need not be mentioned.

It might seem that the way to measure school effectiveness would be to compare the school's objectives with its performance. However, this has not been done directly, presumably because the school's objectives have not been clearly stated in measurable terms. In the Coleman survey, "equality of educational opportunity" was posited as a school objective, but neither the precise school goals nor their actual accomplishments in this context were quantified. Rather, the school-output measure was one of students' scholastic "achievement," narrowly defined in terms of performance on standardized tests of ability and attainment; implications for equality were then deduced from observations about variance in scholastic achievement and verbal ability between schools. Since such variance was small, it was deduced that schools were not differentially effective. By the same token, however, it could be argued that since all schools achieved at more or less the same level, all were equally effective.

On examination, it can be seen that the Coleman Study, and many studies like it, do not really address the question of school effectiveness at all.* They are, in fact, more properly regarded as studies of the rela-

---

*Although we believe this to be so, we will throughout this book continue to use the term *school effectiveness* in the loose sense in which it has been used in the context of studies such as the Coleman Report.

tionship between input factors and output measures of the school. This comes close to the economic concept of efficiency. That is, the question is not whether schools achieve what they set out to, but rather how particular resources are related to particular outputs. By implication, the concern is with costs and efficiency. Is the provision of certain facilities worthwhile in terms of improved output? If money is spent on compensatory education, what is the payoff in terms of pupils' ability to read and write? Will the provision of a school library improve students' reading or general knowledge? Will the provision of a language laboratory improve students' language knowledge?

Since efficiency is concerned with the minimization of cost for a given output, compensatory education should, presumably, not be provided if the recipients do not learn any more as a result, nor should libraries or laboratories be set up if these have no effect; and indeed, this is precisely what many people said following publication of the results of school-effectiveness studies.

The efficiency model, derived from economics, has its limitations in thinking about schools. For one thing, industrial models of efficiency are based on the operation of a competitive market system (O'Donoghue, 1971; Pincus, 1974). Obviously, schooling does not operate in such a system, since public-sector financing will ensure that schools will be provided even if costs are very high. This is not to say that costs are not taken into account in the allocation of resources; the policy of amalgamating small schools into larger units has been carried out largely in the belief that costs per pupil are lower in a large school. The idea of allowing schools to compete for personnel and to sell their service to pupils, however, occurs only in the private sector of educational systems, and even then there are constraints on the operation of competitive open-market principles.

Another problem in applying the input-output efficiency model to education is that its operation assumes a clear definition of the output or product (O'Donoghue, 1971). In industry, it is necessary to consider the demand for a number of products before deciding which is most likely to meet consumers' needs. One may then proceed to estimate the costs associated with the production of each product. In the absence of clear definitions of the product of schools, however, assessments of efficiency in the field of education can only be carried out at a very crude level.

Despite these difficulties, there is still a sense in which a consideration of schooling in terms of inputs and outputs is appealing, perhaps because economic terms are so familiar. Certainly many recommendations for educational improvement, such as proposals to provide language laboratories or to reduce pupil-teacher ratio, are based—implicitly at any rate—on the assumption that the available resources affect educational outputs. Such a view seems implicit in the minds of policymakers and of the public.

CONCLUSION

Concern over how our schools are working is not new. As long as public education has existed, government officials, administrators, parents, and researchers have, from time to time, questioned the efficacy of certain school practices. However, for a number of reasons, concern with schooling and its consequences reached major proportions in the 1970s. Not least among the reasons prompting this concern was a growing pressure to use schools to contribute to the attainment of equality of opportunity for all citizens.

The U.S government's concern received concrete expression in its commissioning a survey of the American school system in 1964, the report of which was published under the title "Equality of Educational Opportunity" (Coleman et al., 1966). Around the same time, compensatory education programs were instituted for poor and minority children. The results of both these efforts provided new material for the school effectiveness controversy.

One might have thought that research evidence would have helped resolve a debate between those who argued that schooling had an important role to play in social reform and those who claimed that schooling was a rather ineffective vehicle to achieve anything, much less contribute to major social changes. For a number of reasons, the research evidence was of limited value in the debate.

School effectiveness, though often spoken about, was never clearly defined. If a school is to be regarded as effective, then it must achieve the objective it sets out to achieve. Unless the objectives of schooling are clearly stated, the school's role in attaining them cannot be assessed. "Equality of opportunity" was posited by some commentators as an objective of schooling. However, if at least five different definitions of the term exist, it is obvious that this objective leaves much room for disagreement.

Indeed, at the root of the problems in interpreting research on school and program effectiveness is the question of the objectives of schooling and the methods of assessing them. Methods for assessing school and program outcomes in the cognitive area have changed, in a way that is seldom adverted to, over the last 70 years. When assessing schools and programs in the policy-oriented investigations of the 1960s, investigators used the methods that were readily available to them, without giving serious consideration to their adequacy. Obviously, the value of a school-effectiveness study will stand or fall on the adequacy of its measure of the school's efforts.

In the hustle and bustle of research commissioned by policy makers, researchers did not have much time to consider this issue. Neither did they have much time to consider the precise school-based factors which might contribute most to scholastic achievement or the analytic models that might best represent how schools actually function. If they had looked for a body of knowledge about the workings of schools that would have guided them in these matters, their search would have been in vain. At this stage in the debate, it seems reasonable to explore such issues.

chapter 2

Empirical Studies

INTRODUCTION

This chapter provides an overview of the major school-effectiveness studies carried out in recent years, the findings of which underlie the growing controversy in this area. The most influential of these studies was the "Equality of Educational Opportunity" survey, which was sponsored by the U.S. government and was reported by Coleman and his colleagues in 1966. A number of important reanalyses of the data collected for this survey, in which alternative analytic procedures were employed, followed.

Studies of compensatory education also provide a major source of evidence in recent controversy about school effectiveness. Several such studies were commissioned by the U.S. government. Their findings relate particularly to the school's role in the education of poor and minority group students.

The findings of both types of study, taken together, present a fairly pessimistic picture and seem to provide a basis for a denial of traditional beliefs in the efficacy of schools. A final verdict on this issue, however, should be reserved until we have carried out a closer examination of methodological procedures used in the studies in later chapters.

THE "EQUALITY OF EDUCATIONAL OPPORTUNITY" SURVEY

In carrying out this nationwide survey, Coleman et al. (1966) addressed four issues. First, they sought to determine the extent to which racial and cultural groups were segregated from one another in the public schools. Second, they surveyed the facilities and resources available in schools attended by different racial and cultural groups in an attempt to determine the extent to which equal educational opportunities, in the form of resources and facilities, were offered. Third, they investigated how much students learn in school, as measured by standardized-test performance. Fourth, they attempted to identify the relation between students' achievements and the resources and facilities present in the schools they attended.

To answer these questions, the largest survey of American public education in history was mounted. Nationwide, 645,000 pupils, categorized into six racial and cultural groups, were administered standardized ability and achievement tests. Pupils in grades 1, 3, 6, 9, and 12 were included in the survey. About 60,000 teachers completed questionnaires about their educational backgrounds, experiences, and attitudes. Information on a host of facilities, ranging from average teacher salary to age of textbooks in particular subject areas, was collected from over 4,000 schools.

The final report from the survey, popularly known as the Coleman Report, was published on the eve of July 4, 1966, with little publicity and no fanfare. The occasion did not seem to warrant either. A study that had started out to document what most people assumed was reality—that the inequality of resources in American schools was taking its toll on students' scholastic development—concluded that "school brings little to bear in a child's achievement that is independent of his background and general social context" (p. 325). For a society that believed in the importance of the school as an agent in reducing inequality, this finding proved distinctly uncomfortable.

Essentially, Coleman's survey denied the efficacy of schooling as a powerful equalizer in American society. "Equality of Educational Opportunity" did demonstrate, ten years after the decision outlawing so-called separate but equal education, that racial separation still characterized the vast majority of American schools. Some 80 percent of all white pupils in the first and twelfth grades attended schools in which the student body was over 90 percent white; 65 percent of all black first grade students attended schools which were over 90 percent black, while 48 percent of the black twelfth-graders attended schools in which half or more of the students were black. However, despite conventional wisdom to the contrary, the physical facilities, curricula, and teacher characteristics in black and white schools were similar—much more similar than Coleman, Congress, and most Americans had believed. While there were gaps in resources and facilities between predominantly black and predominantly white schools, these gaps were generally small. For example, more secondary schools classified as white indicated on the questionnaire that students had access to an accelerated curriculum; such access was possible for 66 percent of the predominantly white schools and 61 percent of the predominantly black ones. In some categories, such as access to remedial reading teachers, black schools had small advantages over white ones.

The survey, not unexpectedly, did reveal differences in scholastic performance among racial and cultural groups. Utilizing standardized tests of reading and mathematics achievement and verbal and nonverbal ability, Coleman documented sizable differences between white students and other racial or ethnic minorities studied. As the report states, "With some exceptions—notably Oriental Americans—the average minority pupil scores distinctly lower on these tests at every level than the average white pupil" (p. 21). Moreover, the disparity between "majority" and "minority" pupils' test scores seemed to increase at progressively higher grade levels. This was interpreted as indicating that minority pupils fell farther and farther behind their white counterparts the longer they remained in school.*

Of all the findings reported in "Equality of Educational Opportunity," the one which most surprised the authors, educators, and the American public had to do with the relation between the resources present in a school and pupil achievement as measured by standardized tests. When home background variables were controlled, school characteristics and resources such as per-pupil expenditure, teacher experience, number of books in the school library, presence of science laboratories, curricular differences, and a host of similar variables appeared to make little difference in students' measured levels of achievement. For example, after controlling six student home-background variables in an attempt to assess the effects of school resources independently of students' social class, Coleman found that district per-pupil instructional expenditure for Northern blacks and whites in grades 6, 9, and 12 accounted for less than 1 percent of the observed variation in school achievement. The report did tentatively suggest that some school factors—the school's social-class composition and the teacher's verbal ability the most prominently mentioned—could make a difference in pupils' achievement.

Yet what mattered most, according to the report, was not the material quality of the school at all, but students' home backgrounds *prior to*

---

*This conclusion is a function of the metric (in this case, the grade equivalent) which is employed. The use of percentile ranks does not reveal an increase in score disparity over grade levels (Coleman & Karweit, 1972).

entering school. Coleman found that the largest differences in measured achievement occurred among students within the same school rather than between students in different schools. That is, students in the same school, with presumably equal access to facilities and resources, differed much more in achievement among themselves than did the mean performance of students in different schools which possessed different resources and facilities. For some portions of the student population studied, the performances of students within the same schools were nine times more different than the average performances of students in different schools. Thus the most crucial finding of the report was that if quality of schools is assessed in terms of access to materials and facilities, the measures most commonly used by educational reformers and school administrators, then the quality of schools bore virtually no relationship to students' measured achievement. It is this finding which has received the most attention. Its implications were bluntly spelled out in the report:

> Schools bring little influence to bear on a child's achievement that is independent of his background and general social context; . . . this very lack of an independent effect means that the inequalities imposed on children by their home, neighborhood and peer environment are carried along to become the inequalities with which they confront adult life at the end of school. For equality of educational opportunity must imply a strong effect on schools that is independent of the child's immediate social environment, and that strong independent effect is not present in American schools (p. 325).

"Equality of Educational Opportunity" had two major effects on the school-effectiveness controversy. First, by virtue of its magnitude, timing, and conclusions, it did much to precipitate the ensuing debate about the effectiveness of schooling. The finding that school characteristics alone accounted for very little of the large differences in pupils' achievement indicated, in the words of one social commentator, "that professional practice in a major social institution was not nearly so efficacious as had been thought" (Moynihan, 1968). Such a conclusion would hardly be welcomed by the educational establishment, which predicated its practices on the belief that facilities are strongly related to school achievement. Second, and of equal significance, the Coleman Report did much to alter the prevailing conception of equal educational opportunity. Before the survey, equal opportunity was generally meant to mean equal access to the inputs of schooling: good teachers, libraries, textbooks, classrooms, and the like. When the report showed that the relative equality of these inputs across different types of schools did not lead to equal achievement, the conception of equal opportunity shifted to an emphasis on tested achievement (Bell, 1972; Coleman, 1972). Schools would be regarded as affording equal educational opportunity when different pupils in different schools manifested similar achievement.

There are several reasons why the findings of the Coleman survey, despite the fact that it essentially replicated those of numerous other studies, had a considerable impact. Its sheer magnitude was far beyond the scale of any similar study performed before or since. On this score alone it was more likely to receive public attention. Second, the study looked explicitly at disparities among racial and ethnic groups. At the time the study was performed, the problems of the poor in general and the black poor in particular were of primary social concern in America. Any study which explicitly examined racial and ethnic disparities in resources and achievement and concluded that school resources and facilities were unrelated to achievement was bound to have significant impact. Third, since the study was commissioned by the U.S. government, it was very likely that its findings would be significant in determining national educational policies. A study which might influence such policies would surely be closely scrutinized.

Despite this, reaction to the report was at first very limited. Its lack of promulgation may have contributed to this situation. Three separate summaries of the report were prepared before the final version was released at a press conference. No press release accompanied the summary document, which was not available to the press until just before the news conference. Further, the report was allowed to go out of print after the initial printing was exhausted. The summary highlighted racial segregation and downplayed the lack of resource differences and low relation between resources and pupil achievement. Only a few academics recognized and commented upon the import of Coleman's survey (Jencks, 1966; Moynihan, 1968). Two years after its completion, "Equality of Educational Opportunity" had had no apparent effect on federal programs for education. Had conventional wisdom triumphed, with a little help from its supporters?

The Coleman Report might have languished in obscurity had it not been for a series of events which refocused attention upon its findings and their import for educational reform. In January 1969, a new administration took power in Washington, one considerably more conservative than its predecessor and with its own ideas about federal educational-intervention programs. Vociferous and articulate spokesmen for this administration, most notably Daniel Moynihan, did much to publicize Coleman's findings within the administration and in Congress (Grant, 1973). Indeed, President Nixon's message on Educational Reform in March 1970 was a primer on Coleman's findings. Commenting upon the presumed relationship between school facilities and achievement, the president concluded

> Years of educational research, culminating in the 'Equality of Educational Opportunity' survey of 1966 have, however, demonstrated that this direct, uncomplicated relationship does not exist.

It must also be noted that during this period a "guns or butter" debate was underway in Washington. Pressures on the federal coffers as a result of the Great Society's domestic commitments were clashing with pressures from the expensive war in Southeast Asia. The administration, locked into many of the domestic programs by law or political exigency, viewed education as one area where expenditures might be reduced. Moreover, additional negative evidence on school and program effectiveness was gradually becoming available as a result of evaluations mandated by Congress during passage of the Elementary and Secondary Education Act of 1965 and the Economic Opportunity Act of 1964. In virtually all cases, the evidence confirmed or supported the Coleman Report's conclusions. Not only did reanalysis of the Coleman data prove the initial findings to be quite robust (Jencks, 1972; Mosteller & Moynihan, 1972), but studies of compensatory-education programs revealed no consistent or sizable benefits to pupils enrolled in such programs (Averch et al., 1972; Cicirelli et al., 1969; Glass et al., 1970; Picariello, 1968; U.S. Office of Education, 1970).

The availability of new evidence on school effectiveness, the advocacy of the Coleman findings by individuals within the Nixon administration, and, most of all, efforts to use the report to justify reorientation of federal government's educational priorities and programs did much to bring the Coleman study to the center of attention. Some three or four years after its rather obscure initial release, "Equality of Educational Opportunity" became a source of controversy. The challenge to conventional wisdom about school effectiveness was acknowledged, and the school-effectiveness debate began in earnest.

Reactions to the Coleman study in the academic community were varied and critical. Criticisms ranged from relatively minor ones related to procedural and mechanical errors in handling data (Bowles & Levin,

1968b; Smith, 1972), to major ones that perceived the findings as "near-racist" (cf. Moynihan, 1968). In between, critics pointed to problems pertaining to nonresponses and selective participation (Hanushek & Kain, 1972; Jencks, 1972b) and to possible defects in the report's method of analysis (Bowles and Levin, 1968a; Smith, 1972). This latter point has perhaps received the most attention. It has been pointed out that by carrying out separate analyses for regional and ethnic groups, Coleman reduced the heterogeneity of schooling and achievement, thus also reducing the likelihood of finding relationships (Dyer, 1968). It has also been noted that a severe reduction in sample size followed stratifications for analytic purposes; while the number of students included may have remained large, the sampling unit was the school. Naturally, the number of schools was considerably fewer than the number of students, which affects the statistical inferences that can be made (Hanushek & Kain, 1972). Coleman's failure to distinguish between different kinds of high school (trade, vocational, academic, and comprehensive) or between tracks or classes within schools might have led to a confounding of factors relating to school and achievement and the selection of students into different tracks (Smith, 1972). And it has been argued that the study's analytic model underestimated the role of school resources, since school factors were introduced into the analysis only after student-background factors had been "controlled" (Smith, 1972; Mayeske et al., 1972; Wiley, 1976).

A perusal of related studies carried out before or about the same time as the Coleman study does not present a picture that differs essentially from that provided by Coleman. Earlier univariate studies did not show consistent and significant relations between any school variables and achievement, as measured by standardized tests. More recent multivariate studies carried out in the United States and in Europe provide basically similar results (e.g., Benson, 1965; Burkhead, Fox, & Holland, 1967; Goodman, 1959; Kiesling, 1969; Mollenkopf & Melville, 1956; Peaker, 1967; Sohlman, 1971). But it was the Coleman Report which brought home to the educational community just how unimportant variations in school facilities might be.

SOME REANALYSES OF THE "EQUALITY OF EDUCATIONAL OPPORTUNITY SURVEY" DATA

The richness of the Coleman data, together with the impact of the study on the educational community led to a number of reanalyses. Smith (1972) selected subsamples of Northern students in the sixth, ninth, and twelfth grades and carried out reanalyses in the light of errors in, and criticisms of, the original study. In particular, he questioned Coleman's implicit model of the educational process and his choice of statistics. The Coleman approach assumed that five sets of variables determine a student's achievement: home background, characteristics of the student body, school facilities and curriculum, teacher characteristics, and other unmeasured factors of heredity and environment. The five factors were treated in the analyses as if they were additive. Coleman argued that since background factors operate prior to school experience, their influence on variance in students' test performance should be examined prior to examining the influence of school factors. This, Smith (1972) points out, has the effect of assigning to background factors the explanatory power that they possess uniquely as well as the explanatory power they share with school resources.

Despite differences in approach, Smith's reanalyses basically confirmed Coleman's findings. A very large proportion of school-to-school variation in achievement on standardized tests was attributable to differences in home background—over 66 percent for white secondary students and about 33 percent for black students, figures which are much higher than those reported by Coleman. The relations between school resources and verbal ability, on the other hand, were found to be very slight. Smith concludes on the pessimistic note that "the myth that the reallocation of conventional inputs will lead to a redistribution of achievement outputs can no longer be accepted" (p. 315).

A major difference between the Coleman analysis and the reanalyses of Mayeske and his colleagues (Mayeske, Wisler, Beaton, Weinfeld, Cohen, Okada, Proshek, & Tabler, 1972; Mayeske, Okada, Cohen, Beaton, & Wisler, 1973) was that the latter adopted a symmetric variance decomposition method that allowed the relationship between school factors and student achievement to be shown without first allocating all of the shared variance to the home background of the student. The method attempts to determine unique contributions of variables to variance as well as the common contributions of sets of variables.

Mayeske's reanalyses also modified the Coleman data. In particular, a new criterion measure of school outcome was constructed. An overall achievement composite based on a factor analysis of five measures (general information, reading comprehension, verbal ability, mathematics achievement, and nonverbal ability) was used in place of the single measure of verbal ability used for the most part in the Coleman analyses. Furthermore, a method of criterion scaling was employed in which measures of the input or independent variables were scaled against the output or dependent-variable measure. One effect of these modifications was the demonstration of greater between-school variance than the 10 percent Coleman had found. For the twelfth-grade sample, Mayeske reports that 34 percent of the total variance in the composite measure was associated with the schools which students attend; the figure for ninth-grade students was 37 percent. When attainment was related to school variables (facilities, special programs, teachers' training), however, it was clear that the unique contribution of these school variables to achievement was low; what did seem important, in terms of achievement, was the influence of home and school factors acting *in consort.* Thus Mayeske's reanalyses had the effect of considerably changing Coleman's inferences about the singular importance of home background. Mayeske emphasized a combined effect of home and school factors on achievement. For reasons that are not clear, Mayeske's findings have received little attention.

THE IEA STUDIES

Although not directly related to the Coleman study, the projects of the International Association for the Evaluation of Educational Achievement (IEA), which have been concerned with the study of educational achievement in a variety of subject areas (mathematics, science, reading comprehension, literature, civic education, French as a foreign language, and English as a foreign language) across twenty-one countries, are worth considering since they provide data on school systems and environments. The IEA research had as its aim the identification of the factors accounting for achievement differences between countries, schools, and students (Postlethwaite, 1975). Achievement tests suitable for different countries were specially constructed for the projects.

While the proportion of variance in achievement accounted for by the school was on the whole larger in the IEA studies than in the Coleman study, the fact remains that home-background variables consistently accounted for more of the variance in achievement than did school-based variables. The average contribution of home-background variables to total variance in between-student analyses ranged from 1 to 29 percent for fourteen-year-old students; the average for science, reading comprehension, literature, French reading, and English reading was about 15 percent. Previous schooling (type of school and/or type of program) showed a greater range, from 0 to 52 percent. However, on the average, previous schooling contributed less to the explanation of between-student variance than home background. The average contribution of "learning conditions" (amount of prior instruction, teacher characteristics) was similar to that of previous schooling (Postlethwaite, 1975). It should be noted that these figures are based on regression analyses in which, as in Coleman's analyses, blocks of variables were entered chronologically on the assumption that earlier events in an individual student's life influence later events in his or her life and schooling. Thus again, variance jointly shared by home and school factors was uniquely ascribed to home background.

The IEA studies, by virtue of the fact that they were carried out in several countries, can provide information of a kind that studies confined to one country cannot. Take, for example, the question of "elitist" versus "egalitarian" education, in which "elitist" is taken to mean a system in which school-resource allocation is associated with socioeconomic status as happens in England, Germany, France, the Netherlands, and the United States, while "egalitarian" means one in which there is not a significant relationship between expenditure per student and socioeconomic background, as is the case in Israel, Japan, Scotland, and Sweden. The IEA data indicate that whether a school system is elitist or egalitarian is not related to level of achievement or variation in achievement (Noonan, 1976).

The IEA studies revealed quite remarkable differences between countries in the relation between attainment and home and school variables. For example, the proportion of variance in achievement accounted for by school factors (as compared to the proportion accounted for by out-of-school factors) was much greater in developing countries than in industrialized developed countries. This finding seems to be a reflection of the fact that school conditions vary more in underdeveloped countries than in developed ones, while the converse is true for home conditions (Walker, 1975). Because of the method of variance decomposition used in the IEA studies, there are difficulties in interpreting observations on the relative contribution of background and school variables to variance in achievement. However, this finding does suggest that it may be dangerous to base conclusions about school effectiveness on studies that have all been carried out in the same country, where variance in any of the independent variables may be very limited. Given different home conditions and a different school system, the findings may be much altered.

HEAD START AND TITLE I EVALUATIONS

Another major source of evidence in the school-effectiveness controversy in the United States comes from evaluations of Head Start and Title I compensatory-education programs. The evaluations of these programs employed a variety of designs. Those that attempted to compare the performance of children with school experience to that of children without it come closer to answering questions about the absolute effects of schooling—albeit for a limited section of the population and for a limited time period—than the surveys that have thus far been considered. Because of various defects in design and execution, however, they do not answer the question unambiguously.

By congressional mandate, a proportion of the funds allocated to each local project was to be set aside for a study to assess the project's effectiveness. However, it was not until 1968 that reasonably reliable evidence on the extent to which compensatory-education programs were narrowing the achievement gap between disadvantaged and advantaged pupils began to become available. There were three reasons for the delay.

In the first place, emphasis at the local level, where compensatory-education programs were conceived and carried out, centered upon action and the disbursement of services to pupils, rather than upon the systematic evaluation of program effectiveness (Murphy, 1971). It was at the local level that the problems of the disadvantaged students were most pressing; given the choice of devoting resources, including money, to the program itself or to evaluation of the program's effectiveness, most educators and administrators chose the former.

In the second place, federal guidelines requiring formal evaluation of program effectiveness caught most school districts unprepared to muster the expertise required to carry out such evaluations. In fact, one might argue reasonably that it was the evaluation requirement which provided the major impetus for the sudden growth of evaluation research and theory in the 1960s. Not only were local school districts caught unaware, but so also, for the most part, were the universities, which heretofore had been the major suppliers of evaluation expertise to the educational system at large. The late 1960s saw many universities institute or enlarge training programs in educational evaluation. Until expertise became available and the government bureaucracy showed that it was serious about the evaluation provision in contracts awarding funds for compensatory-education programs, the quality of local-level evaluations was shamefully poor (Averch et al., 1972; Wargo et al., 1972). One commentator, looking back on the early years of Title I indicated that

> Title I requires local districts to make annual evaluation reports to the states, including "appropriate objective measurement of educational achievement." Unlike previous federal programs, the provisions called for the public display and disclosure of the information which schoolmen knew would be used against them. . . . The evaluation provisions also put strain on many local school districts and state departments of education which had little evaluation experience. It is no wonder that from the start there has been reluctance and resistance toward fully implementing this provision of Title I, and a tendency toward obfuscation. After all, to the extent that evaluations do not disclose meaningful information on program results, local districts can meet their own priorities without being subject to challenge based on evidence of failure. (Murphy, 1971, pp. 55–56)

In the third place, Congress's emphasis on evaluation at the community level made it difficult to obtain a nationwide overview of the effectiveness of compensatory education. Different programs, designed to meet the needs of different communities, keyed to different instructional approaches and varying widely in the adequacy of their evaluation activities, were not conducive to obtaining national policy insights into the efficacy of compensatory education. In the initial three years of Head Start and Title I, due to a combination of federal and local inertia in implementing rigorous effectiveness studies at a level that would make policy decisions possible, little useful evidence about the programs was forthcoming.

In 1968, however, the federal government undertook large-scale investigations of compensatory-education programs. By that year, financial pressures led to a closer inspection of the efficacy of various domestic social and educational programs. The more conservative administration added additional impetus to the call for program accountability.

The nature of these studies differed from that of the "Equality of Educational Opportunity" survey, which was concerned with the relation between a wide array of school facilities and student achievement. By contrast, the compensatory-program evaluations focused primarily upon a single resource—the compensatory program—and its effect on achievement. The programs themselves generally sought to increase substantially the resources devoted to each pupil by lowering class size, adding additional instructional personnel, or individualizing instruction.

While the specific features of the programs varied from community to community, primary attention was paid to whether compensatory-education programs in general, regardless of their particular characteristics, successfully increased achievement in the target population. For the most part, this determination implied comparing the performance of compensatory-program participants with the performance of an equivalent group of nonparticipants. If the groups were approximately similar in all regards except exposure to the program, an accurate assessment of the program's effects could be obtained. Higher achievement among program participants would imply that compensatory education could increase pupils' performance; similar achievement by the participant and nonparticipant groups would imply that the program was not successful in raising performance levels among the treated pupils.

In practice, owing to the relatively poor plans for local evaluations, researchers rarely were provided with instances in which a comparison could be made between a treated and an equivalent untreated group. So in most cases, they were forced to survey the best of local programs across the nation and to strive to synthesize the results of these programs into a general statement about the effectiveness of compensatory education. As both investigators and critics were quick to point out, these surveys were also subject to whatever methodological limitations existed in local evaluations.

Several large surveys of Title I programs were commissioned or performed by the United States Office of Education. In general, these surveys selected samples of Title I programs in which a fairly rigorous evaluation plan was carried out and similar or identical measures of achievement were used to assess participants' learning. The surveys were quite consistent in their findings.

An analysis of the reading achievement scores of 155,000 participants of 189 Title I projects during the school year ending in June 1967 indicates that a child who participated in a Title I project had only a 19 percent chance of a significant achievement gain, a 13 percent chance of a significant achievement test loss and a 68 percent chance of no change at all. This sample of observations is unrepresentative of projects in which there was a higher than average investment in resources. Therefore, more significant achievement gains should be found here than in the more representative sample of Title I projects. (Piccariello, 1968, p. 1)

It will be noted in the following reports of analyses that all outcome data indicated a distinctly higher than average reading gain for nonparticipants than for participants. (Glass et al. 1970, p. 63)

> For participating and nonparticipating pupils, the rate of progress in reading skills kept pace with their historical rate of progress . . . Compensatory reading programs did not seem to overcome the reading deficiencies that stem from poverty. (U.S. Office of Education, 1970, pp. 126–127)

> Although each LEA [Local Education Authority] reported some reading improvement for the students in our sample, most of the students were not reading at levels sufficient for them to begin to close the gap between their reading level and the national norm. The gap between the reading level of the educationally deprived children and that of average children of the same age generally increased while the students were in the program. (United States: Comptroller General, 1975, p. 6)

While the conclusions of these surveys are qualified by the authors, who cite a number of methodological problems, the findings of large-scale evaluations of Title I programs are quite consistent. The programs appear to have had very little effect in narrowing the achievement gap between advantaged and disadvantaged pupils' achievement. In March 1973, a former Commissioner of Education, in an appearance before the House Subcommittee on Departments of Health, Education and Welfare Appropriations, summed up the impact of Title I:

> I would have to say at the present stage after seven years of Title I, while many good things can be said about it in terms of attitudes of teachers, parents, and in some cases of children, the bottom line does not show very much. In other words, the measurable conditions . . . do not make a strong case yet for saying that the $8 or $9 billion which have gone broadly to the disadvantaged have yet made a sweeping difference. (quoted in United States: Comptroller General, 1975, p. 10)

At about the same time as the initial large-scale surveys of Title I effectiveness were being carried out, the Office of Economic Opportunity commissioned a nationwide study of Project Head Start, the preschool program for disadvantaged youngsters. This study, the most comprehensive and systematic up to that time, was carried out jointly by the Westinghouse Learning Corporation and Ohio University (Cicirelli et al., 1969). The Westinghouse/Ohio University study selected at random 104 of the more than 12,000 Head Start centers throughout the nation for investigation. All children who had been eligible to enter a center were identified. For each center, a group of eight pupils who actually participated in the Head Start program and eight pupils who were eligible but did not participate were selected. The nonparticipating children were matched to the participating children on seven variables: continuity of residence in the target area, eligibility for Head Start, equivalent school experience, no other Head Start experience, gender, racial and ethnic identity, and whether kindergarten was attended. Since the study was performed ex post facto—that is, after the pupils had completed their Head Start experiences—it was possible to select pupils who were currently in the first, second, or third grade. A variety of achievement and attitudinal instruments was administered to the participating and nonparticipating groups at each center.

The report found little to celebrate in preschool compensatory-education programs. In the first grade, children who had spent a full year in Head Start (but not those who had taken part only in summer programs) performed better than the nonparticipating group on one achievement test, but by the time they had reached second grade the advantage had been lost. On the other measures administered, both cognitive and affective, Head Start children did not differ appreciably from their school peers who had not attended Head Start.

This study has been subjected to a great deal of methodological criticism. It has been criticized for being too narrow in scope, focusing only on cognitive and affective outcomes to the exclusion of other worthy Head Start goals in the areas of health and nutrition. (Smith & Bissell, 1970). It has also been argued that the investigators failed to pay adequate attention to variation among Head Start programs. Further, the sample of centers and participants selected has been criticized for being unrepresentative and too small to provide confidence in the study's findings (Madow, 1969; McDill et al., 1972; Smith & Bissell, 1970; Williams & Evans, 1972). These criticisms were responded to by the study's authors (Cicirelli, 1970; Cicirelli, Evans, & Schiller, 1970; Evans, 1969; Evans & Schiller, 1970). Overall, political and methodological issues surrounding the Westinghouse/Ohio University evaluation of Project Head Start conspired to limit the evaluators and to diminish the quality of the data they gathered (Datta, 1976).

When all was said and done, however, the fact remained that the results of this and other evaluations could not be considered encouraging to those who had reasoned that the malleability of children in their early years presented a golden opportunity for intervention to overcome the effects of early childhood experiences in disadvantaged areas. Studies of the effectiveness of Title I and Head Start programs did not provide much reassurance that enhancing the school environment of disadvantaged children by means of extra expenditures, smaller class sizes, additional teachers, or enrichment activities would result in either substantial or lasting achievement gains.

FURTHER EVIDENCE

By about 1970, the results of "Equality of Educational Opportunity" and the large-scale compensatory-program evaluations began to receive wide circulation, and the lines for the school-effectiveness controversy were drawn. On one side were those who concluded that schools are not important since they demonstrably contribute little or nothing to scholastic development. On the other side were people who could not accept the research evidence since it ran counter to long-held beliefs in the efficacy of schooling.

With the battle lines forming, additional research was released which seemed to entrench more firmly the attitudes of the two sides. Arthur Jensen in 1969 published "How Much Can We Boost of IQ and Scholastic Achievement?" in which he argued that ability is largely inherited. Jensen started his now-famous paper with the words "Compensatory education has been tried and it has apparently failed" (Jensen, 1969), and concluded with the argument that 80 percent of intelligence was genetically determined. It was one matter for researchers to claim that social class and home background were more powerful in influencing attainment than school resources or programs; such a conclusion at least left room for the social meliorists to envision changes in children's early environmental experiences. To claim that the bulk of intelligence was genetically determined left little room for melioration of any sort.

In 1972, David Armor published the much-criticized, widely circulated article "The Evidence on Busing." Citing evidence from the Metco Project in Boston, as well as reports on four other busing programs in New York, Michigan, California, and Connecticut, Armor concluded that busing does not raise black students' standardized-test performance. Moreover, black pupils' self-esteem, race relations, and success in higher education were not enhanced by busing. Integration, at least as defined in terms of voluntary busing of black students, did not appear to raise achievement.

In 1972 also, *Inequality: A Reassessment of the Effect of Family and Schooling in America* (Jencks et al., 1972) was published. Jencks and his colleagues undertook a more ambitious task than simply relating school resources and home background to measured achievement; they sought to look also at economic success in later life. Jencks identified three basic assumptions upon which the educational-reform programs of the 1960s were based. The first assumption was that eliminating poverty was primarily a problem of helping children born into poverty rise out of it; once families escaped from poverty, they would not regress back into it. The second assumption was the the principal reason poor children cannot escape the shackles of poverty is because they lack basic cognitive skills such as reading, writing, and calculating. The final assumption was that education was the best avenue for overcoming poverty. Each of these assumptions was tested and found to be erroneous by the authors of *Inequality*. Extending Coleman's conclusions, Jencks and his collaborators indicated that although background factors are more related to school achievement than school resources or facilities, school achievement has little relation to economic success, measured in terms of job-salary level. The authors concluded:

> Our work suggests, then, that many popular explanations of economic inequality are largely wrong. We cannot blame economic inequality primarily on genetic differences in men's capacity for abstract reasoning, since there is nearly as much economic inequality among men with equal test scores as among men in general. We cannot blame economic inequality primarily on the fact that the parents pass along their disadvantages to their children, since there is nearly as much inequality among men in general. We cannot blame economic inequality on differences between schools, since differences between schools seem to have very little effect on any measurable attribute of those who attend them. (p. 8)

CONCLUSION

Taken altogether, the Coleman Report, the nationwide studies of compensatory education, the Jencks study, and Jensen's theory appeared to constitute a powerful denial of the traditional belief in the efficacy of social reform through emphasis on more and better educational programs. Each investigation appeared to further erode the veneer of confidence Americans had placed in their schools. Coleman seemed to be saying that the path to equality of educational attainment was not through the quality of the resources and facilities schools offered their students, since these bore little relation to achievement once students' home backgrounds were taken into account. The Title I evaluations and the Westinghouse/Ohio University Head Start investigation appeared to argue against the efficacy of compensatory-education efforts, whether carried out prior to or after school entrance. Jencks extended the argument further by concluding that neither schooling nor home background was substantially related to job income in later life; even if schools were effective there was no necessary carry-over from the educational to the economic sphere. While no one quarreled with the basic premise that all persons in the society should be afforded equal opportunity, the findings of these studies were interpreted to indicate that schooling—the most time-honored and politically viable means of insuring equality—now appeared to be incapable of providing such equal opportunity.

Dissenters to this pessimistic conclusion were quick to take up the gauntlet. The research is defective on many counts, they argued; as subsequent chapters will show, they were correct. The researchers themselves were often the first to point out the flaws in their work. The central question, however, was whether these flaws were sufficient to negate the seeming consistency of the results obtained in numerous studies. Further research was undertaken to test the validity of previous research, and then more research was undertaken to test the validity of the latest research. Arguments ranged from polemical to technical and statistical. However, insights into the schooling process itself and the way in which that process is best viewed were often slow to emerge. Much of the debate has overlooked questions about schooling and school effectiveness and the most useful manner in which to conceptualize these concepts. The development of these concepts is most important, since it can help to demythify the black boxes of schools and schooling research, while at the same time enriching our perspective of what is reasonable to expect from our schools.

chapter 3

Strategies and Analytic
Procedures in Investigating
School Effectiveness

INTRODUCTION

In considering what empirical research studies have to say about school
and program effectiveness, it is necessary to identify initially the questions various studies were capable of answering. There are, of course,
many questions one might ask about schooling and its effects, and it is
clear that the prevalent methodologies used to examine school and program effectiveness are not capable of answering a number of these questions. In this chapter we shall show that of the two general questions of
interest, one related to the absolute effect of schooling and the other to
the relative effect of varying quantities of a given school resource, studies to date have focused on the latter. We shall then describe three
different strategies which may be used to examine school and program
effectiveness, paying particular attention to the real-life problems which
have arisen in their use. We shall show that as the research strategy
adopted makes greater and greater accommodations to the realities of
the context in which it is carried out, the analytic problems associated
with that strategy multiply.

ABSOLUTE EFFECTS OF SCHOOLING

The importance of identifying the type of question research studies are
capable of answering is clear when one considers the conclusions which
have been drawn from school and program-effectiveness research, both
in the popular press and the technical literature. Levine and Bane (1975),

for example, conclude that "the bulk of research indicates that schooling does relatively little of what it always claimed to do—foster the cognitive abilities of students and thus assure them a productive niche in the economy" (p. 19). Note that the conclusion refers to "schooling." It does not say that certain types of schools may do little but that other types may do a lot, or that schools with more of a particular resource or facility may enhance pupils' cognitive achievement to a greater extent than schools with less of that resource or facility. The judgment it makes about the effects of schooling is absolute. Implicitly, Levine and Bane set up a comparison between schooling and no schooling and conclude that schooling does little to foster pupils' cognitive abilities. There is no clear evidence of an empirical nature to substantiate this view. And what evidence does exist tends to contradict the conclusion that schooling, as opposed to no schooling, has but little effect on students' cognitive abilities.

To determine the absolute effect of schooling, one would need data on the attainment level of a group of children that had attended school and a comparable group that had not. Differences in attainment between the two groups would then provide evidence of the absolute effect of schooling (Smith, 1972). This is not the type of evidence most school and program-effectiveness studies provide. There is, however, some evidence based on data gathered in circumstances that approach this ideal. For example, to avoid integration, public schools in Prince Edward County, Virginia, were closed from 1959 to 1963, and the majority of black children received no formal education during this period. Compared to children who did attend school in an adjacent county, the cognitive performace of nonattenders was found to be severely retarded; intelligence test scores were depressed by fifteen to thirty points (Green, Hofman, Morse, Hayes, & Morgan, 1964). These findings are reminiscent of early findings reported for children with poor attendance. Gordon (1923), who investigated the achievement- and ability-test performance of a group of English canal-boat children who attended school only about 5 percent of the school year, found that performance on the Stanford-Binet Intelligence Scale decreased with age. The mean IQ of children from age four to six years was ninety; for children over twelve, it was sixty. H. Gordon also reported that IQ and actual school attendance were positively correlated (.37).

In a study in the United States, Wheeler (1942) tested the intelligence of children living in an isolated mountain area in Eastern Tennessee in 1930, at the depth of the Depression. Ten years later, he administered the same tests to children in the same area. During this time, school facilities, such as libraries and teacher qualifications, had improved in the area. Wheeler found that the children's median IQ had increased by ten points over the ten years. Furthermore, the average child was eight months younger chronologically and nine months superior in mental age for his or her grade than the average child in 1930.

While suggesting the importance of schooling, these studies do not control for the operation of other factors which might have affected children's performance. All the studies involved naturally occurring situations; none allocated some children randomly to a school-treatment group and others to a non–school-treatment group, a necessary condition to determine unequivocally the absolute effect of schooling. Further, the canal-boat children lived in impoverished homes; their decreasing performance on tests of intelligence was, no doubt, in part a function of such an environment.

Similar comments apply to studies, carried out in Africa, which have attempted to compare the development of the cognitive abilities, such as conserving and categorizing strategies, of children who attended school with those of children who did not (Greenfield, 1966; Greenfield, Reich, & Olver, 1966). Using Piagetian tasks to test children's perceptions of the equivalence of continuous quantities which varied in their perceptual presentation, it was found that the differences in conservation ability were greater between unschooled and schooled West African children from the same rural village than between urban and rural children. These studies again cannot be accepted as providing unequivocal evidence regarding the effects of schooling. In the first place, it is not known why some children attended school and others didn't. Besides, in the African context, differences in performance on cognitive tasks have been reported for children living in different environments, even when both sets attended school (Kellaghan, 1968). To confuse the matter further, it may be that the quality of schooling covaried with the quality of the home environments. Overall, the results suggest but do not prove that school affects cognitive development.

A further source of evidence of the effects of school attendance is found in evaluations of early intervention projects for children in disadvantaged areas. In this context, it is sufficient to note that while the long-term effects of preschool experience on achievement have not been marked, there is a good deal of evidence that children exposed to particular types of preschool experience exhibit increased levels of performance, particularly in the short term, on intelligence tests and other school-related measures (Bronfenbrenner, 1975; Kellaghan, 1977c).

There are two final sources of evidence which may be cited in considering the absolute effects of schooling. Both are historical. One relates to the expansion of education in the last century in Western countries and in this century in developing countries. Such expansion was paralleled by increases in literacy. It might again be argued that such an interpretation does not take account of the role that extraschool factors played in extending literacy; however, it is hard to identify what factors outside the school would have contributed significantly to such development.

The other source of evidence is the test performance of students over periods of time, and here the evidence on school effects is far from ambiguous. Burt (1969), for example, has cited data on median levels of school attainments of ten- to eleven-year-old children in English schools for the period 1914 to 1965. The Plowden Report (Great Britain: Department of Education and Science, 1967) also cites data over time on performance in the basic school subjects. The Plowden Report points to a general improvement since the end of World War II; Burt, on the basis of a longer time series, suggests an overall decline in standards, using as a baseline the pupil standards in 1914. In the United States, data to support the idea of declining standards have also been reported. For example, evidence exists that since the mid-1960s, mean levels of performance on the Scholastic Aptitude Test, the American College Test, the Iowa Tests of Educational Development, and the Iowa Tests of Basic Skills have all dropped (Beaton, Hilton, & Schrader, 1977; Harnischfeger & Wiley, 1975).

On the basis of this kind of evidence, inferences have been made about the effects of schooling. If standards are declining, the schools are blamed; if they are rising all is well in the school. The arguments may be interpreted in terms of the absolute effects of schooling, or as relating to the effects of particular school practices. For example, the debate about rising or falling standards is often carried out in the context of the so-called traditional-progressive debate in education. Supporters of traditional teaching, in which emphasis is placed on the three R's, have frequently attributed a purported decline in standards to a shift to the more open, less structured child-centered approach of so-called progressive education. However interpreted, inferences from such data are always hazardous. Based as they are on the interpretation of trends over time, problems arise which relate to possible differences in the populations compared and to the appropriateness of tests for different generations of students (cf. Great Britain: Department of Education and Science, 1975). While the source of the data (test scores) may appear more empirical than estimates of literacy or teachers' judgments, this may only give the conclusions a spurious validity.

To add to the complexity of the situation, it does not follow that whatever effects schools might have would be similar in all situations. Deprivation of schooling for middle-class children at the elementary level might not have very serious effects. Given a relatively poor home environment vis-à-vis scholastic development, the school's impact may be relatively great; in a rich home environment, the schools impact may be slight. It is unlikely, however, that these relations would continue to hold at levels above elementary school. While home-based attitudes might still be important in learning science or a foreign language, it is difficult to envisage how the formal instruction required for such learning could be provided in the home.

Overall, the sources of evidence relating to the absolute effects of schooling, taken singly, may not be very convincing. The presence of possibly confounding variables renders impossible the drawing of un-ambiguous causal inferences from the available data. Furthermore, the range of output measures examined is limited. Taken together, however, the studies do point toward a school effect. School attendance, as opposed to non-school attendance, is beneficial to pupils' cognitive ability. Certainly the studies reviewed provide no support for Levine and Bane's (1975) conclusion that schooling, in the absolute sense, is ineffective.

For the most part, available empirical studies are not capable of an-swering unequivocally the question "Does schooling make a differ-ence?", even if common sense indicates that it does. Rather, available studies by and large are directed toward examining the relative effective-ness of particular school resources and programs. Thus, studies pose and seek to answer such questions as: "Does greater teacher experience, per pupil expenditure, or classroom space relate to higher pupil achieve-ment?" "Do smaller class size, newer textbooks or more remedial pro-grams contribute to achievement?" Note that the comparisons implied are not between teachers versus no teachers, textbooks versus no text-books or remedial programs versus no remedial programs; rather they are between the effectiveness of different amounts or qualities of a given resource or facility. Thus, far from being capable of providing evidence about the absolute effect of school attendance, most studies can only provide evidence about the relative or differential effectiveness of differ-ent quantities of a given school input.

Potentially, at least, it was possible for studies of compensatory edu-cation to provide evidence on the absolute effect of preschool programs on pupil achievement; the performance of preschool attenders could have been compared to the performance of nonattenders. However, while such information would have been useful, it would not have shed a great deal of light on the absolute effect of regular school attendance. Further, as we shall note later in this chapter, a variety of circumstances prevented the evaluation of preschool programs from providing the desired evidence on the absolute effect of schooling.

In sum, it is clear that one must be careful to avoid reading into empirical studies of school and program effectiveness conclusions about issues the studies were not designed to deal with. After many years of research we know little about the absolute effect of schooling as compared to no schooling; most studies were concerned with the relative effectiveness of varying quantities and qualities of given school resources on pupil achievement. In considering these studies, we shall examine three strategies which have been used to examine differential school and program effectiveness.

THE EXPERIMENTAL APPROACH

Given a choice of design, most researchers would probably choose the experiment to examine school and program effectiveness. However, "true" experiments have not been carried out for this purpose. For if experiments are desirable because they provide the strongest grounds for causal inferences about variables and their effects, they do so only by imposing stringent requirements on the conduct of the research. True experiments must satisfy three conditions. First, a single, well-defined population of subjects which has not had prior exposure to the inputs or programs under study must be identified. Second, samples must be selected at random from this population. And third, inputs or programs of interest (the so-called treatments) must be allocated to the different samples. In the simplest case in which a single input is under study, two randomly selected samples would be drawn from the subject population. One sample would be exposed to the input while the other would not. The second, untreated sample of subjects would then serve as a control for the sample which had received the treatment. When these conditions are satisfied, a comparison of the performance of the treated and untreated groups on some outcome measure (e.g., an achievement test) at the conclusion of the treatment would be interpreted as providing evidence of the treatment's effect.

The underlying rationale of the experimental approach is that random selection of subjects from a single, well-defined population should produce groups which are equivalent on all relevant variables. By treating differently groups which are initially equivalent and by observing their respective performance at the conclusion of the experiment, it can be inferred that particular treatments were the causes of any performance differences observed between the groups, since the only way in which the groups differed was in the treatments they received.

The situational demands and control required for the conduct of true experiments has placed them beyond the realm of possibility for most school- and program-effectiveness studies. The conditions required for systematic experimentation rarely occur spontaneously and must therefore be externally imposed. Further, this imposition must take place prior to the actual application of the treatment variables of interest. This requirement in turn demands that the investigator have sufficient control over the conditions under which the research is carried out so that he or she can randomly select units and assign treatments to them. For a number of reasons, large-scale studies of school and program effectiveness have not been able to fulfill these conditions.

A primary obstacle is the fact that schools are created and maintained to deliver a service, not to facilitate comparisons of effectiveness among varying combinations of input variables or program characteristics (Airasian, 1974; House, 1973a; Riecken, 1976). The sanctity of local school control, coupled with fears of federal encroachment on this control, have made it virtually impossible for researchers to implement the large scale, random selection, and systematic treatment variation required for nationwide experiments of school effectiveness. Schools are ongoing enterprises with a complex array of concerns, orientations, and problems. For most school personnel, these take precedence over random allocation and systematic examination of the effectiveness of resources or facilities. The researcher, by the very nature of the task, questions the value of a particular school input or innovation. School personnel, as practitioners, tend to believe in what they are doing (Jackson, 1968; Good & Brophy, 1973).

The likelihood of meeting the conditions required for true experiments was potentially greater for evaluations of compensatory-program effectiveness. These programs were virtually nonexistent prior to 1960. When compensatory programs came into being they did so as an adjunct, or separate feature, of most traditional school programs. Thus, conducting true experiments to study the effectiveness of such programs appeared quite feasible, since no great intrusion into the day-to-day functioning of the regular school program was required. However, even with compensatory-education programs, the notion of local control was considered crucial; the choice of a particular program, its goals, methods, and clientele were left to the discretion of local authorities. Moreover, compensatory education quickly became a symbol for the war on poverty; the idea was simply too attractive and generated immediate national support. In the conflict between popular and political support for launching remedial-education programs (however poorly formulated) and the desire for systematic social experiments not necessarily in tune with the perceived needs of the clientele, there was little question which strategy would prevail (McDill et al., 1969; Moynihan, 1973; Rossi, 1972).

Intimately related to the realities of local control, political popularity, and the primacy of delivering services is the fact that not all variations in educational inputs and programs are perceived to be equally valuable. An experiment requires that the investigator randomly form groups and systematically provide different treatment to these groups. The fact that different groups receive different treatment—and that this treatment is determined by the experimenter's using random-selection techniques—is generally perceived by parents and school personnel as unfair (Rivlin, 1976). Parents may complain that the treatment tried in one school is better than the treatment tried in their child's school. Teachers may argue that they are more comfortable using an approach or facility different from the one arbitrarily imposed on them by an experimenter. It is reasonable to question whether it is right—or possible—to deny pupils or teachers a school resource they perceive as valuable simply becasue their names were not drawn out of a hat at the time when that resource was being allocated. Preconceptions about what are effective educational variables and strategies have made it difficult and of questionable ethical merit for researchers to engage in the systematic selection and manipulation of school inputs and programs for the purpose of performing true experiments.

A second major factor which has precluded the use of true experiments in school- and program-effectiveness studies is lack of knowledge about the critical variables in the educational process. Experiments are predicated upon treatment and control, which are in turn predicated upon knowledge of or strong hypotheses about variables that contribute to achievement. If the experimenter is to treat groups differently and observe the effects of this differential treatment on group performance, he or she must have a clear idea of which variables should make up the various treatments. Moreover, he or she must "know" the variables sufficiently well to control and manipulate them, not only in the particular setting of the experiment but in future replications of it.

Unfortunately, conceptualizations of the school variables which may affect pupil achievement have been so broad and inclusive that meaningful measurement and comparison of them has precluded the use of experiments. For example, in identifying the school inputs which might affect pupil achievement, Coleman (1966) compiled a list of 400 variables. The recently completed International Study of Educational Achievement (Comber & Keeves, 1973; Purves & Levine, 1975; Thorndike, 1973) measured more than 700 student, teacher, and school characteristics hypothesized to relate to pupil achievement (Burstein, 1976). The picture has not been much brighter for studies of compensatory-program effectiveness. Here, given local control and inclination, scores of different aims, emphases, orientations, methods, and materials have been proposed, singly and in combination, as important antecedents to increased pupil achievement (Averch et al., 1972; Bronfenbrenner, 1975; McDill et al., 1972).

A final factor which has frequently prevented the use of experiments in studies of school and program effectiveness is that as new innovations, strategies, and programs have become available in education, they have often been seized upon and implemented as though they were certain to be successful. In a sense, the public has been so bombarded by new programs and approaches, each more elaborate than its predecessor, that false expectations have been created. New programs or variables are often perceived as being good simply because they are new; for many, new is by definition better. It can be extremely difficult for educators and politicians to withstand pressure for making programs or innovations available to all who wish them (Airasian, 1977).

This has been particularly true with respect to Project Head Start and other compensatory-education programs. Initially, Head Start was to be an experimental program reaching a limited number of disadvantaged children. The idea was so politically and educationally attractive, however, that the program received immediate national support and quickly expanded into a nationwide program available to virtually all who wanted it. The attractiveness of the program, coupled with the perceived certainty that it would make substantial inroads into the problems of disadvantaged youngsters, led its supporters to place widespread availability above the need for systematic examination of program effectiveness.

Finally, in order to conduct experiments, there must be a sufficient commitment to experimental evidence to call upon the services of the experimenter before the treatments are implemented. Historically, a variety of political and educational motives associated with getting a program quickly into the field have taken precedence over the preplanning, random selection, and control required for experimental trials. Fast and broad implementation has been valued more than slower experimental approaches. The question of effectiveness most frequently has arisen after a program or innovation has already been underway and has failed to reach the optimistic expectations held for it at its inception. However, when the question of effectiveness is posed after widespread program adoption, a true experimental design is precluded. Therefore, although an experimental design is desirable because it permits causal inferences to be made, it is virtually unattainable as a practical strategy in large-scale school- and program-effectiveness studies.

APPROXIMATIONS TO EXPERIMENTS

As we have seen, a series of factors has limited the use of true experimental designs in studies of school- and compensatory-program effectiveness. In the place of experiments, researchers have turned to other strategies in an effort to identify the antecedents of pupil achievement. One of these strategies has been the quasi-experiment, which essentially represents an after-the-fact attempt to mirror a true experiment (Campbell & Stanley, 1963; Cook & Campbell, 1975). Generally this involves the comparison of nonrandomly selected groups or the identification of a control group after the treatment has been completed (Riecken & Boruch, 1974). Most conditions of a true experiment are satisfied, except for random selection of groups from a single population.

Quasi-experiments have been used most often in evaluations of compensatory-education programs. Although the initiation of such programs might have provided the opportunity for true experimentation, we have identified a number of reasons why this was not so. Freedom to devise programs locally resulted in a great variety of programs and objectives; the emphasis was on action, on problem solving, not on research; school personnel were reluctant to accept the constraints required for a true experimental evaluation if they were perceived to interfere with attempts to grapple with educational problems; evaluation findings might be threatening, since it was recognized that they could be used in political decisionmaking; and programs were launched so quickly and local expertise in evaluation and research were so limited that even if the will to experiment had been present, the opportunity and means to do so were not. In the circumstances, a quasi-experimental approach seemed the only viable alternative.

Unfortunately, a number of disadvantages associated with quasi-experiments conspire to reduce confidence in compensatory-education studies which have used this approach. Several problems arise from the inability of investigators to assign children at random to a treatment (intervention) or nontreatment group. In the absence of a control group constituted in this way, other procedures have been adopted to establish a criterion against which the performance of children in intervention programs might be assessed. For example, children from the same areas in which projects were implemented who had not taken part in the project were identified and used for the purpose of comparison. Since the most needy children were likeliest to have been enrolled in the program, the children remaining in the comparison group have usually been higher achievers than, and almost certainly different in other ways from, the program participants. The two groups are different from the outset: how, then, is e to interpret differences in performance between the two groups after the treatment of one of them? Are such differences related to program participation or are they a function of differences which predate the program?

The answer to these questions is complicated by the operation of statistical regression to the mean. When a group of low-scoring children is retested, there is a tendency for their mean score to increase from initial to final testing (Campbell & Erlebacher, 1970). This increase, a statistical artifact associated with the unreliability of test scores at low and high extremes of the score distribution, will occur regardless of a program's effect on participants. Thus, there will be a tendency for children in compensatory programs to show improvements on test scores independently of the program's impact.

The same tendency will occur in a control group. Unfortunately, if the characteristics of this group differ from those of the program participants, regression effects will differ for the two groups; scores will regress toward two different means, since in fact the groups have always had two different means (Campbell & Erlebacher, 1970).

Other techniques, such as analysis of covariance, are sometimes used to statistically equate groups which are known to differ. However this procedure does not entirely solve the problem of making comparisons between nonequivalent groups, since group differences typically are only partially removed; differences between groups on variables other than those covaried may continue to exist and influence test performance differences.

A procedure of matching children has been adopted in some evaluations of compensatory programs. For example, in Cicirelli's (1969) evaluation of Head Start programs, children who originally had been eligible to participate in the program were identified, and then those who originally had actually participated in a Head Start project were matched on the basis of age, gender, race, and socioeconomic status to eligible children who had not participated. The investigators tried to emulate a true experimental procedure by starting with a single population of children (those initially eligible for Head Start) and dividing these into two groups (participants and nonparticipants) in which characteristics of one group were matched to characteristics of the other. All of this, however, took place after the fact, after the program's termination. Hence, although participants were matched to nonparticipants on a number of variables, there was no way of knowing whether the two groups were similar on other variables not included among the matching criteria. For example, one important variable omitted in identifying the two groups was ability.

In evaluations in which no comparative group was available, other strategies have been adopted to assess the performance of program participants. In some cases, participants' performance is compared to the normative data provided by test publishers; this in effect, means that the sample used to standardize the test is used as a control group, with all the disadvantages that the practice implies. In cases where longitudinal data on program participants are available, effectiveness is often determined by inspecting "gain" or "change" scores from a pre-test to a post-test. However, the meaning of "change" scores has been seriously challenged "primarily because such scores are systematically related to any random error of measurement" (Cronbach & Furby, 1970).

In sum, quasi-experiments endeavor to approximate a true experimental strategy so that causal inferences about treatments may be made with confidence. However, in accommodating to the conditions in which they are carried out, quasi-experiments are confronted by methodological problems which weaken the inferences they engender. In particular, inability to constitute experimental and control groups by means of random selection and allocation raises problems in the interpretation of observed differences in the groups that are compared.

SURVEYS

In lieu of true experiments or approximations to them, an investigator may turn to survey research to examine the differential effects of schools and programs on student achievement. This in fact has been the most widely used technique in this area of investigation. It has been used in many studies of school systems, in the "Equality of Educational Opportunity" survey (Coleman et al., 1966) and in several smaller, non–policy-oriented investigations.

The survey is attractive because, unlike the experiment, it requires no prior random allocation of subjects to groups. Further, the situation as it exists is taken as the starting point of the investigation and the survey is designed to obtain information about that situation. Thus the researcher does not intervene in the situation being studied to control or to manipulate variables. Practically speaking, it is simpler to obtain a description of the functioning of a school than it is to adopt or change particular school practices. However, the inferences which can be made about relationships between variables observed in this way are correspondingly limited.

Surveys of school effectiveness have taken a variety of forms. They vary in the type of data they employ—the main distinction being between cross-sectional and longitudinal data—and in the extent to which adjustment is made for students' initial status. For example, in a longitudinal survey it may be possible to obtain a measure of students' performance before and after they have been exposed to a learning situation. In cross-sectional data, aptitude scores or a measure of socioeconomic background collected at the same time as the outcome data may be used as proxy data for initial status (cf. Marco, Murphy, & Quirk, 1976).

Some studies of school effectiveness in which longitudinal data are obtained are rather similar to some of the examples of compensatory-education evaluation which we considered in the previous section. The main way in which the studies considered in this section differ is not so much methodological, though the two types of study are characterized by rather different analytic procedures, as it is in terms of the problem investigated. In the previous section, we were primarily concerned with evaluations of compensatory programs; here our concern is with studies which relate school, teacher, and pupil input factors to pupil achievement in ongoing school systems.

Most of the investigations considered in this section make use of regression models in their data analyses. Regression is based on correlational data, and herein probably lies the major weakness of survey research: the presence of a correlation does not necessarily imply causation. The justification for interpreting a correlation causally has to be found outside the correlational data. Very often, the additional information required to support a causal inference is not available. This seems especially true as far as knowledge of schooling is concerned; in this context, Campbell and Stanley (1963) have made the point that in research on teaching, the causal interpretation of correlational data has been overdone rather than underdone.

To interpret changes in one variable as the cause of changes in another, it is necessary to satisfy three conditions (Cook & Campbell, 1975). First, temporal precedence of the causal factor to the observed effect must be demonstrated; the effect cannot be present prior to the application of the causal factor. Second, the causal factor must be related to, or correlate with, the observed effect. If the causal agent and presumed effect do not vary in concert with each other, one could not be the cause of the other. Third, there must be no plausible alternative explanation for the observed effect other than the causal factor.

The results of pupils' performance on standardized scholastic-achievement tests, administered as part of an ongoing testing program, have long been used for measuring the effectiveness of school systems. The traditional procedure has been to compare the performance of pupils in a system with a national average or norm; the discrepancy between the scores is considered a measure of the system's effectiveness. This approach, however, fails to take account of the pupils' entry characteristics or the conditions in which the educational endeavor is carried out (Dyer, Linn, & Patton, 1969).

In many cross-sectional surveys, the limit of knowledge is the correlation between two variables, with perhaps some supporting evidence from other sources. Correlations based on cross-sectional data cannot provide evidence of temporal precedence. Partly for this reason the need for gathering longitudinal data has been stressed by several commentators (Bowles & Levin, 1968b; Hanushek & Kain, 1972; Rivlin, 1971), and, indeed, the findings of school effectiveness studies based on such data have been found to differ considerably from findings based on cross-sectional data (Dyer, Linn, & Patton, 1969). Since the longitudinal approach obtains measures on the same set of students at different times, it would seem to possess a number of attractions which the cross-sectional approach does not share. First, some measures of students' initial status may be obtained so a base line is available to measure "growth" or "change." Second, the approach permits greater awareness of cumulative processes.

A number of procedures, which involve obtaining a measure of development or growth, have been suggested to provide indexes of school effectiveness from data collected in ongoing school testing programs (Dyer, Linn, & Patton, 1969; Hilton & Patrick, 1970). Data have also been gathered over time in a number of research studies. The most extensive and ambitious of these has been Project Talent (Flanagan & Cooley, 1966), data from which have been used a number of times to estimate school effectiveness (Jencks & Brown, 1975; Shaycroft, 1967). Studies of this nature have attempted to determine whether achievement in a school system was above or below expectation. Sometimes difference scores (posttest minus pretest) have been used, but more usually deviations between scores actually achieved and scores predicted from earlier performance are used. This involves regressing posttest scores on pretest scores and then calculating residuals. A number of variations are possible. In some studies, the school was used as the unit of analysis: mean scores were entered in regressions, and school residual scores calculated. In other studies, the individual was used as the unit of analysis; individual scores were regressed and individual residual scores estimated. While the different procedures yield indexes that are highly correlated, they are different enough to indicate that they do not assess effectiveness in the same way (Marco, 1974). And even within one method, the size of the deviation that one regards as significant can vary with the test of statistical significance used (Convey, 1977).

Apart from technical problems of this kind—which after a period of relative neglect have been receiving increasing attention in recent years—there are other hazards in using data which have been collected over time to examine school effectiveness. There is the problem of sample attrition; students move from one class to another, from one school to another. Indeed, if the student body is unstable, findings from longitudinal studies may be misleading (Marco, Murphy, & Quirk, 1976). This is so whether data are "matched" (only students for whom complete information is available are included) or "unmatched" (all students for whom measures were obtained at any point are included).

There is a further problem if the school is used as the unit of analysis in longitudinal studies. Although one of the method's attractions is that it makes cumulative processes visible, students within a school are not all exposed to the same environmental conditions. The possible effects of such variety may be lost, even in a longitudinal study, unless a unit less inclusive than the school is used.

In summary, because surveys are descriptive, involve no direct intervention into the situation being studied, and typically include a large number of variables, they are subject to a number of methodological problems. The following section will deal with the major problems in this area, particularly those arising from the Coleman Report.

Hazards in Survey Data Collection

Surveys are usually large-scale efforts and many factors which might contribute to their success or failure are far beyond the investigator's control.

A basic problem relates to the extent to which the sample responding represents the population of interest. In the Coleman study, the high proportion of school districts which refused outright to participate or did not return the mailed questionnaires has been a basis for criticism (Armor, 1972; Bowles & Levin, 1968b; Hanushek & Kain, 1972; Shea, 1976). Nonparticipation can arise for any number of reasons. Some districts in the Coleman study, notably large school districts such as Chicago and Los Angeles, refused to cooperate because they were afraid that the federal government would utilize the data to prove they were discriminating against minority students (Jencks, 1972b). In the end, complete data were received from only 60 percent of the schools in the original sample. Some investigators have attempted to analyze differences between responding and nonresponding schools to determine whether the data reported in "Equality of Educational Opportunity" are biased. While Jencks (1972b) concludes that no such bias exists, the point is still debated. It is clear that at least one characteristic—willingness to respond—differentiated responding and nonresponding schools.

Issues relating to data gathering and the preparation of data for analysis are likely to arise in large-scale surveys. Again, we may take examples relating to the Coleman study. Bowles and Levin (1968b) point out that in coding the data for analysis, missing data points were coded at the mean score of the individuals responding. A more accurate technique, they argue, would have been to establish a separate category for nonresponses. Further, information provided by the superintendents, principals, teachers, and students surveyed may not have been accurate (Bowles & Levin, 1968b; Jencks, 1972b; Mosteller & Moynihan, 1972). Children, especially those in primary grades, who were asked to report on such matters as "father's education" had high rates of nonresponse (50 percent for first graders). The accuracy of the information supplied by students who did respond may therefore well be questioned. What one may infer from this criticism is that research conducted on a large scale in the real-world school setting is likely to encounter numerous handicaps which can affect the quality of the samples studied and the data gathered. It is unreasonable to expect ideal data-collection procedures and perfectly representative samples from studies which rely upon the cooperation and methodological sophistication of local school personnel who see rendering instructional services or bureaucratic control as more important than the demand of any research methodology (Airasian, 1974). When studies are conducted at a national level, the difficulties inherent in a single school or school district are compounded many times over. It seems very unlikely that any large-scale study of school effectiveness would end up with a perfect data set.

Interpreting Data: Between- and Within-School Variance

A not unusual way to examine school-effectiveness data is to separate variance on a criterion measure of achievement into within-school and between-school components. The within-school component is a measure of the extent to which individual students differ from the average student in their school; the between-school component is a measure of the extent to which school averages differ from the mean score for the total sample. It is argued that the between-school component provides some index of the differential effectiveness of schools, since if between-school variance in achievement did not exist, there would be no point in looking for possible effects of different schools on achievement. Furthermore, since factors other than school characteristics can contribute to between-school variance, "variation in achievement that exists between schools represents an upper limit to the effect of factors that distinguish one school from another in its ability to produce achievement" (Coleman, 1966, p. 295).

Here we may recall that Coleman was concerned with input differences between schools and how these differences related to pupil achievement. As a consequence, his focus was on between-school variance, not variance associated with differences among pupils within a school. This latter component of variance was treated as unsystematic or "error" variance in his analyses.

When variance in achievement between schools is compared with variance within schools, the within-school component is normally larger. Thus, if schools are defined as effective only if large proportions of between-school variance are observed, then studies to date would indicate that schools are not very effective.

However, this conclusion may not be warranted. Take, for example, the case in which children entering one school differ very much at the time of entry from children entering another school. Suppose also that both schools have a uniform effect upon their pupils so that the initial differences among the pupils attending particular schools are mirrored in the pupils' achievement-test performance. Large proportions of between-school variance will be observed in this situation. However, the observed between-school variation is largely attributable to differences between the types of pupils who attend different schools, not to school-specific factors. Thus, the magnitude of the between-school variance observed is not in itself a sufficient indicator of differential school effectiveness.

Or let us suppose that different types of pupils attend different schools, but that some schools are more successful than others in bringing about pupil changes; suppose further that the successful schools are the ones with the lower-achieving entering pupils. A measurement of pupils in these schools would produce small amounts of between-school variance, since some schools have been successful in overcoming the entering handicaps of the poorest potential achievers. The lower-achieving entering pupils had caught up with the initially higher-achieving ones and in the process had reduced achievement variance between schools. Schools would have had an effect in this situation, but a definition of school effectiveness based on proportions of between-school variance would not have detected it.

The division of variance into within- and between-school components also fails to take cognizance of the fact that within most schools, students, even at the same age level, are grouped in one way or another—into groups within a class (reading groups) and into classes or tracks (college preparatory, business, general). It is naive to think that all groups are treated in the same way. Clearly, each group had different teachers, may follow different curricula, and may also receive differential amounts of the school's physical resources (library, laboratories, etc.). Using a single estimate to describe the performance of all students in a school—a mean or an estimate of within-school variance—scarcely does justice to this situation.

There is the further point that individual students and schools interact in a highly complex and dynamic way:

> Children and teachers are not disembodied intelligences, not instructing machines and learning machines, but whole human beings tied together in a complex maze of social interconnections. The school is a social world because human beings live in it (Waller, 1932, p. 1).

There is a wide range of individual differences between students entering school; in their readiness to learn, in their motivation to learn, and in their learning aptitude. If one accepts Carroll's (1963) view of aptitude as the amount of time required by the learner to attain mastery of a learning task, and if one assumes this aptitude is more or less normally distributed, then a measure of achievement at any single time is likely to show considerable variance within a class. Apart from individual differences in students' cognitive and motivational characteristics, the environment of school and classroom, including peer and teacher interaction, may all affect students in a highly idiosyncratic way. Because students interact differentially with school characteristics throughout their school life, it would be surprising if the variance within schools—or within classes, for that matter—on almost any outcome measure were not found to be large. But it is not justifiable to conclude that such variance is independent of the effects of the school environment on the individual students in it. Rather, it seems more reasonable to conclude that at least some within-school variance should be attributed to the effects which schools have had on individual students.

In mentioning the need to consider the possibility that differences in achievement exist between classes in a school, we are raising the issue of the appropriateness of using the school as the unit of analysis, as has been the case in most school-effectiveness studies (cf. Burstein, 1976). It has been shown that when correlation analysis is used, correlations based on within-aggregate, between-aggregate and total-group aggregate can vary considerably. When correlations based on units within a group (e.g., classrooms within a school) differ greatly, correlation analyses at a total group level may have limited usefulness (Knapp, 1977). Likewise, when the variances of definable groups within an aggregate (such as classes within a school) are heterogeneous, variance estimates calculated for a total school group may fail to reveal information that would be of considerable value in assessing school effectiveness.

A number of investigators have taken up this issue and proceeded to divide the within-school component of variance into between-class and within-class components. Rakow, Airasian, and Madaus (1978) analyzed eighth, tenth and twelfth grade data in mathematics collected in the IEA study and found that considerable components of variance traditionally defined as within-school variance were, in fact, associated with differences between classes. Similarly, in studies carried out in Ireland at both elementary and high school levels, using standardized tests and examinations geared to specific syllabi, considerable portions of within-school variance—as high as 73 percent—were found to be more correctly assigned to between-class differences than to individual variation (Kellaghan, Madaus, & Rakow, 1979; Madaus, Kellaghan, & Rakow, 1976; Martin & Kellaghan, 1977).

If the existence of between-unit variance is accepted as evidence of the unit's differential effects, then these findings provide strong evidence of the differential effects of classes within schools. Certainly, they indicate that the existence of large amounts of within-school variance cannot automatically be attributed to individual differences between students or to error and therefore interpreted to indicate the absence of school effectiveness. Taken in conjunction with our other comments on the interpretation of components of variance as indices of school effectiveness, these findings suggest caution in interpreting studies which make a too-ready translation of estimates of variance components into statements about school effectiveness.

Regression

Regression has been the statistical model most frequently used in school-effectiveness studies. We will discuss problems in the use of the model to represent the functioning of schools and present a series of specific procedural problems associated with the use of the model.

Regression attempts to analyze the collective and separate contributions of two or more predictor or input variables (e.g., school resources) to the variation in a dependent, criterion, or outcome measure (e.g., school achievement) (cf. Cohen & Cohen, 1975; Kerlinger & Pedhazur, 1973). The variation in the outcome measure can be separated into three parts: that which can be attributed to the predictor variables individually, that which can be attributed to the predictor variables as a group, and residual variance unexplained by the regression. The first two parts comprise the total amount of variation explained by the regression (Wisler, 1974). Coleman (1966), for example, having examined between- and within-school variance in achievement measures, attempted to predict achievement variance from information about the home and school characteristics of students.

$$Y^1 = a + b_1 x_1 + b_2 x_2 + \ldots + b_k x_k + e$$

The general regression equation for any number of variables is shown above: Y^1 is the predicted score, a is an intercept constant, b is a regression coefficient or weight, x is the score on an independent or predictor variable, and e is error, or that portion of Y^1 which cannot be explained in terms of the independent variables (cf. Kerlinger & Pedhazur, 1973). Combinations or blocks of independent variables may be used in place of single variables; in the Coleman survey, this was in fact the case. Thus for example, x_1 would represent a block of variables representing the student's home background; x_2, the student body block, x_3, the school facilities block, and x_4, the teacher characteristics block. Coleman's task was to determine the contribution of each of the four blocks to the explanation of achievement variance.

The use of a regression model to represent the operations of school makes certain assumptions about how the variables represented in regression equations are related. Basic assumptions refer to additivity and linearity. Additivity assumes that a student's achievement may be determined by a simple summing of the contributions of home background, school facilities, peer influences, and teacher characteristics. If the simple additive models holds, the value of a predicted measure (e.g. achievement) should not alter if a decrease in the value of one predictor term is compensated for by an increase of similar value in another. For example, a decrease in the predictor variables of three home "units" could be compensated for by an increase of three school "units." It may be that compensatory action for the disadvantaged which attempted to compensate for deficits in the home by increasing resources in the school was based on the assumption that home and school variables contributed to achievement in an additive fashion. However, it is unlikely that the factors that affect achievement act in this way.

Linearity assumes that the relation between pairs of variables can be represented by linear functions; that is, an increase in one variable leads to a corresponding increase in another. Thus if the relation between variables is interactive, curvilinear, or of a threshold nature, the linear regression model will misrepresent it unless one includes special terms in the regression model to represent these relations, which is rarely done.

We have reason to believe that the assumption of linearity does not hold, at least in the case of some school variables. For example, teaching experience may not be linearly related to effectiveness. It may be that a teacher requires a certain amount of experience to reach his or her highest level of effectiveness, but that after a period of time, effectiveness begins to deteriorate (Armor, 1972; Spady, 1973). Thus the relation between teaching experience and effectiveness would be curvilinear rather than linear.

The effect of other variables on achievement may be of an asymptotic nature. The presence of a given amount of a resource (for example, certain equipment or books) may have a positive effect on student achievement, but the addition of units beyond a particular amount may have no further effect. Treating such a variable as linearly related to achievement would again misrepresent the true situation.

Another basic assumption in the use of the regression model is that one can specify the direction of relations between variables at least between independent and dependent variables; otherwise one could not decide which variables should be designated dependent and which independent. However, the direction of relations is not always clear in studies of schooling. Problems in the specification of causal relationships are exemplified by Coleman specifying a verbal-ability measure as a measure of school outcome. Is verbal ability a result of schooling, and so correctly regarded as a dependent variable; or is it a cause of school achievement, in which case it should be regarded as an independent variable? Or is it both? Many research studies use a verbal-ability or intelligence measure to predict attainment, and teachers, in general, would seem to be in agreement with this interpretation. However, the relation between verbal ability and school achievement may be more complex; empirical evidence indicates that the direction of causality may not be consistent or clear-cut for all samples of individuals (Crano, Kenny, & Campbell, 1972; Kellaghan, 1973).

Again, is "attitude to school" something a student brings to school and which contributes to achievement, or is it a result of the student's experience of schooling, including past achievements? Or is it one thing for one student, and something else for another?

Regression analyses cannot decide matters like this; the decision has to be made before the analyses are carried out. The decision that is made can have serious implications for the interpretation of findings. It is salutary to bear in mind that not enough is known about schooling to be able to posit the direction of relations among many of the variables which have been used in school-effectiveness studies.

Multicollinearity

Another problem in the use of regression analysis arises when one is dealing with a large number of independent variables which are highly intercorrelated. The term *multicollinearity* has been used to describe this situation. An examination of the correlation matrices derived from school-effectiveness studies makes very clear that variables used in the studies typically exhibit such collinearity (Mood, 1971).

High collinearity, unfortunately, has the effect that one obtains high standard errors in one's regression coefficients; furthermore, minor changes in the pattern of intercorrelations can result in major changes in coefficient magnitude (Bowles & Levin 1968a; Pedhazur, 1975). It is also difficult to interpret the import of observed relationships.

Two issues have received attention in this context. One concerns procedures to group kindred variables into blocks; the other concerns the order of the entry of the variables into the analysis. The problem of grouping has been dealt with in several studies by the establishment of sets or blocks of variables; each block is made up of a set of variables which are perceived as conceptually similar to one another and conceptually distinguishable from variables included in other sets. Conceptual appropriateness is a basic prerequisite for inclusion in a block. In addition, the empirical relations between variables are usually taken into account. This involves the screening of input variables on the basis of their partial correlations with outcome variables; input variables are retained insofar as they have significant partial correlation coefficients with a given number of outcome variables.

In general, blocks have been constructed to represent home background factors on the one hand and school factors on the other. Further specification has varied from study to study. For example, the IEA studies used four blocks: home and student background, school placement variables (type of school and type of program), recent school treatment or learning conditions (instructional or quasi-instructional variables), and personal attributes (Thorndike, 1973). Coleman (1966), who also used four blocks, constituted them somewhat differently: home background, student-body characteristics, school facilities and curriculum, and teacher characteristics.

Blocking has certain obvious attractions. Methodologically, the handling of a very large number of variables in a single analysis may be extremely cumbersome, if not impossible. Conceptually, too, there are attractions. It is easier to think in terms of broad categories of variables which represent the home or the school than it is to think in terms of a multiplicity of variables, each of which may represent a very restricted sphere, but which at the same time are known to be related. Blocking becomes necessary when a partitioning of variance is planned, since a large number of variables will result in a proliferation of higher-order commonalities. For example, Pedhazur (1975) has pointed out that the use of four independent variables (or blocks) gives rise to fifteen elements; four are unique, six are second order, four are third order, and one is fourth order. The interpretation of higher-order elements can be little more than guesswork.

The disadvantages of blocking, however, should also be borne in mind when evaluating school-effectiveness studies. First, there is the possibility of error in assigning variables to blocks; this is obvious when dealing with variables that are highly intercorrelated. Second, the fact that clusters of variables are entered into analyses creates problems in identifying the effects of specific individual variables (Spady, 1973). Third, the statistical screening of variables for inclusion in blocks makes use of stepwise regression analysis to achieve maximum prediction with a minimum of variables. However, if the investigator is concerned with the explanation of phenomena related to school effectiveness, rather than mere prediction, he or she may be left with a situation in which important explanatory variables have been screened out of the analysis. Finally, the use of blocks limits one to a variance-partitioning analysis, since unless one derives an overall single measure for a block (for example, a factor score), it is not possible to obtain regression coefficients (Pedhazur, 1975).

Once blocks are established, the next decision concerns the order in which the blocks will be entered into final analyses in which the relation between the blocks and a measure of school output will be estimated. In regression analysis, the first independent variable entered in the equation contains all the variance which that variable can explain in the dependent variable, regardless of what common contribution that variable or block shares with other variables or blocks subsequently admitted to the equation. In other words, it contains variance which overlaps with all other input variables or blocks with which it is correlated. Each additional variable or block which is added likewise preempts the variance it has in common with subsequently entered variables or blocks. Only the last variable or block contributes uniquely to the explained variance.

The major analytic problem in using regression analysis in educational policy-related studies is how to separate the part of the variation in achievement due to variation in school resources from the parts due to variation in students' backgrounds or peer-group influences. In investigations such as those carried out by the IEA (Comber & Keeves, 1973) and by Coleman (1966), the problem was solved by assuming a causal model for relationships between the blocks. Coleman argued that

> . . . since the student's background is clearly prior to, and independent of, any influence from school factors, these background factors can and should be held constant in studying the effects of school variables. Thus the variation in achievement and attitudes to be explained by school is that left after variation explained by family background differences is taken out. (Coleman et al., 1966, p. 330)

Each block is added in turn (there is some variation in the order of entry of the school blocks) and as many variables within a block as add to prediction at a specified significance level are included. The independent variables are treated as if their effect were additive; achievement is determined by adding the effects of school variables (facilities, curriculum, and teachers) to the effect of background experiences.

This procedure is justified if home factors are, in fact, independent of school resources and facilities; if no relation exists between home background and school variables. However, it is unlikely that the home background children experience is unrelated to the types and quality of resources they will find available to them in school. The quality of school resources, whether teacher, peer, or facility characteristics, vary with the class background of the neighborhood or community. Thus, pupils' home backgrounds tend not to be independent of school factors, but rather are reflected in the quality, cost, and quantity of the resources available in the schools pupils attend. There is, in essence, an overlap or relation between home and school input variables (Hanushek & Kain, 1972, Madaus, Kellaghan, & Rakow, 1975; Mayeske et al., 1972).

When blocks are related, the home block, since it was entered first in the regression, will contain not only all the variance it uniquely accounts for in pupil achievement but also the variance it shares with other blocks. Thus the family background block is assigned the explanatory power which it possesses uniquely and the explanatory power it shares with other blocks. The school blocks, on the other hand, are assigned none of the variance in achievement for which they account jointly with family background. It has been argued that the end result is in an overestimation of the effect of home background factors on achievement and an underestimation of the effect of school-based factors (Bowles & Levin, 1968b; Hanushek & Kain, 1972; Michelson, 1970; Wiley, 1976).

The adequacy of the partitioning approach we have been considering depends on the purpose of the investigation and the inferences that one wishes to draw from the data. For some purposes, a form of asymmetric variance decomposition may be appropriate, though there are certain inferences which the technique does not permit. For example, Coleman (1975a) points out that the procedure does not permit the kind of inference made in the IEA studies about the relative effects of home and school variables. The Coleman (1966) study, though it used the same basic analytical procedure, focused on the relative size of the effects of different school variables, rather than on the relative size of home and school variables—though it is this latter point that has often been emphasized in subsequent discussions of the report. If one confines oneself to an examination of the effects of school variables in the Coleman data, the limitations of asymmetric variance decomposition are not so serious, since various orders of entry of the school variables were used.

To overcome problems associated with techniques of asymmetric variance decomposition, a method of symmetric variance decomposition has been suggested (Beaton, 1973, 1974; Mayeske et al., 1972; Wisler 1974). The method has been used in the reanalyses of the Coleman data carried out by Mayeske and his colleagues (Mayeske, et al., 1972, 1973; Mayeske & Beaton, 1975). Its purpose is to partition "explainable variance in a dependent variable into the portions attributable to each independent variable and to all combinations of independent variables in order that we may better understand the interactions of predictors in estimating the criteria" (Beaton, 1974, p. 63). A major virtue of symmetric variance decomposition is that the partitioning of variance is not dependent on the order in which variables are entered. Thus, for example no *a priori* decision is taken to assign to the home variance which is jointly attributable to home and school factors. Specifically, this kind of analysis allows the expression of the overlap between blocks of independent variables in explaining variance in the dependent variable. The squared multiple correlation is broken into elements which are assigned to each individual regressor and to each possible combination of regressors (Beaton, 1973). The commonality of background and school factors can be expressed as the squared multiple correlation (R^2) of the background and school factors combined, minus the unique variance explained by each of these factors. Given the reality of the relation between home and school variables, such a procedure seems preferable to one that assumes that home factors only operate prior to schooling and do not continue to interact with school factors when the child goes to school.

A number of reservations have been expressed about the use of symmetric variance decomposition. Wiley (1976), for example, notes that the technique does not solve the basic problem of high collinearity among the input variables. Since the various home and school variables are highly correlated, it is not possible to arrive at an unambiguous interpretation of the importance of particular variables.

There is in fact a danger, as indeed exists when other forms of analysis are used, that unjustified causal inferences will be made because of limitations of the analysis employed. Since commonality is based on regression analysis, it shares the problems associated with that technique. For example, the addition or deletion of variables can easily change unique and common values. Commonalities, in particular, should be interpreted with caution. Higher-order ones, according to Pedhazur (1975), will almost always elude explanation.

It may seem appealing at times to draw inferences from commonality data about interactions. After all, the high commonalities between home and school factors which a number of studies have reported would seem to confirm our everyday observations that school and home interact in a dynamic way. Home background continues to exercise an influence throughout the student's school career. The school in turn may affect the student's work habits, attitudes, and aspirations. While all of this appears reasonable, high commonality values cannot automatically be accepted as providing confirmation for it. A commonality of itself, when used in a nonexperimental design, cannot unambiguously be interpreted as an interaction. Several other possible relations may be represented by it: one set of variables may be the cause of the other or both may share a common cause. As holds true for any method of analysis, findings must always be interpreted in the light of other information about the phenomena under investigation.

CONCLUSION

In this overview of the strategies which have been used most frequently in the analysis of school effects, we have raised several issues. First was the consideration of the type of questions about school and program effectiveness which studies were designed to answer. We saw that few studies provide evidence on the absolute effects of schooling, that is, the effects that schooling, as opposed to no schooling, have on pupils. Recent large-scale studies of school effectiveness speak to the differential effects of schools and school programs rather than to the effects of schooling per se. From these, all we can get is some indication of the effect on pupil achievement of differing quantities and qualities of such inputs as physical resources, faculty qualifications and program characteristics.

We also considered three approaches to investigating school and program effectiveness—experiments, approximations to experiments, and surveys. Problems relating to the real-life world in which studies are carried out arise when one attempts to impose the control on ongoing school situations that are required in the use of the experimental approach.

The survey seems more manageable and thus more attractive, as its frequent use suggests. However, its relative manageability should not obscure its shortcomings. A survey that is cross-sectional, for example, cannot tell much about how the past characteristics of a system affect the present behavior of students. Neither can it tell how factors that are not present in the system might affect it if they were to be introduced in the future.

There are also many methodological problems associated with current school-effectiveness assessment procedures which use the survey approach, whether cross-sectional or longitudinal. These refer to the model of schooling implied by the use of certain analytic techniques, particularly regression, as well as problems relating to the handling of large numbers of correlated variables. While these problems are becoming more explicit and attempts are being made to develop more acceptable procedures to deal with them, much still remains to be done in this area.

In the light of the problems associated with survey research, one may be tempted to suggest that greater efforts should be made to carry out true experiments in schools. In theory, there can be little doubt that such a course of action would be desirable. However, it seems that experimentation in any critical areas of schooling will have to await not only the development of better research tools, but also a realization among policymakers, school personnel, and the general public that our present knowledge of schooling is inadequate and that that inadequacy should be remedied. While this is happening, students of education might give more time than they have in the past to the development of their understanding of the workings of schools. The availability of better theories of schooling and of theoretically, as well as empirically, based hypotheses on the role of variables in the school context would mean that future researchers would not have to operate in the largely theoretical vacuum in which the strategies which we have considered in this chapter have been employed.

chapter 4

School Inputs, Processes, and Resources

INTRODUCTION

Despite the many problems associated with using the production model of inputs and outputs to conceptualize schooling, the "Equality of Educational Opportunity" survey, as well as several other important school-effectiveness studies, nonetheless considered the school in such terms. As a consequence, the language of much of the ensuing debate over the inferences drawn from these studies has been couched in terms of the relation, or lack thereof, between inputs to school and outputs of schooling. While we are not happy with using what is essentially production-model language to describe schooling, we shall for convenience retain the terms *inputs* and *outputs* in this chapter. We shall use *inputs* to describe the resources (fiscal, physical, individual, and instructional) associated with schooling, and *outputs* and *outcomes* interchangeably to describe school achievement, that complex result of the interaction between the learning experiences provided and the pupil's reaction to those experiences.

We shall address three general areas in this chapter. First, we shall examine the nature of input variables used to characterize schools and programs in effectiveness studies. Second, we shall describe a range of problems associated with the selection and measurement of input variables. Finally, we shall provide a brief overview of research findings on the relation between input variables and student achievement.

INPUTS

Inputs and outputs can receive different emphases by people examining the functioning of schools. For example, some have focused primarily on outputs, as in the evaluation approach (Averch et al., 1972) exemplified in many studies of compensatory education. Others have looked exclusively at inputs, as was often the case when government commissions in Europe or regional accrediting groups in the United States examined educational systems (Kellaghan, 1977a).

Some commentators using the term *inputs* have attempted to make a further distinction between inputs as resources applied to students from outside the school (e.g., expenditure, physical plant and teacher characteristics) and processes within the school, "the process by which the resources are applied to the students and the response of the students to the process" (Averch et al., 1972, p. 6). For the former type of variable, the school is regarded as a "black box" and no attention is paid to what is actually going on inside it; the latter type of variable, on the other hand, is intimately concerned with activities in the box.

While the distinction may be of some value in categorizing research studies, it does not seem to be particularly useful in attempting to assess the factors that may contribute to school effectiveness. An obvious disadvantage is the conceptual difficulty of assigning variables to an extraschool status ("input") or to an in-school status ("process"). Are such variables as "amount of homework," "tracking," "proportion of slow-learners," "proportion of students who have read more than sixteen books," "proportion of students who are members of a debating club"— all variables used in the "Equality of Educational Opportunity" study— to be regarded as in-school or out-of-school variables? If one accepts the distinction, they will be regarded as out-of-school variables. And how is one to regard students? Are they inputs? In particular, what does one say of student intelligence and motivation, significant variables omitted from the "Equality of Educational Opportunity" survey?

Since it is extremely difficult to draw a clear line between physical facilities, personal characteristics (of students and teachers), and what actually goes on in schools, in this chapter we shall regard all of these as input. The decision was not made simply to avoid the task of attempting to draw difficult conceptual distinctions. There was the additional consideration that focusing on one type of variable might result in neglecting more important ones. Indeed, part of the problem of previous school-effectiveness studies is that their preoccupation with variables which were relatively easily measured and which could be relatively easily manipulated by policymakers may have resulted in failing to identify variables which contribute most to the attainment of the objectives of schooling. Besides, given the complexity of schooling, one might expect interaction between variables inside and outside the school, and between variables traditionally regarded as status and process.

Considering, as we do in this chapter, a number of conceptual and methodological issues relating to input variables in studies of school and program effectiveness, it is well to bear in mind that a discussion of input variables on their own introduces a rather artificial distinction. The adequacy of inputs cannot really be considered in isolation. Inputs are judged to be relevant or irrelevant only in the context of the outputs they are presumed to affect (Guttman, 1969). The situation is made somewhat easier for us by the fact that most school-effectiveness studies have employed norm-referenced standardized measures of scholastic achievement or verbal ability as their measure of school output. Less frequently, other measures, such as students' aspirations and plans and postschool destination, have been used. We shall also refer to measures of scholastic achievement which differ from traditional standardized ones. For the most part, and unless otherwise stated, the outcome measures matched to the inputs we consider in this chapter will be norm-referenced standardized tests.

In considering the results of studies of school and program effectiveness, we should be alert to the fact that the failure to find a strong relation between inputs and output measures does not necessarily imply a criticism of the choice of input variables. It may be that the inputs chosen are strongly related to some other, unmeasured outputs. Schooling outcomes are many and extend far beyond the types of skills and abilities measured on the standardized achievement and ability tests that have been used in virtually every study of school and program effectiveness. If we find, for example, that there is no relation between class size and pupils' measured achievement or ability, this does not mean that class size is an unimportant educational variable. It simply means that class size and standardized-test performance are not highly related to one another. Class size may be related to other school outcomes, such as social development or dropout rate.

Moreover, we must be careful not to single out the input variables as the primary cause of the disappointing finding of school- and program-effectiveness studies, for the problem may lie not with the inputs but with the measures of school output used. This theme will be explored in detail in succeeding chapters; suffice it to say that inferences about the effects of schooling on adult occupational opportunities have been shown to be a function of the measure of adult occupational success employed (A. Schwartz, 1976). Thus, Jencks et al. (1972) found no relation between educational factors and occupational success as measured by income. Blau and Duncan (1967), on the other hand, defined occupational success in terms of the perceived status of the occupation an individual engaged in. Using this criterion, they found a high correlation between education and success. Clearly, varying the outcome measure can result in different inferences about the effectiveness of school resources (cf. Shea, 1976).

Schools are complicated institutions with a variety of intended purposes. A given school or program input is potentially related to many outcomes, only a few of which have been measured. The conclusion that school or program input variables have little effect on pupils' standardized-test performance does not mean that such variables may not be important for attaining other outcomes. It may be that class size, remedial teachers, and new texbooks are important educational inputs for heretofore unmeasured outputs. We really know very little more about this after publication of studies of school and program effectiveness than we did before. The critical point is that the validity or importance of particular school and program inputs should not be determined on an absolute basis, but rather in relation to the particular school output measure they were used to predict.

Choice Of Input Variables

As a starting point in considering the input variables studied in school- and program-effectiveness research, it is reasonable to inquire what prompted their selection in the first place. In answering this question, one is quickly confronted with the fact that the rationale underlying the selection of input variables for studies of differential school effectiveness is somewhat different than the rationale which guided the selection of inputs for the evaluation of compensatory-education programs. In the former case, the inclusion of information on physical and structural characteristics of schools seemed dominant; in the latter, greater consideration was given to the nature of the curricular offerings associated with various programs.

In retrospect, it might seem that the variables used in "Equality of Educational Opportunity" were poorly chosen. After all, it would seem that a cursory review of prior school-effectiveness studies would not have led to any great confidence that the measures of school resources and facilities which were chosen would be found to be closely related to attainment as measured by standardized tests. The input variables are not readily classified. They cover home background status characteristics (parental occupation, family size, and possessions such as television sets and automobiles) as well as variables on parental interest as perceived by the pupil (how much the student talked with parents about school). A large number of items relate to school and teacher characteristics. Information on schools was obtained on such factors as curriculum comprehensiveness, extracurricular activities, science and library facilities, age of texts in use, number of days in session, length of academic day, and expenditure. For teachers, information was obtained on their backgrounds (including socioeconomic status, academic degrees, experience), verbal ability, perceptions of student and school quality, preferences (for example, as to type of students), and salary. Student-body characteristics assessed were the extent of problem behavior in the school (property destruction, stealing, drinking), dropout rate, and aspects of academic environment (inferred from numbers going to college, overall grade average in school, interest in school, and reading). Such variables are generally interpreted as representing status characteristics of the school (Averch et al., 1972) rather than as processes which operate within the school. However, some of the variables, particularly those relating to student activity, can hardly be said to fit readily into a status category.

It is clear that many of these variables had been used in prior research on school effectiveness. The Coleman survey does not review such studies. Why were these variables chosen? We suggest three reasons. First, the study was intended to describe the status of schools attended by various racial and ethnic groups in the United States. Because it was a survey and because of its scope and size, the researchers were subject to certain constraints in selecting variables for study and in choosing methods of gathering data about these variables. The sheer magnitude of the study meant that input and output data had to be collected in comparatively easy ways. The researchers could not visit every school, observe each teacher, and record the physical, cognitive, and affective performances of each pupil. In the end, mailed questionnaires were used to gather the bulk of data about school, teacher, and student inputs. The teacher questionnaire contained more than seventy questions dealing with professional training, experience, type of school and pupil preferred, and problems existing in the school. A thirty-item vocabulary test designed to measure teachers' verbal ability was also included in the teacher questionnaire. The bulk of information about school resources and facilities was obtained from the principal questionnaire, which asked questions about facilities, staff, program, curriculum, racial composition, and other school characteristics. Superintendents provided additional information about the school system itself and system expenditures. Student questionnaires obtained information on student's home background as well as attitudes toward school, race relations, and life in general.

For the most part, the questionnaires captured information about the status of the resources and facilities existing in a sample of American schools. While information on school size, age, and expenditure is relatively easily obtained (although as we shall see this ease sometimes results in the information lacking validity), it is considerably more difficult to appraise more process-oriented school and teacher variables such as teaching style, grouping strategies, and the like. Also, the accuracy of the latter type of data, had it been based upon observation and impressionistic interpretations, might have been highly suspect. Obviously, it was much simpler to obtain descriptions of the status of pupils, teachers, resources, and facilities in the schools than to characterize processes and interactions within schools.

A second reason for Coleman's choice of variables was that, since the study was carried out in the context of possible government policy formation, the input variables chosen would have to be amenable to manipulation by policymakers. Schools which had less of a resource that might relate to pupil achievement could be given more of that resource in the expectation that student achievement would increase. The ability to intervene and change input variables that appeared related to pupil performance was thus a consideration in the selection of the school resources and facilities to be studied (Coleman, 1975a). It may be interesting to know, for example, that teacher's personality characteristics or classroom management techniques are highly related to pupils' achievement test performance. However, even with such knowledge, how one would proceed to bring about basic and nationwide changes in such teacher characteristics is unknown. On the other hand, if differences in pupil achievement were found to be associated with manipulable inputs such as per-pupil expenditure, age of textbooks, or class size, policymakers would have had a fairly straightforward strategy for attacking the problem of improving pupil achievement.

Third, it was generally believed that financial and other status variables of the kind employed by Coleman *were* indeed important determinants of educational achievement. This belief seems to have been based largely on the knowledge that standards of attainment varied throughout the country; northern students did better than southern ones, and white students did better than black ones. Results from school districts that administered standardized tests documented these regional and racial differences in attainment. It was also known that expenditure on education varied in a similar fashion. For example, Armor (1972) reports that mean per-pupil expenditure for teachers' salaries in metropolitan Middle Atlantic schools with mainly white students was $284, while in predominantly black schools in the South it was $163. The observed covariation of expenditure and educational attainment led to the conclusion that level of attainment was a function of expenditure. This, in turn, led to a further relatively simplistic inference: that if expenditure were increased, the level of attainment of pupils would be raised.

This line of thinking received support from a number of studies of black migration from the South to the North. Klineberg (1935), for example, examined the relation between test scores of southern-born blacks who had emigrated to the North and their length of residence in the North and found a positive relation. Lee (1951) showed that on entering Philadelphia schools, southern-born black children scored lower on intelligence tests than children born locally. However, the southern-born children showed consistent year-to-year increases in mean IQ scores, while the local-born ones did not. Findings such as these were attributed not only to a generally more stimulating northern environment, but also to the better quality of school in the North.

A basic problem in accepting data from school districts as evidence that higher attainment is a function of "better" schools and, in particular, of expenditure on schools, was that the covariation of expenditure and other factors that might contribute to attainment was ignored, particularly such factors as pupils' entry level of ability and attainment and the quality of out-of-school support provided by parents or the community during the school years. Many studies have shown that major forces associated with educational attainment are to be found within the children's home. This finding applies to disadvantaged as well as to more general populations (Kellaghan, 1977b). Wiseman (1967) claims that "home" variables should be assigned nearly twice the weight of "neighborhood" and "school" variables in accounting for attainment. Peaker (1967) goes further and identifies parental attitudes (inferred from the initiative shown by parents in involving themselves in their children's education, as evidenced by assisting in homework and visiting the school) as an important component in the home environment. Variation in such attitudes, he points out, can account for more of the variation in children's school achievement than can either the variation in home circumstances (physical amenities of the home, parents' occupation and income, family size) or variation in schools (school size, staff experience, competence of teachers as assessed by inspectors).

It was perhaps findings such as this that led Coleman to control stringently for home factors in the analyses of his survey data. This was achieved by entering home factors in regression analyses prior to school-based ones in predicting standardized-test performance. This strategy, however, excluded the possibility of demonstrating the effects of interactions between school and home—interactions that may well be more important than the unique effects of either the home or the school (cf. Mayeske et al., 1972).

The variables studied in the evaluation of the effectiveness of compensatory education for disadvantaged children differed in many respects from those used in surveys of school effectiveness. It may be that investigators regarded many of the variables used in the latter as irrelevant in dealing with compensatory education, particularly during early childhood. School and home conditions could be considered as more homogeneous in programs for the disadvantaged; variables such as laboratory and library facilities would have less relevance in early-childhood education. More basically, however, compensatory programs were thought of primarily as action and development enterprises; thus research relating to them was carried out less in the context of input-output studies than in the tradition of the evaluative approach, which attempts "to analyze the effectiveness of broad educational interventions that are directly related to large issues of social policy" (Averch et al., 1972, p. 9).

During the 1960s, when compensatory education was introduced on a large scale, emphasis on the flexibility of development in early childhood and the belief that critical periods of learning may exist early in life—both of which positions received support in the work of psychologists and ethologists (Kellaghan, 1977c)— seemed to assume that providing a stimulating school environment, without too much concern about the nature of the stimulation, was sufficient to result in improved pupil attainment.

Given the optimism with which compensatory programs were launched and received, it is possible that the perceived certainty of success that accompanied the programs made evaluation perfunctory or unimportant. In such a situation one would not expect the evaluation of program effectiveness to be taken very seriously (Datta, 1976; Murphy, 1971).

Looking at existing studies of compensatory education reveals serious design problems that tend to make interpretation difficult. In the earlier studies of this kind, little attention was paid to the different aims, methods, or intents of the local programs that were examined (Picariello, 1968; Cicirelli et al., 1969). In most cases, such studies involved little more than compilations of local-level effectiveness studies. Since the nature of the local programs, as well as the outcome measures used to assess their effectiveness, differed drastically, it is difficult to know the precise input or output variables that were examined in these general studies. Cicirelli et al. (1969), for example, administered a battery of cognitive and affective tests to a number of comparison groups; all pupils were examined on a common outcome measure. However, types of Head Start programs attended by the children— whether the program had primarily health orientation, cognitive orientation, or affective orientation—were not distinguished. In these circumstances, the value of a common outcome measure is diminished by a lack of information about the nature of the input variables operating in different programs. Where program variables cannot be identified, the most one can say is that the input investigated was the presence of a Title I or Head Start program, or the application of increased funding for the disadvantaged. Inputs specified at this level of generality are rarely helpful because they hide more than they reveal about particular variables or approaches which might be related to increased achievement.

Other compensatory-education studies sought to define input variables more specifically. Generally, this involved focusing investigation upon a particular type of program categorized in terms of either input or output factors (cf. Bissell, 1970; Glass, 1970; Rivlin & Timpane, 1975; U.S. Office of Education, 1970). Hawkridge and his associates (Hawkridge, Chalupsky & Roberts, 1968; Hawkridge, Tallmadge & Larsen, 1968), for example, first identified successful compensatory programs and then attempted to identify factors which most frequently discriminated between successful and unsuccessful programs. This strategy led to a description of programs in terms of the type of objective pursued by the program (cognitive scholastic or socioemotional), the use of individualized instruction, and the provision of teacher training. Similar efforts have been reported by McDill, McDill & Sprehe (1969) and Posner (1968). This approach, however, is limited by the fact that the examination of program features is generally *post hoc*, requiring that inferences be derived largely from testimony based on the recollection and perceptions of program participants. Moreover, salient contextual features, specific to certain locales or programs, are often overlooked in focusing on program characteristics.

More recent studies of compensatory programs have adopted a more experimental approach as well as attempting to define compensatory-program characteristics in greater detail. In the Head Start Planned Variation Study, which began in 1969, programs are classified under three main headings (Bissell, 1973): preacademic programs (fostering the development of such skills as number and letter recognition), cognitive discovery programs (promoting the growth of basic cognitive processes such as categorization, differentiation, and abstraction), and discovery programs (fostering learning as part of the growth of the "whole child" through free exploration and play). While the classification is useful in terms of general description, it does not take into account the fact that within any type of program, great diversity may exist. Classification of programs in broad terms does not tell us a great deal about what goes on in particular schools. Nor does it tell us whether what was reported to be in a program was actually implemented. There is ample research which documents the problem of trying to infer from the reports of local-level administrators the nature of the actual compensatory experience participants received (Averch et al., 1972; Elmore, 1975; Haney, 1977; Lukas, 1975; Nay et al., 1976).

Input variables studied in compensatory-program investigations are fraught with limitations. The trouble is not that investigators are unaware of the problem; it is simply that the diffuse, community orientation of compensatory-education programs present what have thus far been insoluble difficulties for researchers. There is little question that whatever theoretical rationale might have guided the study of input variables in evaluations of compensatory-education programs has been effectively subverted by a long list of practical constraints stemming largely from the emphasis on local control of program planning and implementation and the post-hoc nature of most evaluations.

Problems In The Selection And Measurement
Of Input Variables

The selection and measurement of input variables give rise to a variety of problems which no school-effectiveness study to date has satisfactorily solved. The problems range from how to measure input variables to how to analyze the data. Problems which arise from high correlations between input variables pertain not only to the selection of variables but to analytical methodology. In considering a further set of problems relating to input variables, we are inevitably forced to consider basic concepts of schooling and the model which, explicitly or implicitly, we are using to represent the process of schooling.

Many of the issues which we will consider have been raised in the numerous critiques that have been made of the Coleman Report and similar studies. Our objective is to provide an overview of the major issues as they relate to the selection and measurement of input variables in school-effectiveness studies. To the extent that the problems which we consider are related to school-effectiveness studies that have been carried out to date, our confidence in the findings of such studies must correspondingly be weakened.

Delineation of Input Variables

Variables which are selected to represent reality always involve some degree of abstraction. Furthermore, there is a limit to the number of variables one may select, if only to make research practical and manageable. The selection of variables is predicated on the existence of some prior knowledge about the phenomena to be investigated. In the absence of such knowledge, one would have no basis for choosing variables at all. The kind of knowledge that can guide the selection of variables can come from several sources: the findings of past research, deductions from a theory, or the existence of a prevailing conventional wisdom. If prior research, theory, or conventional wisdom is erroneous, or provides a poor representation of the classes of variables which are important, the variables identified as salient will not be very useful in explaining and understanding the phenomenon of interest.

These considerations, when applied to school-effectiveness studies, give rise to questions regarding the adequacy and validity of the input measures which have been used. The first thing we may note is the limitation in the available knowledge about schooling. While many empirical studies of schooling have been carried out since the turn of the century, up to the 1950s most such studies were based on the examination of the possible effects of single variables (though some did attempt to control for factors such as intelligence and student background). It was not until the 1950s that developments in computer technology made possible studying large numbers of variables simultaneously.

Investigators in the large-scale studies of the 1950s and 1960s were faced with problems of limited scientific knowledge in the selection of variables. There was relatively little empirical data available and even less in terms of comprehensive theories or models of schooling. Getzels (1969) has attributed the noncumulative nature of research on the classroom, on teaching, and on teacher-pupil interaction to the paucity of integrative concepts available to investigators. One could add the relatively small number of well-designed studies, either correlational or experimental, in explaining this poor state of knowledge about schooling (Rosenshine & Furst, 1971). Given this situation, investigators such as Coleman were forced to rely more on conventional wisdom in selecting their measures of school inputs than were investigators in other disciplines.

It is not surprising that, with hindsight, it is possible to make many criticisms of Coleman's choice of variables. For example, one could question the decision to employ variables which represented primarily status characteristics of schools while largely ignoring more process characteristics. The selection of variables for which data are relatively easily obtained and which are relatively easily quantified may be a short-sighted policy, since it may preclude "the clear specification of influence mechanisms and social processes" (Spady, 1973, p. 171). Several critics have voiced their opinions on this point, arguing that if the transactions, interactions, and processes which occur during schooling were the focus, the relations between school inputs and student achievement would be higher. But as always, the validity of this conclusion depends on how student achievement is defined and measured.

Measurement of Input Variables

Problems associated with the actual measurement of the variables also arise. Suppose, for example, that on the basis of prior knowledge one is led to expect that teacher characteristics are related to schooling outcomes; to carry out empirical reseach it is necessary to make operational the concept *teacher characteristics* in measurable terms. This involves devising a technique which will provide a valid and reliable index of the variable one is interested in.

In many cases, the variables measured were high-inference ones; the specific constructs measured by the variables are not clear. For example, Rosenshine and Furst (1971) point to the difficulty of determining what exactly is meant by "clarity of teacher presentation" or "teacher enthusiasm."

An apparently more straightforward input variable, per-pupil expenditure, may also represent a variety of factors, covering salaries for teachers, administrators, supervisors, clerks, librarians, instructional aides, and janitors, as well as expenditure on physical plant, heating, books, and equipment (Klein, 1976). However, superintendents and principals vary in their rules for resource allocation (Luecke & McGinn, 1975; Owens, 1972). Thus a knowledge of gross expenditure does not reveal how funds are actually distributed. Does it, in fact, make any difference to school outcomes whether money is spent on school buildings, on library facilities, or on teacher salaries?

Many of the variables measured in studies of school effectiveness may be regarded as "proxy" measures. That is, it is not expected that the age of a school building, the age of a textbook, or the number of books in a school library are important in themselves in determining achievement; rather, it is assumed that some factor or factors associated with such variables, though not directly measured, are instrumental in affecting achievement. For example, an obtained measure of the teacher's verbal ability is presumably a proxy for such variables as the teacher's ability to communicate effectively and grammatically. In this situation, the identification of the causal agent becomes difficult, since one does not have the opportunity of directly observing possible relations between causal agents and effects, but rather must view them through the intermediate proxy variable used to represent the direct causal agent.

A basic validity issue underlying measurement in any study pertains to the ambiguity of the construct being measured. An ambiguous definition of the construct most often has an adverse impact on the reliability and validity of the ensuing measure. This is an issue that has not received a great deal of attention in school-effectiveness studies, though it seems particularly relevant to school-input measurement which tends to rely heavily on the use of questionnaires. Dyer (1972), for example, used the example of an apparently straightforward variable "total enrollment in the school" to point up the problem of ambiguity in questionnaire responses. In any school, the total enrollment fluctuates from day to day. It is influenced by pupil absence as well as the movement of families in and out of the school catchment area. In some urban school districts, pupil turnover can be very high, while in rural areas it is generally low. When asked on a questionnaire to indicate the total enrollment in his school, a principal may be hard put to provide a straightforward reply. Is he or she to provide total enrollment on that day or total enrollment averaged over the previous year? In some states, total school enrollment is defined as the number of pupils enrolled in the school as of a particular date, regardless of enrollment prior to or subsequent to that date.

Other states or localities use different formulas. Whatever the procedure used, the single number reported will hide some variation in the day-to-day school enrollment.

The fact that many input variables have been considered proxies for more complex variables detracts from both the reliability and reality of the measure. In addition to the normal error to be expected in the measurement of any variable, there is an additional source of error in the measurement of proxy variables, since the variable being measured is itself a measure of another variable (Kellaghan, 1977a). Given the vulnerability to error of measurement techniques in social science studies, Walberg and Marjoribanks (1976) express the view that causal relations may appear weak not because they are weak but because the constructs underlying the variables used in studies are ambiguous and hence unreliable. There is an obvious need to attend more closely to the validity and reliability characteristics of variables in school-effectiveness studies.

Problems of input-variable ambiguity which characterize studies of differential school effectiveness are small compared to those which characterize compensatory-program evaluations. Part of the ambiguity arises from the fact that federal guidelines for compensatory education left the practical details of programs to the community. Hence, a variety of programs have been offered to pupils under the general classification Head Start or Title I. Some communities have stressed remedial work in the three R's; others have emphasized enrichment; still others have emphasized goals related to altering pupils' attitudes and values. And it is not unusual to find the same community drastically shifting its program orientation from year to year. Moreover, instructional strategies and materials even within the same program emphasis have varied widely. In some communities instruction has been highly structured and cognitively oriented, while in others more open, unstructured arrangements have prevailed. Moreover, students in different localities have been taught by regularly employed classroom teachers, teacher's aides, other students, and machines.

The diversity of program inputs across compensatory-education programs would not necessarily create a problem of ambiguity were the diversity not compounded by poor program specification at the local level (Averch et al., 1972; Nay et al., 1976; Rivlin & Timpane, 1975; Rotberg & Wolf, 1974; Wargo et al., 1971). Nay *et al.* suggest that this lack of specificity may, in large measure, be due to problems in program management at the national level. In an article entitled "If You Don't Care Where You Get To, Then It Doesn't Matter Which Way You Go," they argue that the typical federal program, including compensatory-education programs, are unmanageable for any one of the three reasons: (1) the program lacks specific objectives related to the overall program goals; (2) the program lacks testable assumptions which link program activities to the achievement of program objectives, and (3) managers lack the motivation, ability, or authority to manage (p. 98). With these circumstances prevailing at the federal level, there was little incentive for local authorities to attend to detailed program specification (Murphy, 1971; Timpane, 1970). Unfortunately, as the need for program specification became clear in the early 1970s, federal efforts to evaluate the impact of Title I and Head Start all but ceased (Timpane, 1976).

Exacerbating an already difficult problem is the fact that the compensatory programs actually implemented at given sites are not necesarily isomorphic to the originally intended program plan. In assessing the effectiveness of compensatory education, it is not sufficient to focus attention exclusively on the planned input variables; it is also critical to determine what inputs actually become part of the program (Fullan & Pomfret, 1977). How did the planned inputs change in practice? Plans which appear adequate on paper can, in practice, be watered down or poorly administered. If evidence on program effectiveness is to be credible, it must be shown that the intended inputs were actually implemented. (Elmore, 1975; Rivlin, 1976). Such evidence is difficult to obtain. Even the comparatively sophisticated and closely monitored Head Start and Follow Through Planned Variation studies (Bissell, 1973) produced evidence showing that most of the variance in the degree of program implementation for the different Head Start models examined lay *within* particular models (Lukas, 1975; Rivlin & Timpane, 1975). Most implementation differences were found among teachers using the same compensatory approach rather than among teachers using different approaches.

In a broader sense, program definition and implementation are critical from the point of view of replication. If a compensatory education program were found to be successful, we would want to capitalize on the important features of that program in planning new programs. However, if the program were so poorly defined or haphazardly implemented that it was virtually impossible to identify its relevant inputs, it obviously would be difficult to re-create it for succeeding groups.

In light of the ambiguities often associated with program specification and implementation, the compensatory-program evaluator is typically faced with the problem of determining what is the essence of the program being evaluated; what are the input variables being examined? Even studies which have endeavored to examine programs with a single emphasis (e.g., improve reading performance) have been faced with ambiguity in defining input variables (Glass, 1970). Often, a broad program label such as "Title I" or "Head Start" is, as noted above, the only reasonable input label under which to characterize many local programs. The use of broad program labels, however, really tells little about the particular inputs examined. In a figurative sense, generalizing across existing diverse programs is akin to examining apples, oranges, cherries, pears, and plums and releasing one's conclusions under the general category "fruit." In the end, we are left with conclusions about compensatory-education programs where the input is defined no more specifically than "preschool experience" or "extra within-school instruction," regardless of the aims, nature, or characteristics of this experience or instruction.

Effects of Aggregation

Given the difficulties we have observed in interpreting the precise meaning of variables used to describe schools in both the traditional school-effectiveness context and in compensatory programs, it is surprising that many investigators have tended to confound the issue further by their methods of data aggregation. In a sense this is a data-analytic problem, but since it also relates to the interpretation of the meaning of input variables, it will be considered here. Many analyses, by their choice of unit of analysis (class, school, district), assume that inputs as distributed by the system are isomorphic with inputs as received by the student (Coleman, 1972). This assumption is implicit in studies which have aggregated properties of students to the classroom or program level (Cicirelli et al., 1969; Iwanicki, 1974; Walberg, 1969), the school level (Katzman, 1968), the district level (Kiesling, 1969; Bidwell & Kasarda, 1975), the state level (Walberg & Rasher, 1974) and the national level (Bidwell, 1975). This assumption also underlies studies in which teacher characteristics have been aggregated to the school level, as has been done in virtually every study of differential school effectiveness (Coleman et al., 1966; Comber & Keeves, 1973; Husen, 1967; Jencks et al., 1972; Levin, 1970; Mayeske et al., 1972; Michelson, 1970; Smith, 1972; Thorndike, 1973). Thus, the measures of teacher characteristics used in data analysis are *averages* across all teachers in a school.

One must expect to find aggregations of data in studies of school and program effectiveness, if for no other reason than that schools and programs are aggregates of teachers and pupils and classrooms are aggregates of persons and processes (Burstein, 1976). However, the unit of grouping may have important implications for the construct validity of input measures and consequently for the inferences made about school or program effectiveness. Indeed in some cases the choice of a particular unit may have the effect of obfuscating efforts to identify important relations among variables.

The use of the school or school district as the unit of analysis assumes that all students in a given school or school district are exposed in the same way and to the same degree to all resources measured. That this assumption may serve to conceal the role of school variables in affecting achievement is clear if we consider two school resources generally considered to be important: teachers and physical facilities.

In the case of teachers, parents are aware that differences exist among the teachers at their neighborhood elementary school. Teachers have different reputations and parents may spend a great deal of time and effort endeavoring to place their child with a certain teacher because he or she is warm, concentrates on basic skills, runs an open classroom, or instills discipline. Certainly teachers are different, and if their different reputations are deserved, it is probable that pupils with one type of teacher will be treated differently from pupils with a teacher of another type. Parents' perception that individual teachers' personal characteristics do make a difference to pupil outcomes motivates their placing their children with one or another teacher. While these outcomes are not exclusively restricted to the outcomes measured on standardized tests, it is logical to assume that some individual teacher characteristics are related to pupil test performance. Such characteristics are lost when they are submerged into a school-level index of average teacher experience or quality. No pupil is exposed to the school's average teacher experience or quality; rather, he or she is exposed to particular teachers, each with unique attributes.

Similarly, within schools, pupils receive differential exposure to school resources and facilities (Averch et al., 1972). Students in some school tracks or programs never use the language or science laboratory, participate on athletic teams, or take books out of the library. Some pupils in some courses always use second-hand texts, while others in the same school invariably receive new textbooks. The dollar cost of educating pupils within a school differs according to the materials, resources, and facilities students need to complete their particular course of study. An index of average district or school per-pupil expenditure fails to take such differences into account. Assigning the same school mean on a resource, facility, or expenditure input variable to all pupils in a school assumes that all have equal access to the inputs. This obviously is not the case, yet information about the effects of differences in the allocation of inputs to pupils within a school cannot be examined when data are aggregated to the school level.

The problems associated with the level to which data are aggregated may be more critical at some levels of education than at others. Thus, while the failure to tap within-school or program diversity in the application of input variables is characteristic of most school- and program-effectiveness studies (Burstein, 1976), the problem may be most severe at the high-school level. It is in the high school that the differentiation of pupils into tracks or courses of study takes on its most visible and rigid form. The intended aims of these tracks differ greatly, as do the nature of the courses, resources, and experiences to which pupils in the tracks are exposed. Such differences also exist at the elementary-school level, but not in as overt a form as at the high-school level. Within-school differences in access across pupils in various tracks are pronounced on almost any input variable one might consider. The lack of uniformity in pupil access to school inputs in the same school makes the aggregation of data to the school level of questionable validity. Moreover, differences among pupil access to specific resources within a school have an important bearing on the relevance of the standardized tests used to measure school effectiveness.

Problems in Grouping Input Variables

School-effectiveness studies have tended to use a large number of input variables to describe schools, partly perhaps from an appreciation of the complexity of the phenomena and partly since it was not known which variables were critical, it was hoped to avoid the mistake of omitting ones that might be important. The use of a large number of variables, however, creates its own problems, not the least of which is how to handle so many variables parsimoniously in analyses, though behind the methodological problem there are often important substantive issues of variable selection.

Partly because of the limitations of analytical procedures, individual input variables are sometimes categorized into superordinate categories called blocks. Thus, one set of variables may be grouped as referring to the students' homes, another group to the student body, another to teachers, another to curricula and school facilities. Initial classification is usually done on the basis of the conceptual similarity of variables. The appropriateness of the classification may then be checked empirically. However, this procedure is not always as straightforward as it may appear. For one thing, input variables in studies of schooling tend to be related, often closely, and the relations cross any obvious conceptual categorization that one may impose on the variables. If two variables are closely related, can one unambigously assign one to the school (because it is physically present there) and another to the home? For example, the correlation between the socioeconomic status of the community and the volumes per student in the school library may be high. Yet in assigning variables to blocks, number of volumes per student in the school library would be categorized as a school facility while socioeconomic status would be categorized as a home background variable. The problem is particularly acute where variables seem to be surrogates for other underlying factors. Such underlying factors may represent aspects of different parts of the environment which can readily be differentiated at one level (for example, home and school), but may not be so readily differentiated in terms of values or attitudes.

The initial assignment of variables to categories can affect the course of any analyses that are performed as well as the results. It is clear that an initial incorrect assignment may provide very misleading conclusions.

Problems With The Amount Of Variance Associated With Input Measures

A final point in considering input variables is the variance that exists in input measures. In general, one can say that reduction in variance on a variable reduces the chances of that variable showing relations with other variables. This is so for statistical reasons; but selecting conditions in which variance is limited for some variables will increase the probability that observed relations between other variables will be more marked. Thus, if we examine the relation between school inputs and student achievement only within very homogeneous student populations (e.g., upper-income whites attending suburban schools), we would in effect be curtailing the home-background variance in the group studied. By curtailing home-background variance, relations which exist between school inputs and achievement are more likely to be evidenced.

Whether reduction in variance is a good or bad thing will depend on the object of one's investigation. Obviously, one would not wish to reduce variance in a variable that one wished to show to be effective. If, on the other hand, one wanted to show the influence of certain variables, one might take steps to reduce variance in variables which might interfere with a demonstration of the desired effects.

Most school-effectiveness studies have been carried out in the United States, where variance in input measures may be rather limited. The IEA studies, in contrast, permitted comparisons among countries; it is of interest that quite remarkable differences were found among countries in the relation between attainment and home and school variables (Postlethwaite, 1975). For example, when home background and school resources are aggregated to the school level (neighborhood effect), home background accounts for 80 percent of between-school variance in science achievement in Scotland, while in Sweden the figure is only 8 percent. Conversely, school factors make a large contribution to variance in achievement in Sweden, but not in Scotland. As an explanation, it is suggested that since school neighborhoods are more homogeneous in Scotland than in Sweden, there is greater between-neighborhood variance in the former. Because of the method of variance decomposition used in the IEA studies, there are difficulties in interpreting observations on the relative contribution of background and school variables to variance in achievement. However, this finding does suggest that it may be dangerous to base conclusions about school effectiveness on studies that have all been carried out in the same country, where variance in any of the independent variables considered may be very limited. Given different home conditions and a different school system, the findings may be very different. Findings from surveys in developing countries indicate that this is indeed the case. For example, no relation was found between socioeconomic background and academic achievement, as measured by the Primary Leaving Examination and Cambridge School Certificate examinations (neither of which is a norm-referenced test), for Ugandan students (Heyneman, 1975). On the basis of a review of a number of studies in developing countries, Simmons and Alexander (1975) also conclude that home conditions are not related to scholastic learning; however, neither do they find that facilities such as "high quality" teachers or more expensive plant contribute to increased achievement.

It is, of course, possible to restrict variance within one country on certain variables by selecting subgroups of a population. On the assumption that the effects of schools on students may not be the same for all subgroups of students in the school, Frederiksen & Bolt, Beranek, and Newman (1975) further stratified populations of sixth-grade students who had taken part in the *Equality of Educational Opportunity* survey on the basis of race and home background, and then proceeded to carry out separate analyses of school effectiveness for each group. By restricting analyses to one subgroup at a time, individual family-background factors were held constant. The authors found that among schools attended by children of the same socioeconomic background or race, it was possible to identify some that were consistently "effective" or "ineffective." In ineffective schools, it was estimated that the mean normative grade equivalent was 2.5 years, while in effective schools it was 4.8 years. In considering the school characteristics associated with effectiveness, it was necessary to distinguish between characteristics consistently associated with effectiveness (those that shared a consistent relation in the case of all subgroups of children) and ones that were not consistently related. Examples of the former were a number of teacher characteristics (e.g., had been educated in a teacher's college rather than a liberal arts college), school characteristics (lack of ability grouping and special programs for the mentally retarded). There were also teacher characteristics (race, attitudes toward social class, and compensatory education) and school characteristics (availability of reading materials within a school) which were related to school achievement for some groups but not for others.

In two school-effectiveness studies carried out in England and Ireland (Madaus et al., 1975, Brimer et al., 1978), the fact that students in secondary schools in those countries are more homogeneous in background than students in the less selective American schools was regarded as an important factor in being able to show strong effects of school-based resources on student achievement. It seems reasonable to suppose that restricting variance in factors in the home environment related to staying in school would have the effect of making it more likely that the influence of school-based variables would be demonstrated. By the same token findings from studies carried out with selected groups of students obviously cannot be applied to other groups of students without first obtaining other evidence.

An implication of these findings is that variables may operate differently in different contexts. Further evidence is to be found in Hanushek's (1970) study of different ethnic groups. In this study, while differences in teachers and classrooms are found to be related to the achievement of white elementary school children in a school district in California, this was not found for Mexican children. In general, analyses of the "Equality of Educational Opportunity" data suggest that school resources and verbal achievement are more strongly related in the case of blacks than whites. These two findings may not seem to complement each other; however, they do indicate that different sets of students may react differently to resources.

In summary, problems in the selection and measurement of input variables cause difficulties in interpreting the results of studies of school and program effectiveness. The problems range from the choice of variables which primarily define status rather than process characteristics to the ambiguity of the variables. In many cases, it is not possible to describe the inputs about which conclusions regarding school effectiveness are based. Despite these problems, there is an emerging body of research concerning the impact of particular types of input variables on student achievement; it is this research which we will now consider.

EMPIRICAL RELATIONS BETWEEN SCHOOL VARIABLES AND ACHIEVEMENT

A systematic review of empirical studies of the relation between school variables and achievement will not be attempted here. Rather, we will attempt to provide a picture of the types of variables that have and have not been found to be related to school attainment. Our brief review will be selective; it will be concerned more with variables that have been found to be related to school attainment than with those that have not. Reference will be made to small-scale studies as well as to the more recent large-scale ones, which have contributed most to the debate on school effectiveness. We shall also refer to studies which have been carried out since the Coleman survey which, in our view provide some of the strongest evidence relating to the influence of school factors on achievement.

School Facilities

Much of the discussion following Coleman's study has centered on the role of per-pupil expenditure, class size, school organization, school libraries, and laboratory facilities as predictors of standardized test performance. These aspects of schooling, and many more, had been related to various measures of school achievement in countless studies (cf. Stephens, 1933, 1967). On the whole, the results of the studies underline what Stephens (1967) has called "the constancy of the school's accomplishment" (p. 71); school outcomes do not vary markedly or consistently with variations in school characteristics. Some studies, for example, find that expenditure is related to attainment (Mollenkopf &

Melville, 1956; Goodman, 1959); others, that it is not. The general conclusion of commentators is that while most studies have identified some status characteristics of schools that are related to student outcomes (test scores or educational plans), the relations tend to be weak. Furthermore, there is little consistency across studies in the variables that appear significant (Averch et al., 1972; Jencks & Brown, 1975).

Time Devoted to School Subject

This school input, which intuitively seems critical for student achievement, is so obvious that it can easily be ignored. If a high school did not offer physics as part of its curriculum and students spent no time studying the subject, one would hardly bother to assess student performance on a physics test. In a broader context, Wiley (Wiley, 1976; Wiley & Harnischfeger, 1974) has argued that since schooling can only influence a child who is actually present, exposure to schooling is an important variable in the study of school effectiveness. The evidence on exposure to schooling, however, is ambiguous, and studies which included as a variable the length of time school is in session (Jencks, 1972a) or the amount of time devoted to a particular subject (Martin & Kellaghan, 1977) have not shown time to be an important predictor of achievement.

One possible explanation of this finding is that once schools offer a subject, they may not differ greatly in the amount of time they devote to it. If variation between schools in time devoted to teaching a subject is not great, obviously one would not expect such variation to be a key factor in explaining achievement in that subject. Or it may be that schools *do* vary in the actual amount of class time in which students are actively working on a subject, though measures derived from timetables may not reflect such differences. Bloom (1975) has observed in connection with the IEA studies that in some countries, students appear to be actively engaged in learning for 90 percent or more of class time, while in other countries, students are so engaged only 50 percent of the time. Measures such as "hours of school year" will provide some index of exposure, but may be an inaccurate index of content or intensity of treatment (Spaeth, 1976).

In the absence of direct measures of the actual amount of time spent working on a subject, the variable "opportunity to learn" may provide a rough indication of a school's emphasis and time allocation. In the IEA studies, for example, teachers were asked to estimate the proportion of their students who had covered the topics measured by the test items

(Husen, 1967). Such a measure, it will be noted, is not a measure of time or of opportunity. Nevertheless, in a number of studies (including the IEA), correlations between measures of reported opportunity to learn and student achievement have been found to be positive, significant, and consistent, varying between .16 and .40 (Rosenshine & Furst, 1971).

Teacher Characteristics

Several studies point to the importance of teacher variables in school effectiveness. It is not so much that teacher variables have been found to contribute significantly to achievement, but rather they appear, in one form or another, in studies and evaluations of school and program effectiveness with considerable consistency. It is reasonable to expect that the teacher is a key factor in student achievement, and indeed in the Coleman survey there was evidence that teachers' verbal ability was related, albeit not very strongly, to student achievement. One looks in vain however, for evidence of a consistent and significant relation between any teacher trait and student achievement. Moreover, the teacher characteristics traditionally regarded as important may in fact not be so. For example, many school systems pay more for teaching experience and graduate education, from which one may infer that these are thought to relate to student achievement. However, at least in California, Hanushek (1970) has shown that these variables do not relate to student achievement; he found verbal facility and "recentness" of teacher education to be more important variables than experience and degrees earned.

It is possible teachers' cognitive characteristics such as ability, formal qualifications, and experience, are less important than their personality characteristics. Rivlin (1971) has made the point that a "teacher's score on a verbal test may not matter as much as her sympathy, her sense of humor, or her confidence in her students" (p. 75). Alas, the search for the teacher personality characteristics that are consistently related to pupil achievement has not been any more successful than the search for other critical factors in teaching. Getzels (1969) concludes that "It is probably not unfair to say that the inconsistent nature of the results is the single consistent conclusion that can be drawn from the work in this domain" (p. 513).

Quality Of Teaching

A consideration of teachers inevitably leads us to such variables as quality of teaching (Peaker, 1967) and quality of instruction (Bloom, 1976), since in systems of education as they operate, the teacher is a prime source of teaching and instruction. Presumably for this reason and on the basis of the not unreasonable assumption that what teachers actually do is more important than their personal and cognitive characteristics, a number of investigators have looked at dynamic aspects of the teacher's role. While there are many negative, unexpected, and inconsistent findings (cf. Medley & Mitzel, 1963), a number of studies reviewed by Rosenshine and Furst (1971) confirm that quality of teaching is related to student achievement. The kinds of behavior identified in these studies are clarity of the teacher's presentation (making points clearly, explaining concepts clearly, use of a variety of teaching procedures and materials, enthusiasm in presentation as indicated by gesture and voice inflections) and the task orientation of the teacher (focusing on the accomplishment of a definite task). Teachers' behavior, as measured by these variables, probably reflects classroom processes rather than status variables, and indeed these variables seem to have much in common with what Bloom (1976) has termed "quality of instruction."

While conceding that variations in traditional school, classroom, and teacher-status variables do not consistently relate to variation in students' measured achievement, Bloom (1976) suggests that a shift in focus from status input characteristics to process-oriented ones may identify school variables which do relate to pupil performance in a consistent manner. In this view, it is the teaching and not the teacher, the classroom learning environment and not its physical characteristics, that are important for school learning (Crawford et al., 1977; Dunkin & Biddle, 1974; Good, Biddle, & Brophy, 1975; Marjoribanks, 1974; Rosenshine, 1971).

Drawing on Carroll's (1963) work, Bloom's variable, "quality of instruction," is defined as the degree to which the presentation, explanation, and ordering of the task to be learned approach the optimum for a given learner. Essentially this variable concerns the extent to which the instructional process is suited to each learner's needs; it places the emphasis upon a teacher's ability to manage the learning as opposed to managing the learners. Quality of instruction, Bloom asserts, is in turn predicated upon a number of more specific classroom processes. One such process involves the amount of practice and participation students are afforded in learning a task. Another is the reinforcement or encouragement mechanisms teachers use to motivate the student to learn. A third process concerns how a student's learning progress is diagnosed and how this diagnostic information is fed back to the learner to direct future study. Thus, Bloom stresses the relevance of measuring process variables in place of teacher and classroom status characteristics, and suggests that the quality of classroom instruction is comprised of a number of important processes.

> Stripped to its essentials, the *Quality of Instruction* as we define it here has to do with the *cues* or directions provided to the learner, the *participation* of the learner in learning activity (covert or overt), and the *reinforcement* which the learner secures in some relation to the learning. Because much of school instruction is group instruction and because any attempt at group instruction is fraught with error and difficulty, a *feedback and corrective* system must also be included in the quality of instruction. (Bloom, 1976, p. 115)

Bloom concludes that quality of instruction, defined in terms of such processes, accounts for at least 25 percent of the variance in students' achievement. (This conclusion has serious implications for studies of school effectiveness and for teaching and teacher training.)

Student Variables

Students are not always considered as inputs in classic input-output studies of school effectiveness; despite this neglect, evidence on the importance of students' ability predicting attainment is compelling (cf. Cooley & Lohnes, 1976; Getzels, 1969). On the basis of a review and analysis of studies of the prediction of academic performance, Lavin (1965) concluded that measures of student ability generally account for 35 to 45 percent of variation in scholastic performance (as measured, for example, by grades).

A measure of a student's prior achievement in a given subject area is a better predictor of later achievement in that area than a measure of general ability. For example, Jencks and Brown's (1975) examination of Project Talent data led them to conclude that the best predictor of a student's score on a twelfth-grade test is his or her score on an analogous ninth-grade test. However, other ninth-grade scores also contributed to prediction, leading the authors to conclude that "a student's cognitive skill in any given area in twelfth grade depends not only on ninth-grade skill in the same area, but also on some kind of generalized learning capacity that can only be measured using a broad array of tests" (p. 286). Adding other predictive factors that describe the intervening classroom environment to initial test scores, as Bloom (1964) suggested, also improves prediction. In the case of physics test scores, at any rate, about 75 percent of end-of-course test variance can be explained by initial test scores and learning environment measures (Walberg, 1972).

Findings such as these led Bloom (1976) to conclude that student entry behaviors in the cognitive field (generalized behaviors, such as intelligence, and specific behaviors related to a subject area) account for 50 percent of variation in achievement. If this is so, then it is surprising that such behaviors have not always been taken into account in school-effectiveness studies. A number of commentators have pointed to the omission of data on students' ability level in the Coleman survey. Wilson (1968), for example, says that "the most conspicuous determinant of achievement which is not controlled in the analysis presented in the Coleman report is 'ability' " (p. 82). Spady (1973) has noted that the omission of data on student intelligence and motivation "from an educational production function means that the analysis will necessarily provide an inaccurate, incomplete, and even misleading explanation of student achievement" (p. 139).

Evidence on the importance of student personality characteristics for achievement is less compelling. Such factors as social maturity, independence, emotional stability, and achievement motivation were not found in studies reviewed by Lavin (1965) to relate strongly or consistently to achievement. In more recent studies specific school-related affective variables, such as attitudes toward specific school subjects, have been shown to relate more strongly to achievement; in this context, Bloom (1976) has estimated that affective entry characteristics can account for up to 25 percent of variance on cognitive achievement measures.

Peer-Group Influence

The characteristics of students as groups, as well as the characteristics of individual students, may be important in considering school functioning. Within schools, students are formally organized into groups; these groups frequently take the form of classes, which may be organized on one or more of a variety of bases—age, achievement, aptitude, and gender. Evidence relating to the role of these variables in affecting student achievement is not unlike the evidence relating to the role of variables describing the school's physical environment; relations between organizational factors and achievement tend to be inconsistent and not very strong.

Students, however, organize themselves in other ways within schools. Insofar as students look to each other rather than to the adult community for social rewards (Coleman, 1961), we could expect to find an alternative set of subgroups within a school based on student value and reward systems. Some student groupings may coincide with the bases of formal organization in the school—for example, age may be common to both—but the informal student organization is likely to introduce differentiation beyond that employed in the formal school organization; for example, students may not be grouped formally by gender but may form their own subgroups on this basis. They are also likely to form groups on the basis of prestige and leadership qualities as they perceive them among their peers.

Students' value systems were examined by Coleman (1961) in his study of ten high schools in Illinois; he found that they affect students' grades. For example, he found that when academic achievement was highly regarded by the student body, the highest grades were achieved by the most intelligent students. When the student body valued nonacademic achievements (as in athletics) more highly than scholastic success, the most intelligent students were not the highest scholastic achievers. Coleman concluded that "students with ability are led to achieve only when there are social rewards, primarily from their peers, for doing so" (1961, p. 265).

Another aspect of peer-group influence received considerable attention following "Equality of Educational Opportunity." The findings of this study were interpreted to indicate that as the proportion of white students in a school increased, the academic performance of black students also increased. By way of explaining this phenemenon, it was suggested that somehow black students acquired achievement-related motives from their white peers. Armor's (1972) study, in which the school rather than the individual was used as the unit of analysis, confirmed Coleman's finding regarding the relation between the school's racial composition and black students' scholastic performance.

These findings provided a rationale for the desegration policies, including bussing, that were implemented in the United States in the early 1970s. Later studies, however, provided inconsistent findings regarding the effects of transferring students from one school to another (Armor, 1972; Iwanicki, 1977; St. John, 1975). In fact, Coleman (1976) was to disclaim the importance of his earlier finding about racial balance. In particular, it has been difficult to provide evidence that the achievement-related values of middle-class whites are transferred to poor blacks, and that such transfer, in turn, leads to improved scholastic performance of poor black students (Bradley & Bradley, 1977; Gerard & Miller, 1975). It has been argued that unless the school's academic climate is changed, changes in the socioeconomic or racial composition of schools will not affect school achievement (Brookover et al., n.d.)

Process Variables

So far, our review suggests that while "simple one-variable linear relationships are not jumping out of the research data" (McKeachie, 1974, p. 170), perhaps too much emphasis has been placed on this conclusion by commentators on school-effectiveness studies. The finding that some variables seem important for student achievement—even though there may not be consistency in the precise variables which different studies have identified—might lead one to suspect that something is happening which researchers have not been able to capture in their research strategies. Research findings on school effectiveness suggest at least two facts: first, the relations between school input and output variables are complex rather than simple; second, the school variables that seem important in affecting scholastic achievement—however measured—are those that capture the *activity* (processes) of the school rather than those that reflect status variables, such as size or physical amenities. On the importance of status variables to school achievement, we can say at most that they do not relate strongly to standardized-test performance.

This conclusion is hardly surprising given the complexity of the school and what takes place in it. Several commentators have suggested that attention to the transactions, interactions, and processes that occur during schooling rather than to school status characteristics would have provided more striking evidence about the role of school-based factors in affecting achievement (Averch et al., 1972; Bloom, 1976; Bowles & Levin, 1968b; Dyer, 1968; Guthrie, 1970; Haskew, 1973; McDermott, 1976; Smith, 1976). Status variables, such as average number of science courses taught, proportion of students coming from homes with encyclopedias, or teachers' average salary miss the flesh-and-blood dimension of the educative process as it actually transpires in schools and classrooms. Common sense tells us that what people *do* with their resources and facilities is likely to be more critical for student achievement than the mere presence of the resources and facilities, which may not even be used by pupils. In this view, the process through which people interact with their environment is more critical than the physical features of the environment, although one would also expect an interaction between facilities and staff (Spady, 1973). Physical facilities may set limits to the types of interaction that can occur; however, given the presence of encyclopedias, availability of up-to-date textbooks, and science laboratories, how and by whom such facilities are used is of prime importance.

Certainly, in studies of the relation of home background and scholastic achievement, indexes of environmental processes and interactions have been more powerful in predicting student performance, as measured by standardized tests of ability and attainment, than have indexes of home and parent status (Bloom, 1964; Dave, 1963; Linnan & Airasian, 1974; Walberg & Marjoribanks, 1976; Wolf, 1964). For example, while correlations between socioeconomic status, parents' occupation or education and measures of intelligence are generally about .4 or less, correlations of .7 and greater have been found between intelligence and measures of process variables such as parents' strategy of reinforcement, parents' language model and extent of supervision and helping with schoolwork (Bloom, 1964; Fraser, 1959). It may be that more attention to similar process-oriented variables in the school context would increase the ability of school factors to explain scholastic behavior. There are of course serious practical difficulties in measuring process variables, particularly if one engages in direct observational procedures (Cooley, 1974; Porter & McDaniels, 1974). However, questionnaire techniques have been relatively successful in measuring process variables in the home (Bloom, 1964); it may be that similar procedures could be used in measuring the school environment.

To date, attempts to measure processes, transactions, and interactions among people and resources in schools in studies of differential school effectiveness have not been common. As one observer picturesquely noted,

> . . . researchers have measured some school trappings, usually with about the same nose-to-thumb accuracy I employed long ago selling piece goods in a country store. They have *not* measured the essences of quality . . . . The teacher they measure is a degree, a certificate, a length of tenure, and a few other indicators. The methodology they measure is canned something, but the can is not opened to see if its contents match the label. I repeat, it is moral to measure "quality" this way. But it isn't very revealing. (Haskew, 1972, p. 49)

A number of recent studies, however, have paid more attention than usual to the measurement of processes in schools. Brookover et al.

(1978), in a study of elementary schools in Michigan, related school climate variables to students' mean achievement as measured by objective-referenced tests. The climate variables, which were based on perceptions of students, teachers, and principals, described the student climate (student sense of academic futility, student expectations, student perception of teacher "push" and norms), the teacher climate (teacher sense of academic futility, teacher evaluations and expectations for high school completion, teacher-student commitment to improve), and the principal teacher climate (principal expectation and evaluation of students, perception of parent concern, expectations for quality education). The social-psychological and normative variables, based on such measures of school climate, contributed a major portion to the explanation of variance in mean school achievement—as much as 80 percent when climate variables enter first into the regression analyses. The addition of socioeconomic or racial-composition variables added relatively little to the explanation of variance.

The final evidence we shall consider comes from outside the United States. In an Irish study, measures of school climates as well as of other school, teacher, student, and home-related factors were related to variance in achievement on public examinations at two levels—the intermediate examinations, taken when students are about 16 years of age, and the leaving examinations taken at about the age of 18 (Madaus, Kellaghan, & Rakow, 1975; Madaus, Kellaghan, Rakow, & King, 1979). The school climate factors, which were based on perceptions of students and teachers, were complex. They encompassed various components: academic and nonacademic presses of the class, students' concern for and commitment to academic values and pursuits, as well as some features of classroom management.

Considerable variance in achievement was found between classes[*] over a range of examinations (in languages, physical sciences, social sciences, and art)—ranging from 19 to 47 percent at the intermediate level and from 19 to 42 percent at the leaving level. Further, variables related to school climate were found to account uniquely for large proportions of the between-class achievement variance. Among the variables found to be important were teachers' estimates of the extent to which their classes conformed to academic press as well as classes' perceptions of the extent to which teachers expected them to conform to it. Classes which

---

[*]The class rather than the school was used as the unit of analysis.

perceived the level of school discipline as relatively strict (though not necessarily authoritarian) also tended to do well on examinations. Educational aspirations and amount of study were other variables that strongly and positively related to examination performance.

In a similar study carried out in England, variance on eleven London Board O-level examination subjects (languages, sciences, social studies), which are taken by students of about 16 years of age, was partitioned into between and within-school components (Brimer, Madaus, Chapman, Kellaghan, & Wood, 1978). With the exception of one subject area, for which an exceptionally low figure was obtained, the proportion of total variance between schools was found to range from a low of 20 percent to a high of 42 percent. The predictor variables used in the study were not the same as in the Irish studies, but they were similar in many ways. They embraced teacher factors (qualifications, teaching methods, homework expectations), school factors (importance of study, examination orientation, concern with pupils as individuals), family factors, and student factors (students' perceptions of school's emphasis, pressures school brought to bear for academic achievement).

Less between-school variance was explainable in terms of unique factors than was the case in Ireland; rather than the unique contribution of any single block representing a particular source of influence (the classroom, the teacher, or the home), it is the concerted function of blocks of variables that enables achievement to be explained. For seven of the eleven subjects examined, it was the teacher or school variables that made the largest contribution, and for three further subjects it was school press variables. While the teacher variables in the study included reference to supposed teacher virtues such as qualifications and length of experience, actual teaching variables were usually to the fore in explaining achievement variance. The amount of time spent on a course, the adjustment of teaching to the specific characteristics of students, and teachers' belief in the worthwhileness of an examination-oriented approach were among the most specific indications of the ways in which teachers' influences were operative.

These studies provide very strong evidence on the role of school-based factors in affecting scholastic achievement. They further point to the greater ability of process variables rather than status variables to predict achievement. In considering this finding in the context of the two studies, it is well to bear in mind a point we made earlier: school inputs should be considered in the context of school outputs. The school outputs measured in both these studies were examinations that are closely geared to the curricula followed in schools. We shall be taking up the question of the sensitivity of measures of school outcome in later chapters; at this stage we will only note that a combination of process input measures, together with curriculum-sensitive output measures, provides strong supporting evidence for investigators who claim, on the basis of evidence derived from studies that used less curriculum-sensitive norm-referenced standardized tests, that what goes on in schools is a more important determinant of achievement than the physical conditions in which scholastic activity takes place.

In attempting to determine what types of input variables have been shown to work in compensatory education studies, Smith (1976) has identified three variables which relate to student's measured achievement. He called the first "shared purposefulness." In a school which is characterized by such purposefulness, there is a match between parents', students', teachers', and administrators' notions of the important ends of education, and all move toward those ends in a purposeful way. Echoes of Smith's shared purposefulness are clearly to be found in the studies of Brimer et al. (1978) and Madaus, Kellaghan, & Rakow (1975) in which school climate was characterized by social rewards for academic excellence and in which scholastic achievement was valued by teachers and students. Smith's second variable is called "closeness" and applies to the structure and directness of instruction. The concept of closeness suggests that if we wish to teach a child to read, we should concentrate on the reading process rather than on more indirect approaches, such as attempting to change the child's self-concept and through this effect a change in reading. Again, the studies of Brimer and Madaus support the notion that successful schools were working toward the attainment of fairly well defined objectives as set out in school syllabi and as implied by public examinations. The more successful preschool programs for the disadvantaged have also been identified as ones having clearly stated cognitive goals combined with structured attempts to achieve those goals (McDill, McDill, & Sprehe, 1969). And third, Smith names the variable "time," arguing that the more time devoted to teaching pupils the tasks considered important for them to learn, the more likely it is that they will learn these tasks.

Overall, then, the processes, press, and atmosphere of schools and classrooms seem to be more highly related to variation in pupils' measured achievement than does the physical presence of particular types of resources and facilities or the status characteristics of teachers. It is what people do in schools and classrooms—how they reinforce, interact, spend their time, and pursue common goals—which seems to influence performance on specific achievement measures. The fact that process or press variables are more important predictors of achievement than static measures of school and program inputs should hardly be surprising. What might be surprising to some is that the processes and presses which seem to relate to high achievement include classroom and school structure, discipline, purposefulness, time on task, and directness of instruction. Such characteristics are generally considered to comprise a traditional approach to schooling. However, before this observation is taken to be an endorsement of so-called traditional education, it needs to be pointed out once more that the importance of particular input variables, whether status or process in nature, can only be interpreted in the context of the measures which are used to define schooling outcomes. Thus, when school effectiveness is measured in terms of cognitive achievement measures specific to instruction, differences between schools and classes on these traditional process variables are strongly related to differences in achievement between schools and classes. If school effectiveness were measured in terms of creativity or independence, it is possible that non-traditional variables would be found to be more important in accounting for differences between classes and schools.

CONCLUSION

It is clear that efforts to reach conclusions about the effectiveness of school variables must be made with great caution. When we add a consideration of problems associated with the measurement of outputs and with methods of analysis discussed in other chapters to the problems relating to inputs discussed in the present one, any conclusions about the differential effect of schooling or school resources on achievement cannot be regarded as more than tentative.

Perhaps the most striking finding of school-effectiveness studies to date is that variation in such traditional inputs as expenditure, facilities, and teacher qualifications have not been found consistently to explain much of the variance between schools in scholastic achievement as measured by students' performance on standardized tests. Whether the use of more refined measures of such inputs in future research, combined with more sensitive measures of output and methods of analysis, will result in such factors' exhibiting more positive relations to school achievement is difficult to say. It would be difficult on a priori grounds to defend the position that the nature of schools does not condition the effects of instructional methods and their outcomes (Getzels, 1969; McKeachie, 1974). If in future research input variables could be conceived and measured in terms of their mutual interaction to represent the interplay of facilities, students, and teachers, the relevance of such factors as libraries and science laboratories to the educational enterprise might be more obvious.

Common sense and a number of empirical investigations tell us that the most important input is probably the student. If this is so, it does not seem reasonable to exclude a consideration of students' characteristics from studies of school effectiveness. While an arbitrary decision may be made to restrict the term *school input* to physical characteristics or ones that are readily manipulable by policymakers, the exclusion from analyses of an important variable (for example, student ability) must result in a weakening of one's model of the school. Facilities are obviously of little value in themselves; a student must interact with them before they can have any effects. If an important term in the interaction equation is omitted, then information is correspondingly curtailed.

Students also interact among themselves and with other school personnel. It is in such interactions, social-psychological in nature, together with the normative characteristics of subcultures within the school, that the most potent source of differences between schools in students' cognitive performance seems to lie. This is especially true when the measures of school outcomes are sensitive to the content of instructional programs. The importance of process and press variables is also evident, though to a lesser extent, when norm-referenced standardized tests of attainment and ability are used; such tests must be regarded as very conservative measures of the effects of schools, since (as we shall argue in the following chapter) they are probably more correctly regarded as measures of student aptitude than of what students have been taught in school.

chapter 5

School Outcomes: Standardized Tests of Ability

INTRODUCTION

The measurement of school outcomes raises problems that range from the philosophical to the technical. The problems are philosophical in that they touch on issues related to the purpose of schooling. There is, of course, lack of agreement on what the objectives of schooling should be and what balance should be struck between vocational and nonvocational goals, between teaching cognitive material and skills and the personal and social development of pupils.

A discussion of the ends of schooling is beyond the scope of this book. However, omission of such a discussion should not be taken to mean that one's perception of the objectives of schooling is not an important factor in considering the measurement of school outcomes, and any interpretation of studies of the differential effectiveness of schools must involve value judgments about the adequacy of the criterion measures used to define the outcomes of schooling. Does an outcome measure reflect the ends one believes schooling should be devoted to? Individuals will answer this question quite differently in the light of their philosophies of education. Studies of school or program effectiveness, however, have not concerned themselves with philosophical issues concerning the aims of education.

In most large-scale studies of school or program effectiveness there has been little or no explicit discussion about educational aims, and the focus has been on cognitive ends of schooling, perhaps because it was thought that such ends were easier to assess than such ends as social or emotional development, and partly because cognitive factors seem important in the public mind. They are emphasized in teacher-made examinations, and much of the recent criticism of the schools has been that far too many children leaving school are deficient in reading, writing, and computation skills, not that schools do not foster emotional or social development.

Many of those actively involved in education have argued that the goals of their programs were not primarily cognitive but dealt with improving such affective characteristics as motivation, self-confidence, educational aspirations, and the like. These characteristics, it was argued, are prerequisites for eventual success in academic work and later performance in adult life. Consequently it is not fair to evaluate, on the basis of cognitive-test performance, the success of programs which are really trying to develop and/or enhance affective characteristics of pupils and through these, ultimately, cognitive skills (cf. Perrone, 1975; Shapiro, 1973). As noted in the previous chapter, Smith (1976) has called into question the efficacy of this indirect approach to cognitive learning.

While the argument that concentrating on cognitive measures leads one to overlook many important school outcomes is not without merit, it fails to take into account two important facts. The first is political: an important reason for the interest in school effectiveness and compensatory programs in the mid-1960s was evidence that disadvantaged children lacked basic reading and mathematical skills. Since the belief was that children would not be able to hold suitable jobs as adults because of their cognitive deficiencies, it was reasoned that the best hope for breaking the cycle of poverty experienced by these children was to give them, through the schools, these basic cognitive skills (cf. House of Representatives, Hearings Before the Committee on Education and Labor, January 1965). In light of this prevailing attitude on the part of many policymakers, it is naive to argue that studies of school and program effectiveness need not attempt to measure basic reading and mathematical skills.

The second reason for measuring cognitive outcomes is more practical: they are easier to assess than noncognitive ones. Further, on the face of it, there is no reason to believe that noncognitive outcome, such as attitudes, interests, and values, are more susceptible to differences in school resources than they are to home-background factors. In fact, it is probable that basic cognitive skills are more easily taught in schools than noncognitive outcomes. The latter are more likely to be an indirect outcome of the school experience (Madaus & Linnan, 1973). Hence, if we are unable to find direct relations between school resources and cognitive achievement, it would appear that small refuge can be taken in the fact that measures of noncognitive outcomes have been omitted in most studies.

Debate over the "measurableness" of school outcomes is not new, of course. In 1911, Chief Inspector Holmes (1911), recalling his experience in Irish schools during the payment-by-results era, pointed out that

> Wherever the outward standard of reality (examination results) has established itself at the expense of the inward, the ease with which worth (or what passes for such) can be measured is ever tending to become in itself the chief, if not sole, measure of worth. And in proportion as we tend to value the results of education for their measurableness, so we tend to undervalue and at last to ignore those results which are too intrinsically valuable to be measured. (p. 128)

The emphasis on judging school results on the basis of appearance—observable, visible, "measurable" aspects—has been a feature of the technological world view of the nineteenth century, the scientific world view of the 1920s, and the systems-development view of the 1960s and 1970s. On the other hand, there have always been those with a more individual-oriented world view, who have argued that the values undergirding the wide use of tests as outcome measures, or as sorting devices, are antithetical both to good education and to the belief system of teachers (cf. Illich, 1971; Jackson, 1968). While this latter view is perhaps more compassionate and sympathetic, the colder, technocratic viewpoint has generally prevailed.

As a result, those who have criticized the use of cognitive tests to measure school effectiveness are put at an immediate disadvantage, particularly if they attempt to make their argument only on philosophical grounds or on the grounds that "that's not what schools are all about." They might be right to some extent, but, given our technological society, it becomes very difficult to sustain an argument if, as taxpayers and legislators claim, such tests contribute to the efficient use of public monies and, as a corollary, to "good" teaching, to maintaining "standards," to selecting the most "deserving" for further education, and to identifying those who are educationally disadvantaged in terms of basic skills. Part of the problem is that the apparent good sense of these claims preordains the immediate reactions of many policymakers and of the public but tends to suppress the more subtle value assumptions implicit in this orientation. On the other hand, to argue solely that schools really perform more basic functions in society than imparting language, computation, and other cognitive skills, and therefore that effectiveness should be judged on other criteria (or not at all), is to bury one's head in the sand. For some this stance is a subtle effort to avoid accountability or interstate, district, or school-level comparisons.

STANDARDIZED TESTS AS MEASURES OF SCHOOL OUTCOMES

Not only have cognitive outcomes been the focus of most national evaluations of compensatory-education programs and surveys of differential school effects, but invariably the measure of cognitive development used in these studies has been a commercially available, standardized, norm-referenced test (Averch et al., 1972). This choice is understandable since it was generally believed that standardized tests were the correct measure to use in assessing the outcomes of schools. At the same time, investigators were not always happy with this choice of standardized tests, arguing that they did not adequately sample the full range of cognitive objectives that schools attempt to foster (see Smith, 1972; Jencks et al., 1972).

Fitzgibbon (1975a) focused on what is perhaps the central concern in using standardized tests in studies of school and program effectiveness, when he wrote

> Accountability is almost universally accepted in the sense that most of us feel that it's "right." To be against accountability is analogous to being against pollution control, the Fourth of July, and free speech. It's a "good" that one should be responsible for one's actions. The problem becomes, however: who is responsible to whom? And who shall control the instruments and the systems of accountability? Educational tests have been caught up in this issue and are being challenged as to whether they are acceptable for this purpose. In this instance, it is almost always the "standardized test" that bears the brunt of the challenge. (p. 4)

This view touches on an important aspect of the debate over the measurement of school outcomes: who should be allowed to set standards in a system of education that values local control? The real controversy therefore is not over the tests per se, but over who will control education. Proponents of the continued use of standardized tests in studies of school or program effectiveness argue that if such tests are eliminated, either by legislation or some kind of moratorium, then state and local administrators as well as teachers can somehow avoid accountability.

Often, arguments at this level avoid entirely the issue of whether standardized tests are valid measures of school outcomes and rather naively plead that any measure is better than nothing. We suggest that standardized tests, when used in studies of program or school effectiveness, have failed to register what pupils actually attain in schools. It does not follow from this that the use of standardized tests should be abolished. Rather, what is needed are more specific, more sensitive standardized tests for use in the evaluation of schooling. There is nothing inherently wrong with the concept of a test standardized and normed for national or statewide use. The question is what content and constructs these tests are measuring.

Critics of standardized tests should face the fact that some important educational outcomes can and must be measured. Meaningful standards can and must be set; such standards cannot be forever avoided by falling back on the presumed dangers they pose to local control. At some point we must accept the fact that part of the problem in developing better measures of school achievement is directly related to the present structure of American education. Before more sensitive measures can be developed and used widely, vested interest groups will have to come to grips with the need to have agreed-upon standards of excellence at least in the basic school subjects. Furthermore, these groups will need to accept that assessment of these standards will permit interschool, interdistrict, and interstate comparisons of the effectiveness of programs designed to realize these standards.

Large-scale federal involvement in education in the United States began during the past decade in an atmosphere in which there were strong political pressures on schools to reduce disparities between racial and cultural groups in the results of the education process. The involvement also came at a time when legislators and civil servants were becoming increasingly beguiled by systems analysis and the techniques of 'rational' management (e.g., Program Planning and Budgeting Systems—PPBS) based on specification and measurement of objectives. These techniques, perfected for industrial and military application, held out to decision makers the promise of identifying real needs, translating these needs into specific objectives, and checking continually whether the objectives were being realized or could be met in a more efficient way. The end result of the process would be that taxpayers could rest assured of efficiency and value for money.

With hindsight it is easy to point out that this approach applied to education makes unwarranted assumptions about the educational decision-making process. For example, it overlooks the political constraints faced by school administrators (cf. House, 1973b). In addition, it assumes the ability to quantify various outputs associated with the educational process (Campbell, 1976). However, it was only with the passage of time that the weaknesses of the systems approach as applied to education became apparent. Policymakers in the mid-1960s had yet to learn these difficult lessons, and the emphasis on easily quantifiable results was particularly strong.

The concept of demonstrating the *results* associated with a school program was variously embodied in federal legislation and bureaucratic guidelines. Title IV of the 1964 Civil Rights Act mandated a study of the nation's schools and resulted in the Coleman Report, which attempted to document the extent of inequality not only of opportunity but also of results. Title I and Title III of the ESEA of 1965 required an evaluation of the effectiveness of each LEA's program funded under these titles. Tests of achievement and ability often came to be the principal measures of effectiveness used in these evaluations (cf. Wargo et al., 1972). Title VIII guidelines for bilingual programs required the administration of pretests and posttests to measure progress associated with the program. Taken together, these programs represented an unprecedented attempt by legislators and civil servants to pay attention not only to the inputs of the educational system but also to the outcomes associated with education. Furthermore, an effort was made to identify the particular factors that make a difference in improving the scholastic performance of poor children.

In focusing their interest on the results of schooling, both those responsible for drafting legislation and/or guidelines for compensatory programs and those responsible for evaluating the effectiveness of such programs readily accepted commercially available standardized-test data as a criterion measure of school and program outcomes. It is interesting to note that a consequence of this acceptance was that standardized tests became the implicit standard for the evaluation of school performance.

The reasons for the ready acceptance of standardized tests are many and interrelated, but not particularly hard to discern. First, standardized tests had a long history of use, dating to the post–World War I period, when the tests became a key element in efforts to make education "scientific." In time these tests became an accepted part of the educational scene. School administrators generally saw to it that tests were routinely administered every year. As a consequence, most Americans had taken such tests during their sojourn in school and therefore felt that they knew what the tests were all about.

True, there had always been criticism of tests and the testing movement. This criticism might be compared to a tide; advancing, crashing on the shore, and then ebbing. While test criticism is now at flood tide, at the time when Coleman began his survey—when compensatory programs were first evaluated—it was at low ebb. Further, despite the spate of periodic complaints directed at standardized tests (cf. Bollenbacher, 1976; Cronbach, 1975; Madaus, Airasian & Kellaghan, 1971 for a review of this criticism), many laypeople and professional educators at that time uncritically accepted these tests as indicators of important school outcomes.

Second, intervention programs like Head Start and Title I were initially justified on the basis that an "achievement gap" existed between disadvantaged and other children (Biemiller, 1966; Celebrezze, 1965; Marland, 1965). This gap was defined in terms of standardized-test performance levels. For example, in testifying before the congressional committee hearing arguments for the passage of the Elementary and Secondary Education Act of 1965, Anthony Celebrezze, Secretary of Health, Education, and Welfare argued in favor of the bill to aid local schools with compensatory and remedial funds by citing standardized-test performance data.

> You will find that by the end of the third year [grade] this student [in central Harlem in New York City] is approximately 1.2 grades behind the national average and 1.1 grades behind the New York City average. By the time he gets to the sixth grade, he is 2.1 grades below the national average and two grades below the New York average. And by the time he gets to the eighth grade, he is 2 ½ grades below the national average and approximately 2 grades below the New York average. . . . The students continue to get further and further behind in terms of standarized test norms. . . . (Celebrezze, 1965, p. 89)

Documenting the fact that groups already recognized as occupationally and economically deprived were also well below the national average in reading and mathematical skills became an important political lever in the hands of civil rights and labor groups in their arguments that schools could and should be concerned with reducing educational disparities between races and classes. The elimination of educational disparities would, the argument ran, reduce economic disparities separating these groups. It was only logical, having defined the achievement disparity in terms of standardized-test performance in the first place, that efforts to eradicate the disparity be assessed by the same type of criterion measures (e.g., Robert Kennedy, *Congressional Record*, January 26, 1965, p. 513).

Thus standardized tests had an automatic face or political validity. Paradoxically, many individuals and groups who accepted standardized test results as indicative of a pressing need for remedial programs became critics of these tests when they were used in studies which revealed little improvement in pupil performance resulting from compensatory programs. It is interesting to note that for a variety of reasons there has been a double standard of acceptance of standardized tests: results are accepted in the justification but not the evaluation of school and compensatory programs.

Third, standardized achievement and ability tests had, for the most part, well-developed sets of national norms which were generally accepted as providing a reputable "standard" with which school and program outcomes could be compared. While this general acceptance was based on an oversimplification of how such norms could be used and interpreted, nonetheless the performance of the targeted groups had been declared unacceptable relative to the national average, and this low relative standing demanded redress. The norms which accompany standardized tests provided an empirical definition of average performance. The existence of norms, in fact, made the slogan "closing the achievement gap" meaningful. The adequacy of school interventions, policies, and resources was judged in terms of the extent to which such resources enabled students identified as being at low levels on the standardized tests to move to average levels, again as defined by the norms on such tests. Particularly when researchers and evaluators were interested in nationwide performance, standardized test norms afforded a natural comparative criterion, one unavailable with any other type of measurement instrument.

Fourth, many of the individuals commissioned to assess the effectiveness of these programs were trained in the older measurement tradition. In this tradition, standardized tests were the investigator's stock in trade (Madaus, 1973). While some leaders in the measurement field had pointed out weaknesses in using standardized tests for program evaluation (cf. Cronbach, 1963; Stake, 1972; R. Tyler, 1974), most of those engaged in local or national evaluation continued to rely heavily on the standardized test as a principal criterion in assessing program effectiveness. Uncritical reliance on tests was greatly aided by federal and state guidelines which implicitly or explicitly required that standardized tests be used in evaluation (Wargo et al., 1972).

Last but by no means least, like Everest, the tests were there. They were readily and rather cheaply available on the open market. They were familiar to most teachers. They were easy to administer and could be scored rapidly by machine. It would have been surprising if the tests hadn't been widely used, particularly given the fact that budgets for evaluation were quite tight to begin with and that the development and validation of new instruments would have been quite costly. Certainly, given the short time span in which to complete the Coleman study, there would not have been sufficient time to build other outcome measures. Commercially available standardized tests thus became the principal measures of school output in studies of school and program effectiveness.

THE USE OF STANDARDIZED TESTS OF ABILITY AND ATTAINMENT IN MEASURING SCHOOL AND PROGRAM OUTCOMES

Two types of standardized norm-referenced tests have been widely employed as criterion measures in studies of school and program effectiveness: tests of "general ability" (verbal and nonverbal) and tests of "achievement." Tests of general ability (including tests of verbal ability and intelligence) are commonly understood to measure the potential or aptitude of a child to learn; achievement tests are generally understood to measure how well a child has learned the material taught in a specific course. In practice, the correlation between pupils' performance on ability and achievement tests is quite high, of the order of .7 or higher, leading many to doubt the usefulness of a distinction between the two. (Coleman et al., 1966; Kelley, 1927). Despite these theoretical doubts, distinction between learning potential (ability or intelligence) and amount actually learned (achievement) survives.

Some researchers, accepting the view that there is little difference between ability and achievement tests, have suggested that the ability test is the more appropriate measure of school outcomes (Coleman et al., 1966; Cooley & Lohnes, 1976). On the basis of factor-analytic studies of standardized ability and achievement tests, Cooley and Lohnes (1976) conclude that "conventional school assessment is shown to be supersaturated with a general intellectual development factor, despite the variety of names given the variates and the variety of assessment methods involved" (p. 96). Citing Bloom's (1964) analyses in support of the view that intelligence is the most important mental trait developed in any school year, Cooley and Lohnes conclude that a measure of intelligence is the best criterion of instructional successes at both the primary and secondary levels. [It might be noted that Bloom (1976) in his latest book calls for the use of specific achievement tests, not intelligence tests, to assess school effectiveness.]

Certainly some cognitively oriented preschool programs have used an ability test, the Stanford-Binet, as the principal outcome measure to determine program effectiveness. The argument made is that since the objective of preschool education is to teach a "readiness for school" and since scores on the Binet predict subsequent school success, the Binet is a "readiness" measure. Therefore preschools which raise children's IQ scores may be considered successful (Kamii, 1971). The logical criterion instrument in measuring the success of the program therefore becomes the Stanford-Binet, an "ability" or "intelligence" measure (cf. Bronfenbrenner, 1975; Kellaghan, 1977c).

Coleman (1966), on rather different grounds, also supports the idea of using a measure of general ability as a criterion of school effectiveness, citing his own findings as evidence that ability tests are at least as much influenced by school differences as are achievement tests. For the most part, the evidence is based upon the respective amounts of between-school variances associated with the ability and achievement tests used in the survey. For example, the percentage of variance between schools was found to be slightly greater for the ability test than for the achievement tests. This was interpreted to be "indirect evidence that variations among schools have as much or more effect on the 'ability test' scores as the 'achievement test' scores" (Coleman et al., 1966, p. 293).

Coleman presumed that if a school's primary effect is on pupil achievement rather than on ability, then in the higher grades the school-to-school variation in achievement test scores should be larger than the school-to-school variation in ability test scores. However, analysis of his data revealed that the percentage of between-school variance in achievement test scores declined from grade 3 to grade 12.

Finally, when Coleman attempted to determine the amount of variance in individual test scores attributable to school characteristics while holding family background constant, he found that the proportion of test variance explained was greater for the ability test than for the achievement tests. However, on the basis of the observation that ability tests were at least as much affected by school differences as achievement tests, Coleman felt justified in using the general ability test as the measure of school output. In retrospect, one would think that these findings would have made the researchers suspect, and directed them to look more closely at the characteristics of their so-called ability and achievement tests.

There were also, perhaps, less explicit reasons for the acceptance and use of ability test scores as measures of school effectiveness in the Coleman study. It is probably not without significance that the study was planned in the context of equality of educational opportunity and was particularly concerned with the education of children from disadvantaged backgrounds. It was carried out at a time when Head Start programs across the United States were being implemented to raise the intellectual functioning of preschool children (Kellaghan, 1972b). What could be more natural than to focus on ability in a general survey of the educational system also?

As noted in Chapter 2, whether the criterion measure of school outcomes was a test of verbal ability as in the Coleman study or a standardized test of achievement (as in most program-evaluation studies), research resulted in pessimistic findings about the effectiveness of schooling. Simplified, the overall results were interpreted to indicate that once the level of ability and/or home background of students is controlled for, existing differences between school resources, personnel, programs, etc., do not seem to produce a large, consistent, or lasting impact on test scores. Jencks and his associates summed it up as follows:

> There is no evidence that school reform can substantially reduce the extent of cognitive inequality as measured by tests of verbal fluency, reading, comprehension or mathematical skill. Neither school resources nor segregation has an appreciable effect on higher test scores or educational achievement. (Jencks et al., 1972, p. 8)

These conclusions have led some commentators to question the effectiveness of the schools, and others to question the effectiveness of the outcome measures. It is the latter question that we wish to consider in some detail. Basically, we are concerned with a question of validity, a question of the correctness of basing inferences concerning school effectiveness on the results of standardized ability and achievement tests.

VALIDITY OF STANDARDIZED TESTS OF ABILITY AS MEASURES OF SCHOOL OUTCOMES

In considering the validity of standardized tests of ability as measures of school outcomes, we are concerned with two types of validity: content and construct. Content validity refers to the degree to which the behaviors called for in test items constitute a representative sample of the behaviors to be exhibited in the performance domain of interest (American Psychological Association, 1974). To determine a test's content validity it is first necessary to define or specify the behaviors which are included in the domain to be tested. For example, if one were to construct a test to measure students' learning of elementary algebra, one would need to know which behaviors and processes are integral to elementary algebra courses. The second step in establishing content validity involves a judgment to determine whether the test items written are a relevant, representative sample of this domain. The behaviors and content identified as being essential to elementary algebra would be compared to the behaviors and content actually measured in the proposed test to ascertain whether the tested behaviors and content were representative of the essential behaviors and content.

Construct validity, on the other hand, is concerned with the meaning of tests or with the nature of the processes underlying test performance (American Psychological Association, 1974; Cronbach, 1971). The aim of construct validation is to determine the underlying causes or factors which influence individuals' performance on a test. Thus one might ask whether high scores on an elementary algebra test are a function of how much a pupil has actually learned in the algebra course, or a function of some other, independent capability such as the individual's ability to understand complex directions, perceive mathematical relations in spatial terms, or translate words into mathematical relations. At issue is the identification of the construct or dimension underlying test performance. Note that a test may be content valid but construct validation studies may reveal that satisfactory performance on the test resides in some ability or characteristic quite unrelated to the behaviors actually taught in the subject.

Thus, there are two questions which may be raised in considering the validity of standardized achievement and ability tests as measures of school outcomes. First, does the content of the test match the universe or domain of school-based behaviors (content validity)? Second, is there evidence that performance on such tests is related to school-specific learning (construct validity)? We shall now explore these questions for standardized ability tests.

Content Validity

In some respects, the question of the content validity of ability tests relates to a criticism we have already noted: that tests used in studies of school effectiveness did not constitute an adequate sampling of school outcomes, that the behaviors measured in such tests do not represent the full range of outcomes fostered by the school. However, in addressing the question of content validity we are not asking whether Coleman's verbal-ability measure or an intelligence test like the Stanford-Binet adequately sample noncognitive outcomes; but rather, within the cognitive domain, are the types of items comprising an ability test representative of the domain of school learning?

The answer to this question may depend on the level of the curriculum about which one is talking and the characteristics of students the curriculum is trying to affect. For example, a number of preschool programs for disadvantaged children have been designed specifically to raise the level of general intellectual functioning of participants (Kamii, 1971; Kellaghan, 1977c). Given such an objective, it may be legitimate to use a general intelligence test as a measure of program effectiveness. Several studies, in fact, have reported increases in level of measured intelligence as an effect of preschool intervention (cf. Bronfenbrenner, 1975; Kellaghan, 1977c). However, even at the preschool level there are serious issues of content and construct validity associated with the use of an ability test as the principal measure of program effectiveness. Whether raising students' general intellectual ability is the prime school goal for older children is another matter entirely. Certainly, an examination of the activities of schools would lead one to believe that if it is a goal, it is a very remote one. At the elementary level, schools are concerned with reading, grammar, spelling, writing, listening skills, dictation skills, and so on. At the high-school level, algebra, physics, chemistry, foreign languages, commercial, vocational, and industrial arts occupy the curriculum. Contrast the focus of these more specialized courses with the vocabulary, verbal reasoning, and inductive and deductive skills measured by general ability tests and one finds very little congruence.

This is not to deny that general ability or intelligence is not an achievement in the broad sense of the term. Neither does it deny that schools may affect its development. Indeed, we could expect children who do not attend school to have poorer levels of vocabulary and verbal skills than children who do (see Chapter 3). It may even be that differences in the development of verbal ability may be associated with school characteristics.

The point is that schools have a whole host of objectives in the cognitive area which are not represented in a test of general ability.

Even in cognitively oriented preschool programs, the use of standardized ability measures may not adequately sample the specific ways in which a curriculum may alter children's performance. Cazden (1971) shows that the oral language objectives of preschool programs are many and diverse. She argues that

> Because these behaviors probably are affected differentially by particular preschool programs, it is extremely important to test achievement as specifically as possible, e.g., to deal specifically with pronunciation, vocabulary, or question-asking skill. . . .
> The Stanford-Binet must be rejected for our purposes because the only score is a global one which does not separate language from non-language skills, much less permit differentiation within the language area itself. *There is no question of the excellence of the Stanford-Binet for other purposes; it simply cannot function as a test of the achievement of particular language behavior.*
> (pp. 387–88; emphasis added)

Thus Cazden is questioning the content validity (as well as the construct validity) of the Stanford-Binet scale for the assessment of preschool intervention programs.

While it is probably true that general ability cuts across many areas of schooling, the degree to which it is specifically taught in schools is open to serious question. Coleman, for example, suggests that schools only incidentally teach the material covered by ability tests.

> Achievement tests cover material that is nearly the same in all school curriculums, toward which all schools teach alike, while the ability tests cover material that school teaches more incidentally. . . . (Coleman et al., 1966, p. 294)

It seems curious to look for differences between schools on something that is only incidentally taught while ignoring the possible differential success on material that is more specific to school curricula. It would seem more logical to expect differences in expenditures, facilities, curriculum offering, and teacher characteristics to affect and mediate outcomes in those areas for which all schools specifically teach. One would expect financial expenditures and the services and facilities which money buys to have a more forceful impact on the direct instructional aspects of the school than on something which is taught only incidentally. There are thus a number of reasons for questioning the content validity of standardized ability and intelligence tests as measures of school and program effectiveness. Despite this, the tests were used and they provided the principal data for damaging inferences about school effectiveness.

Construct Validity

We turn now to a consideration of the construct validity of tests of general ability in the context of measuring school output. We need to consider what the concept "school achievement" means and what are the implications of using a measure designed to tap the construct "ability" as a measure of the construct "achievement." Is there evidence that schools affect performance on tests of verbal ability, and is there evidence that other factors are more influential? The answer to the first question, in the light of the findings of several studies (Coleman et al., 1966; Great Britain: Department of Education and Science, 1967; Husen, 1967) is that the differential effects of schools on verbal ability is slight. Thus, a test which was assumed to be sensitive to differences between schools, since it was chosen as an output measure in a study of differential effectiveness, is found not to be. When these results became available and were replicated in other studies, the construct validity of ability tests as measures of school outcomes should have been called into question. Instead, however, discussion focused upon the inputs to schooling rather than the adequacy of the output measures. As Levine (1976, p. 228) notes, . . . "the test's validity is not questioned but rather our commonly accepted concepts of what is important for good education: money, facilities, experienced teachers."

The case for the construct validity of ability tests as measures of school effectiveness is further weakened by evidence that verbal ability is strongly influenced by home-background factors—both status and process variables—and that ability is relatively stable during the school years. The substantial influence of home background on the development of "intelligence" as measured by standardized tests, particularly during the preschool years, has been well documented (cf. Bloom, 1964, 1976; Marjoribanks, 1972). Furthermore, given the fact that a large proportion of the variance on "intelligence" at the age of seventeen can be accounted for at the age of eight (Bloom, 1964, 1976), there would appear to be relatively little possibility for schools to have a large independent impact on its development. This is not to deny that school can have a collusive effect with family factors on verbal ability (Mayeske et al., 1972; Brimer et al., 1978), nor is it to say that, given home and school environmental conditions that differ from those that obtain in the United States or West European societies today, "ability" will not be found to be more flexible in later childhood and adolescence. This, of course, is hypothetical. The evidence we do have indicates that under present conditions, measured intelligence or verbal ability is a relatively stable attribute during the school years (cf. Hopkins & Bracht, 1975; L. Tyler, 1976).

McClelland (1973) has pointed out that traditionally the intelligence test has been designed to be relatively stable over time. The reason for this is that the test was designed to measure an innate mental capacity that was felt to be relatively unmodifiable by experience. McClelland argues, however, that this "stability" is only the result of ability tests' measuring behaviors so specialized that they are unrelated to what people have learned (not that people could not learn them).

> . . . Being able to play a word game like analogies is apparently little affected by a higher education, which is not so surprising since few teachers ask their students to do analogies. Therefore, being able to do analogies is often considered a sign of some innate ability factor. Rather, it might be called an achievement so specialized that increases in general wisdom do not transfer to it and cause changes in it. And why should we be interested in such specialized skills? As we have seen, they predictably do not seem to correlate with any life-outcome criteria except those that involve similar tests or that require the credentials that a high score on the test signifies. (McClelland, 1973, p. 8)

This passage raises questions about the content included in such general (specialized) measures and also calls into question whether the construct measured by such tests can be equated with the construct of school achievement. Further, it turns Cooley and Lohnes's argument on its head. Increases in "general wisdom" do not transfer to or modify these general measures, which are not general at all in the sense of being broad-gauged but are instead, in McClelland's view, narrow and highly specialized.

If measured verbal ability is relatively stable and to a large degree a function of the child's preschool background—which includes hereditary, status, and environmental factors—then it seems more appropriate to regard it as a measure of readiness for instruction rather than as a measure of the effects of instruction (Wilson, 1968). One study (Madaus, Kellaghan, & Rakow, 1975) found that the inclusion of the IQ as a school input rather than output had the result of explaining more of the total variance on both standardized attainment tests and syllabus-specific achievement measures (the Irish Leaving and Intermediate Certificate examination in an array of subjects) than was explained when it was omitted, and that the amounts of variance *uniquely* explained by class and individual factors dropped when IQ was included as a separate predictor block. However, the inclusion of the IQ as a predictor of achievement did not alter the fact that for the syllabus-specific measures of achievement such as chemistry, mathematics and French, the class block remained the most powerful of all the predictor blocks in terms of its unique component of explained variance. Interesting also is the fact that when a standardized norm-referenced test was used as the outcome variable instead of the public exam, the IQ block was clearly the most powerful unique predictor. In this study, which was carried out at the secondary-school level in Ireland, home-background factors contributed very little to the prediction of school outcome measures. Pupils in this study were deliberately selected because they were in an academic curriculum and hence were considerably more homogeneous in terms of educational and family background than secondary pupils in the Coleman study, which included all ninth and twelfth graders irrespective of type of high school or curriculum track within school.

Given research on the influence of home and early background on verbal ability, one might consider a verbal-ability score at the age of six to be a surrogate measure of an important aspect of a child's home environment. Indeed, it could be argued that given the nature of his verbal-ability measure, Coleman demonstrated that his family block predicted very well another family variable.

We saw earlier that Cooley and Lohnes proposed a general factor derived from a factor analysis of traditional test batteries (verbal ability and achievement tests) as the principal criterion measure of school effectiveness. Cooley (1976) calls such a factor "general intelligence." Mayeske et al., employed just such a measure in their reanalysis of Coleman's data. While they did find this measure had considerably more between-school variance associated with it than had Coleman's verbal-ability measure for reasons not necessarily having to do with the measure itself (*see* Chapter 2), school factors did not uniquely account for much of this variance. Instead, they found a collusive effect wherein family factors and school variables operating jointly accounted for much of the explainable variance. This finding calls into question Coleman's inferences about the prominence of the family block as well as Cooley and Lohnes's argument that a general ability measures is the correct criterion of school effectiveness. Such measures may in fact assess transfer of learning, but the collusive effect of home and school factors on such measures cannot be untangled, although at present home-background factors appear to be the more important.

Further, Carroll (1976) points out that such a general factor emerges in factor analyses because most cognitive tasks are highly correlated, since they tend to involve a common set of cognitive operations, strategies, and memory stores. It should be noted that such factor analyses generally involve traditional standardized ability and achievement tasks. We shall argue in the following chapter that the traditional achievement tests themselves are general rather than related to specific school learning. Given the general nature of both the ability and achievement measures used, family-background factors tend to remain very important; whatever transfer from specific learning occurs is obscured by this fact.

Moreover, as one progresses through the grades, courses become more specific and pupils taking different courses become more homogeneous with respect to a "general ability factor." At the secondary level, the more specific the course, the less variance there is likely to be in such a general factor for pupils taking the same course. The relative homogeneity of pupil ability within a class suggests that other factors will begin to account for variance on measures of the learnings specific to the course.

Guttman (1969) offers additional evidence that calls into question the use of a general factor as a measure of school effectiveness. When school measures in courses such as German, geography, chemistry, history, and biology are included along with more general measures of verbal and numerical ability in a procedure similar to a factor analysis, different bands of "factors" appear. The analyses showed that school-specific achievement tests (German, chemistry, etc.) were distinct from tests of more general cognitive abilities. Guttman concluded that school specific achievement factors were suitable for use as criterion measures of school achievement whereas the other factors, which loaded heavily on general measures of verbal and numerical ability, were more suitable for use as predictors of school achievement.

Cooley and Lohnes's general factor does not include course-specific measures similar to those in the Guttman analysis, but more general achievement batteries. These, we will argue in the following chapter, are unlikely to be sensitive to the topics covered in specific school subjects.

The relation between increase in general ability and performance on more specific achievement measures is not at all clear. Ebel (1969) has raised questions as to whether broad, general thinking skills will transfer to more specific subject areas. In other words, thinking effectively may differ from subject matter to subject matter or from one area of specialization to another.

At the preschool level, Kamii (1971) points out that it is only an assumption that there is a positive correlation between increase in IQ test score and the amount of learning accomplished in a preschool program. Kellaghan (1977c) found that while it was possible to raise the IQ scores of disadvantaged children, this was not accompanied by corresponding gains in school-related achievements such as reading. Thus justifying the use of general ability measures on the basis of their capability to tap transfer behaviors needs to be reconsidered.

Kamii (1971) makes an additional point related to both the construct and content validity of ability tests when used in preschool program evaluation. Traditional measures of general ability give a single global score because such tests were developed in the absence of a theory which adequately described how children think and develop. Since cognition is now better understood as a structured process, she argues, we need to examine the cognitive processes in the diverse areas of physical knowledge, social knowledge, logical knowledge, and representation. A single global-ability score hides more than it shows about differential cognitive functioning and the effectiveness of different programs in modifying this functioning.

As we saw, many preschool programs do produce gains in general intelligence as measured by tests like the Stanford-Binet. However, the experience has been that this gain washes out relative to control groups who begin school at the usual time. The reasons that the gains of preschool disadvantaged children disappear once the control group enters school are not clear. Two possible explanations can be suggested. First, the gains of the preschoolers are measured relative to a control group that has not had any preschool experience. The children in the experimental program have had instruction that is quite similar to tasks on tests like the Binet. In other words the Binet, when administered at the preschool stage, is not a general test, but one which can be very specific to instruction. As soon as control-group pupils have similar experiences in kindergarten or first grade they erase the gap which existed prior to school entrance.

Karlson gives support to the hypothesis that parts of general intelligence measures can be quite specific relative to the experience to preschool children (Stodolsky, 1972). Karlson found that in a Montessori preschool where the environment was prepared and materials sequenced, there was still a great deal of variation in the activities pursued by individual children in the free play and work which characterized the session. When activities pursued by individual children were identified and the time spent on each activity by individuals noted, it was possible to relate patterns of activities to various subscores on the Wechsler Preschool and Primary Scale of Intelligence (WPPSI), a measure of general intelligence. Differences were masked when all pupils were compared on the measure. However, when specific activities were related to specific subtests, those subtests became specific achievement measures (Stodolsky, 1972).

A second reason the "washout" effect occurs may be that the trait measured in the preschool program is quite different from that measured in the first or second grade. In some ways the argument recalls the finding that creativity test scores declined in the fourth grade (Torrance, 1962). Different theoretical and developmental reasons were offered to explain this apparent decline in "creativity." However, the most likely reason for the decline was that the creativity tests used before grade 4 were individually administered while those given later were group tests. Thus, when the method used to assess creativity changed from an individual to a group test, the scores at first declined but then began to rise from grade 5 on as children became used to group test-taking (Dacey, Madaus, & Allen, 1969; Getzels & Madaus, 1969; Madaus, 1967a, 1967b).

The Stanford-Binet Intelligence Scale (Terman & Merrill, 1960) has an age-appropriate range from two years to adult. As can be imagined, the items for early childhood are vastly different from those at the adolescent and adult levels. There is an interesting difference between early-childhood items (years 2-5) and middle-childhood items (years 6-9). If one categorizes questions on the Binet into manipulative, manipulative-verbal, and verbal, the average numbers of items for early childhood in each category are 2.4 manipulative, 1.8 manipulative-verbal, and 1.7 verbal. The weighting is heavily on the side of manipulative, with a total weighting of 4.2 manipulative, manipulative-verbal and 1.7 verbal. These weightings are completely reversed in middle childhood, when the total manipulative/manipulative-verbal average is 1.75 and the verbal average is 4.25.

The movement to a more verbal mode in the middle childhood years may well account for the washout effect on this test. What has happened is that a *different* trait carrying the same label ("intelligence") as the one measured in the preschool years is being measured in the middle years. Thus, whether there is an actual drop in the trait measured in the preschool years is undetermined, since a different trait is being measured in subsequent years. If this analysis is correct, then it may be that a trait-method interaction effect is responsible for the so-called washout effect.

Present intelligence and ability tests predict well how pupils will perform in school when school performance is measured by standardized achievement tests and teachers' grades. This happens because such measures are used implicitly as entry-level requirements at various grades, and pupils tend to be grouped according to verbal ability; further, all students are treated in much the same way in the instructional process (Bloom, 1976; Crano, 1974; Glaser, 1976; L. Tyler, 1976). Present intelligence tests are not diagnostic; they do not provide data on how a school can help pupils to learn (Bloom, 1976; Glaser, 1976). If schools group or stream pupils on the basis of cognitive entry behaviors which are closely related to the curriculum pupils follow, rather than on the basis of general ability or intelligence tests, alterations in instruction greatly reduce the predictive power of the more general measures of intelligence or achievement (Bloom, 1976). In such a situation general intelligence tests will not predict those who learn best nor will they be valid measures of the processes that contribute to learning in specific school tasks (Glaser, 1976).

CONCLUSION

It seems that whatever construct is measured by tests of general intelligence, it is not congruent with the construct "school achievement"; intelligence and ability tests do not tap specific, course-related student learning. Thus inferences made concerning the differential effectiveness of schools or compensatory programs on the basis of results obtained using a measure of general intelligence, verbal ability, or aptitude possess neither content nor construct validity.

One implication of our discussion is that the choice of tests to measure any construct is extremely important, and one should exercise great care in ascertaining that a test name agrees with the test construct. At the best of times, construct names give rise to problems, since different publics may interpret labels quite differently. Certainly there is a need, often neglected, to decode research language for the public and the policymaker (Lourie, 1976).

Often technical words are taken over by the public with the result that the constructs for which they stand lose their initial scientific sense and become applied vaguely or metaphorically (Greenough & Kittredge, 1961). In the school-effectiveness debate, however, ordinary words such as *achievement* and *ability* have been taken over and used by researchers in such a way that they have lost their common-sense meaning and distinction. Orwell (1968a), recognizing this phenomenon, noted that "abstract words are never coined at all, though old words (e.g., 'condition,' 'reflex,' etc.) are sometimes twisted into new meanings for scientific purposes" (p. 3). He further points out that "when you think of something abstract you are more inclined to use words from the start, and unless you make a conscious effort to prevent it, the existing dialect will come rushing in and do the job for you, at the expense of blurring or even changing your meaning" (Orwell, 1968b, p. 138). Orwell correctly reminds us that the consequences of such a blurring can be serious. "A bad usage can spread by tradition and imitation, even among people who should and do know better" (p. 137).

This is what happened in the debate over differential school effectiveness. Coleman admits that the principal criterion measure often carried the label "intelligence test." Keeping this in mind, consider the semantic problem associated with Coleman's inferences about the factors which explain variation in the criterion measure. "School," the report concludes, "brings little influence to bear on a child's achievement that is independent of his background and general social context" (Coleman et al., 1966, p. 325).

Would there have been the surprise and eventual pessimism associated with their results had they reported that "schools bring little influence to bear on a child's 'verbal ability' that is independent of his background and general social context?" Or that "schools bring little influence to bear on a child's 'intelligence' that is independent of his background and general social context?" If the findings had been reported in one of these alternative forms, one can only speculate on the course the debate—or lack of one—on differential school effectiveness might have taken over the past decade.

In practice, what has happened is that in interpreting the Coleman results, the construct "verbal ability" has become equated with the construct "school achievement," and findings that are limited to conclusions about verbal ability have been generalized to include other school outcomes. Thus, perhaps because general verbal ability is considered so important, perhaps because of the tendency of social scientists to lose sight of the limits of their measures and talk in broader terms or more commonly understood constructs, or perhaps because the media and public needed to simplify complex studies, Coleman's findings have been interpreted in the widest and most damaging possible sense, a sense which extends far beyond the bounds set by the content and construct validity of their principal outcome measures. Unfortunately, it is always easier to tie a knot than to loosen one.

chapter 6

School Outcomes: Standardized Tests of Achievement

INTRODUCTION

While one may see serious difficulties in basing inferences about differential school or program effectiveness on measures of verbal ability or intelligence, the use of standardized norm-referenced achievement tests as criterion measures has failed to radically alter conclusions about the differential impact of schools. In this chapter, we shall argue that the validity of inferences about school or program effectiveness which use standardized achievement-test performance as the criterion of school outcome is also questionable. In particular, we shall argue that traditional, commercially available standardized achievement tests are relatively insensitive to differences between schools, mainly because of their psychometric properties and content coverage. Instead of being measures of outcomes directly related to schooling, these tests are, at best, indirect measures of learning; most probably they measure much the same traits as do tests of general ability, which, as we saw, are closely related to home background and other extraschool factors.

As in the case of ability tests, the issue concerning the use of standardized achievement tests to evaluate schools or programs is basically one of validity; do the tests measure school-specific learning or outcomes that are more dependent upon extraschool influences? It is true that the tests posssess a certain "face" validity; perhaps that is why they have been so widely accepted. Certainly, tests which purport to measure such things as knowledge of basic numerical facts or of reading comprehension would seem to be measuring reasonable outcomes of school instruction. However, such an assumption does not guarantee validity. To establish validity it is necessary to examine the congruence between the objectives of tests and those of schools. When we do, we find that there are many reasons for questioning the assumption that standardized achievement tests adequately reflect the objectives and processes of the school in a manner that would make them sensitive measures of school outcomes. Rather we will suggest that the purposes and methods of construction of commercially available standardized achievement tests and the structure of American education, with its emphasis on local control, produce tests that are relatively insensitive to the details of instructional practices and tend to measure a general achievement factor.

In the United States, there are no agreed-upon and independently determined national criteria for school achievement. Schools may agree on broad goals, such as literacy, but they do not agree on the relative importance of numerous specific objectives which general goals encompass. They do not agree on the relative emphasis to be given specific objectives nor on the order in which they are to be attained. Thus one school, or even an individual teacher within the school might teach fractions at an earlier stage than another school or teacher. In the absence of clear national objectives for various school levels, the constructors of standardized tests set their own. True, they consult with teachers and examine curricula and textbooks, but ultimately the test constructor sets the objectives. Evidence based on direct observation of instruction is never provided to demonstrate that the goals and standards which are embodied in a test reflect the actual goals or standards emphasized in schools. Further, there is no independent check on the congruence between common objectives inferred from an examination of leading textbooks and curricula and what, when, and how the subject matter is actually taught in classrooms throughout the country.

Before considering in detail issues of content and construct validity, we shall consider a number of general points regarding some of the purposes of constructing commercial standardized achievement tests, which suggest the tests may not be appropriate for evaluating program effectiveness. First, standardized achievement tests, like their ability counterparts, are designed for the assessment of individual pupils, not pupil aggregates. Tests designed on an individual-differences model and constructed to maximize differences between individuals present difficulties when used to discriminate between groups, since the distribution of group means will not be the same as the distribution of student scores (Lindquist, 1966).

It is generally assumed that achievement is normally distributed in the population being tested, and test constructors strive to build tests which distribute students on a normal curve. The assumption of normality in itself raises fundamental issues about the nature and origins of achievement. The normality assumption is based on the further assumption that mental traits are the additive result of a large number of independent influences. The fact that testers write items which are scored in terms of one correct answer and the sum of the correct answers is used to represent performance betrays an additive view of knowledge and a philosophy of education predicated upon one correct answer. Certainly the appropriateness of the normal curve to describe school outputs was widely accepted in the post-World War I period, when so many achievement tests were first developed. Writing in 1922, McCall argued that

> The normal frequency surface appears to be Nature's favorite mold. A random sampling of most facts gives the normal surface. Morality, intelligence, the weights and heights of men, the blueness of eyes, and doubtless, the intensity of halos fit the normal curve. It is seldom that mental and educational scores make a perfectly normal surface, but they usually give a rough approximation of it. This is, according to Thorndike, not because nature abhors irregular distributions but because there are usually present in nature the necessary determiners.
>
> Experimental research has isolated these determiners and has found that the measurements for a given fact fit the normal frequency surface when the fact measured is a joint action of:
> (a) a large number of cases;
> (b) causes which are approximately equal;
> (c) causes which are mutually uncorrelated or act independently of each other, i.e., the presence of one cause does not bring with it one other cause.
>
> It is because these conditions are usually present in education that most educational measurements approximate the normal distribution. (in Palmer, 1932, pp. 29-30)

These assumptions, and the characteristics of tests based on them, may be useful when tests are used to make allocative decisions about individuals. For example, if all students attained an identical score on a test such as the College Entrance Examination Board, the test would be useless for making decisions about the selection of students for admission to college. If tests are to be used for placement or selection it is obviously necessary that they produce a distribution of scores which permits comparative judgments to be made about individuals based on their position on the distribution. However, to assume that what is learned in school is normally distributed among pupils is another matter altogether (cf. Bloom, 1976; Fennessy, 1973; R. Tyler, 1974). The assumption derives not only from the individual-differences model but also from beliefs about basic limitations of all children to benefit from instruction; beliefs, it may be noted, in sharp contrast with those underlying most compensatory programs—that all or at least most students can learn and can achieve competency in basic subjects (Airasian & Madaus, 1972). Once one assumes a "mastery" model (Bloom, 1976) for achievement and instruction, the distribution of scores on some real scale of performance in skills being taught would not be expected to be normal but negatively skewed. Further, school learning most likely is not an additive but a multiplicative process, where "performance is not fixed by summing individual, small contributions, but by making just one, then another, and then still another, step along a path where success in each step makes the next one easier or more effective" (Morrison, 1975, p. 37). This does not mean that one should not measure each small step to check on progress or to see where one is going wrong so correctives can be applied. However, it does call into question the assumption of additiveness and independence that underlie the normal curve, which in turn calls into question the way in which standardized achievement tests are constructed.

One consequence of building standardized achievement tests on the assumption that achievement is normally distributed is that the test results derive their meaning from the distribution of the scores of the population who take the test, or more likely from the representative reference population on which the test was "normed." An individual's score is transformed and reported in a form that says something about where that score, and thus an individual, stands in the normal distribution. The relative position of the score in the distribution determines in some sense whether the score is good or bad. Thus, the score does not directly tell anything about what the pupil has actually achieved in terms of content or skills. Certainly, knowledge of an individual's relative standing on an achievement test can be useful; the score can be used for diagnosis, placement, or selection (Bloom, Hastings, & Madaus, 1971). Standardized norm-referenced achievement tests can provide useful information about an individual; but the norm-referenced nature of standardized achievement tests detracts from their usefulness in making inferences about school or program effectiveness, which involve inferences about group performance.

A further point regarding the purpose of commercially available standardized tests suggests they may not be appropriate for program or school evaluation: the tests are designed to have maximum applicability across schools. There are at least two reasons for this. First, the test constructor is concerned with the test's profitability. It makes little economic sense to invest thousands of dollars constructing items, printing booklets, trying out the items, analyzing test data, revising the items, retrying the items, through the many cycles needed to arrive at the final test if it has appeal to only a few school districts in the country.

Second, the test must have maximum applicability if it is to provide adequate norms for comparing the performance of individual students on the test. If a test is to be of use to teachers or researchers concerned with the individual's standing in a particular locale relative to a larger, nationwide student population, the test must represent skills and behaviors stressed at both the local and national levels. In order to provide a true comparison of a student's standing on a trait relative to a national average, the test content must be selected so that it has applicability across many schools; otherwise the norms derived will be too specific for comparisons beyond those few schools for which the test items are relevant. In such a case, the concept of a "national average" or "national standing" would be inappropriate. Hence maximum applicablility of the test meets not only a commercial need, but also the need to provide representative norms to accompany the test.

The objective of producing a test with applicability across a large number of diverse school curricula determines the procedures used in building the test. These procedures in turn serve to limit the usefulness of standardized achievement tests for program and school evaluation. We shall look at two procedures in test development that speak to this issue; the manner in which test content is selected, and the psychometric criteria used to screen items for inclusion in the test. We shall then briefly consider three aspects of standardized achievement tests which may also render them inappropriate for program evaluation: the emphasis on reliability in their construction, the general format of the test, and the use of a total or summary score to indicate performance. We do not wish to imply that any one of these factors necessarily invalidates the usefulness of an achievement test as a measure of school output. We do wish to suggest, however, that the factors in combination contribute to the insensitivity of standardized achievement tests as measures of school output. Taken together, the factors certainly conspire to produce an instrument whose scores do not provide a fair reflection of work and achievement in ordinary classrooms.

CONTENT SELECTION

The procedures used in building a standardized achievement test derive from the need to attain the dual aims of commercial feasibility and representative norms. The first step in constructing an achievement test is the development of a table of specifications. These specifications include a description of the content or topics to be covered and the skills needed in dealing with the content (e.g., recall, translation, application). Often the test constructor will cross the content categories with skills categories; the result is a grid in which each cell can be weighted as to its importance relative to the total test. Of course, certain cells may be meaningless or unimportant to the test constructor. Once the weighting is accomplished, items corresponding to appropriate cells can be drafted.

In selecting content for most standardized achievement tests, it has become common practice to review the ten or twelve most widely used textbooks or curriculum guides in a particular subject in order to obtain a preliminary list of topics or objectives to be tested. The relative weighting, in terms of number of items given to these topics, is also determined. Often, the median number of pages devoted to a topic in the textbooks surveyed is used as a rough indication of the topic's importance (Tinkleman, 1971). Sometimes, a review of popular textbooks is supplemented by a review of the syllabi in the subject area used by a number of large city school systems. As an example, consider the following quotation, which is indicative of the content selection process followed in the construction of standardized achievement tests:

> The process of preparing items for the test was begun by surveying the textbooks and curriculum guides in common use. Teachers and subject-area specialists were also consulted. . . . From a synthesis of data thus outlined, a set of specifications for each test was developed. . . . (Stanford Test of Academic Skills Manual, 1973, p. 12)

After a tentative list of topics and weights has been obtained, teachers and authorities in the subject area generally are asked to review the list and weighting for adequacy and completeness. This review can result in additions or deletions of topics and objectives. It is on the basis of one or more such refinements that the final specification of topics and skills to be tested is made.

The content topics are more easily delineated in certain school subjects and at certain grade levels than in others. At the secondary level, for example in an English literature course, where a fair amount of discretion is allowed the teacher in selecting topics and books and poems to be read, the determination of common content is far from straightforward (Purves, 1971). As one would expect, there are very few acceptable standardized tests in English literature (Purves, 1971); this is true in many subjects at the secondary level, where greater specialization is accompanied by more diversity in content coverage (cf. Bloom, Hastings, & Madaus, 1971). Because of this, studies of school effectiveness at the secondary- or high-school level have been forced to employ general achievement tests modeled after elementary–school test batteries rather than course-specific tests. Yet it could be reasonably argued that it is in specific courses such as French, physics, and algebra that school resources must be expected to have their major differential impact. Unfortunately, however, effectiveness studies have primarily focused on basic reading and mathematical skills because nationally appropriate achievement tests in specific school subjects have been generally unavailable. As a consequence, in the United States, the differential impact of resources on course-specific achievement at the secondary level has remained unexamined, despite the Coleman study.

The test constructor's task is made particularly difficult in the United States by the large differences between schools in the extent to, and time at, which different curricular objectives are included in curricula. Further, as one moves into the secondary schools, offerings become more specialized. For example, tenth-grade students may take accelerated mathematics, college preparatory mathematics, general mathematics, business or commercial arithmetic. Where there is great diversity in courses taught and outcomes desired—even within a single subject area—an achievement test clearly cannot sample from all the objectives taught in all courses. As a result the tests that finally get built for high-school mathematics tend not to be specific to the many math courses taught within a high school, but instead measure more general processes which cut across courses. Moreover, if the test is to be fair to all students, topics on more specialized math courses (such as trigonometry and calculus) tend to be underrepresented in favor of topics from more basic courses, to which most pupils have at least been exposed.

Because they include only common curricular content and objectives, standardized achievement tests often inadequately reflect the specific content and objectives of particular school programs throughout the country. This fact has been recognized by several investigators (Averch et al., 1972; Klein, 1971; Stake, 1972; Stodolsky, 1972) who have attributed the repeated failure to demonstrate the effects of schools and programs to a lack of congruity between test instruments and program content. Furthermore, if a test does not evaluate the learning of idiosyncratic objectives, it obviously will not assess the impact of school resources associated with the learning of these objectives. Since the items should be fair to all of the more widely used curricula, they should not contain subject matter or nomenclature that is specific to one text or approach. Inspection of items in national tests indicates that this goal is usually met. It can be argued that, in light of these factors, the content domain sampled by the achievement test is the wrong domain; the domain should be more specific to the actual instructional process as carried out in different schools.

There is much merit to these criticisms. However, one could argue that a fair assessment of differential school effectiveness needs to use a criterion instrument that includes only common content and objectives. The argument goes this way: if one wished to assess the differential impact of schools on student achievement, then the test should reflect only things common to the schools being compared. Of course such an approach would fail to take into account uniqueness across schools, but it could be considered a fair appraisal of differential school impact on common instructional goals. We feel, however, that the problem is more basic than the fact that only common content or objectives are assessed by standardized achievement tests. As we shall see in the following section, the psychometric procedures used in item selection interact with content selection to favor the choice of test items which measure a general factor—a trait—which in turn is highly related to verbal ability and home background. We may also note that if schooling has a large but fairly even effect on these common content areas or skills, sampled by standardized tests, then differences in the schools will "explain" very little of the variation in outcomes. Other factors because they are more closely related to the remaining variation, will seem to be more important (Smith, 1975).

PSYCHOMETRIC SCREENING

In the construction of a standardized achievement test, once a pool of items reflecting content specifications has been written, the items are field-tested to select the final set of items that constitute the test. In order to obtain a distribution of test scores that approximates the normal distribution, and hence maximally discriminates between individuals, each item included in the test is carefully screened according to its difficulty level and its discrimination index. An item's difficulty is determined by the percentage of students who answer the item correctly. Discrimination is an index of the extent to which performance on a particular item relates to performance on the entire test. An item with a high discrimination index is one which sorts pupils into pass-fail categories in the same way that pupils are sorted into high and low scorers on the test as a whole. Thus the total test score is used as the criterion for item discrimination, and test constructors seek to identify items that measure more or less the same trait as that measured by the test as a whole. In this way, the items selected for the test tend to be homogeneous with regard to a common trait.

In practice, test constructors seek to attain a test which contains items with a modal difficulty of about .625. This value represents 50 percent difficulty level corrected for the possibility of students' guessing the correct answer in the usual multiple-choice format (Carver, 1975; Henrysson, 1971). Items which most or all students answer correctly or incorrectly are discarded or revised, since difficulties of near 0 or 100 percent provide no differentiation between students. Only a very few easy items are included. As early as 1936, Hawkes, Lindquist, and Mann pointed out that one consequence of discarding easy items is that if instruction has been adequate, very important or very fundamental items may have been so thoroughly taught that they have been mastered by all pupils. Such items would be eliminated in item-screening procedures used in the construction of standardized tests.

At difficulty levels averaging .625, variance in test scores is maximized. Since small variances automatically lower the reliability and validity estimates for a test, it is desirable to have maximum test-score variance. Item discriminations in the .3 to .4 range are sought, since they provide dispersion in the scores and consequently maximize differences between students. It needs to be kept in mind that item statistics are based on data derived from individual pupils, not on pupil aggregates. The effect of these procedures is to make the items which survive the selection phase of test development those which maximally differentiate between individual students and which engender a normal test-score distribution.

There is empirical evidence that item selection can influence a test's content validity. For example, Kwansa (1974) developed a pool of items based on an examination of arithmetic texts and classified items according to the skills they measured. The items which survived the tryout phase and item analyses showed distinct departures from the original distribution of skills, with some not being tested at all. This can happen when the test builder routinely discards the items with low discrimination values (Husek, 1966; Cronbach, 1971). Hawkes, Lindquist, and Mann (1936) commented on this interaction between item selection and content validity:

> Because of this necessity [efficient pupil differentiation] it may not be possible to make the content of the items a representative or random sample of the content of the course of study. Certainly, it will not be possible to limit the content of the test to the essential or most important elements in the course. It is no valid condemnation of a general achievement test to find that it contains some items which one does not expect all the pupils or even the typical pupils to have learned. (pp. 31-32)

This warning is similar to the cautions test constructors provide concerning the limitations of their tests. Reputable test publishers have traditionally been quite careful to point out the limits of their measures (cf. Coffman, 1974; Dyer, 1972; Fitzgibbon, 1975b). Unfortunately these admonitions have often been overlooked by test users.

Moreover, if test makers believe that the level of achievement should not differ between two or more groups, they can reject items which are more difficult for one or other of the groups. An example of this practice is found in the discarding of items that differentiate between girls and boys. Items are selected which are equally difficult for both boys and girls so that the end product is a test on which boys and girls perform equally well on average. On the other hand, items may be included which are good at separating groups. For example, if a test is designed to be administered at more than one grade level, other things being equal, preference will be given to items which become easier as the grade level increases.

It has been argued that the selection of achievement test items which maximally discriminate among individuals tends to reduce the usefulness of standardized achievement tests for discriminating between programs or schools. Two consequences of including only items of an intermediate level of difficulty will be considered.

First, in compensatory-education programs, children typically score in the lowest quarter of the distribution of scores on a standardized achievement test. But the exercises found in most of these tests are clustered around the 60 percent level of difficulty. Usually fewer than 5 percent of the items are at the difficulty level which would permit most disadvantaged children to make correct reponses. As the result of psychometric screening procedures there is such a small sample of items of suitable difficulty for disadvantaged children that reliable estimates of changes in the children's performance cannot be obtained, unless the compensatory program effects an enormous improvement in the children's responses. Traditional standardized tests simply were not designed to provide reliable measures of change at the extremes of the distribution (R. Tyler, 1974).

As an example of the second consequence of including only items of an intermediate level of difficulty in tests, consider five schools of about equal size which participate in the item-tryout phase of test construction. Suppose that all students in one school answer a particular item correctly, while virtually all students in the remaining schools answer incorrectly. If the test constructor views item difficulty across individuals, regardless of school, he will conclude that the item is too difficult for inclusion in the test, since only about 20 percent of the students answered correctly. Yet in terms of assessing school or program effects, the observation that every student in one school but no student in the other schools responded correctly is the very outcome sought: the item differentiated between school performance. Note that the same argument holds if all the students in one school answered the item incorrectly and all the students in the remaining four answered the item correctly. The item would still be discarded, this time because it is too easy.

Both these examples illustrate how items which might be useful in assessing school or program differences may be omitted from standardized tests because they do not possess the statistical properties required to maximize score differences across individual pupils. This example also underlines the point that psychometric screening overlooks the fact that some items may simultaneously discriminate between individuals and groups of individuals. The focus on items which maximize differences between individual students, regardless of school group membership, is logical when the purpose of the test is to differentiate individuals in terms of their performance. Critics who argue against the use of standardized achievement tests in program or policy studies cite this fact as evidence of the insensitivity of the tests to group performance differences (cf. Carver, 1975; Porter & McDaniels, 1974). However, this argument overlooks the important point that an item's difficulty and discrimination indexes provide no information about the item's capacity to differentiate between groups. Studies by Lewy (1973) and Airasian and Madaus (1976; 1978) have shown that two items, each with excellent difficulty and discrimination indexes, can function quite differently in terms of group differentiation.

Lewy has called attention to the differences between discriminating among individuals and discriminating among groups, and has demonstrated that the intraclass correlation coefficient (Haggard, 1958) is a useful statistic for identifying test items which differentiated between groups. The intraclass correlation is a measure of the homogeneity of an item's score within groups relative to the total variation among all subjects' scores. The intraclass correlation coefficient is maximized for an item or a total test when all scores within a group are identical and the only score differences lie between groups. Lewy showed that subgroups of items from a total test could be identified, some of which maximized individual differences in achievement but, more importantly, some of which, when scored and treated as a test, also maximized group achievement differences. Scores on the subgroups identified by Lewy using the intraclass correlation method maximized the variance between groups relative to scores on the total set of test items. Extending Lewy's work, Airasian and Madaus (1976; 1978) showed that when all items in a test are summed to form a total score, the power of subgroups with high interclass correlations to discriminate between groups is washed out by the more numerous items which discriminate only between individuals, irrespective of group membership.

Since item difficulty and discrimination indexes are calculated using the individual as the unit, two hypothetical situations are possible: (1) half of all the students in all the schools in the tryout sample can get the item correct, or (2) all the students in half the schools get the item correct while all of the students in the other schools answer the item incorrectly. In both cases the item difficulty would be .50. In the former case the item would not differentiate between schools, whereas in the latter the item would be excellent for detecting school achievement differences. In practice, different variations of these two situations can occur so that an item may be more or less sensitive to group differences. In point of fact, test publishers never consider the item's ability to distinguish between the schools or classrooms of the tryout sample. Thus, critics have argued that because the test items are selected using indexes designed to maximize individual differences, the likelihood of the tests detecting school or program differences is minimized. This may be, but the validity of the assertion depends, at least for the tryout sample, on indexes which are never calculated or considered when selecting items for final inclusion in the test (Airasian & Madaus, 1976).

We have seen that standardized achievement tests are geared to content common across widely used curricula, rather than specific to a particular curriculum. It appears that at the elementary level, the common content is more closely related to home-based than school-based skills (Bloom, 1975, 1976). That is, they emphasize or depend on reading and verbal ability in the content sampled and in the skills measured. School-based subjects begin to appear more clearly at the secondary level; these include algebra, chemistry, foreign languages, and history. While these subjects also depend on reading comprehension and verbal ability, the testing problem is probably less severe, since the pupils electing these courses tend to be more homogeneous (Bloom, 1976; Brimer, et al., 1978).

Item-analysis techniques tend further to exacerbate the emphasis on verbal abilities and reading comprehension. As we have seen, when used to build a test applicable across a wide range of curricula, such techniques tend to purge the test of specific-knowledge items and to select items which measure a general underlying trait. When this happens students can answer items by falling back on more general verbal skills and abilities. Anderson (1972) noted that

> People who do well on a test as a whole will have more verbal ability than people who do poorly. Items selected because they discriminate between these two groups will tend to contain difficult vocabulary or require inferences which are not necessarily critical to an understanding of the concepts and principles being tested. A test constructed to maximize discriminating power will emphasize aptitude and deemphasize achievement. Manipulating tests to control difficulty level and discriminating power tortures validity. (p. 165)

Thus, standardized achievement tests which result from test makers' having to serve the twin demands of widespread content applicability and discrimination among individuals tend to be measures more highly related to general ability and home background than to school-specific achievement.

RELIABILITY

The adequacy of a standardized test is to a significant degree a function of how well it maximizes interindividual differences. The operational index of this adequacy is an internal consistency reliability coefficient (Nunnally, 1975). Although reliability is conceptually defined as the correlation between true and observed scores, it is computationally defined as the degree to which the test spreads scores out over the possible score range; that is, the extent to which the test maximizes interindividual differences.

Internal consistency and stability (reliability over time) are desirable features of any measurement. They are particularly important if decisions are to be made about individuals on the basis of measurement. However, efforts to improve the reliability of measures used for individual assessment may have the effect of decreasing their sensitivity to school or program differences.

In general, internal consistency reliability is dependent on high intraindividual consistency together with high interindividual variation in test performance. If there were no interindividual variation in test scores, the reliability coefficient would be zero. If a test is comprised of easy items, a relatively large number of test items is needed to obtain reliable interstudent differentiation, since a relatively greater number of items are needed to spread scores over the entire score range. The same is true for a test containing fairly difficult items. However, standardized test constructors tend to select items near the midrange of difficulty and with high discrimination, which maximize variation in student scores. As a consequence, standardized tests can attain high reliabilities, in the .9 range, with relatively few items, usually thirty to fifty per subtest. However, this is done at the expense of excluding items of a wide range of difficulty. Since reliability can be attained with a relatively small number of items of similar difficulty level and content, the test constructor may not feel it is necessary or economical to include a large number of items in the test.

On the face of it, differences in outcomes between schools or instructional programs would seem to be more likely to appear if many content and skill areas of varying levels of difficulty were tested. Tests of 100 or 200 items, covering 40 or 50 objectives, would—at least theoretically— appear to offer greater hope of identifying school outcomes which differentiated school achievement and were associated with the availability of particular resources or instructional programs than would tests of 30 or

40 items covering only 8 to 10 global objectives. However, Airasian and Madaus (1976; 1978) have compared the proportions of between-school variance evidenced by the same group of pupils on standardized norm-referenced achievement tests and longer (150 to 200 items) psychometrically unscreened tests in the same subject areas. They found very small differences in the proportions of between-school variance revealed by the two types of tests, despite the large differences in length.

Moreover, there also are problems associated with the measurement of a large number of objectives. First, there is the practical consideration of the time required of examinees. Since individual decisions are not important in program evaluation, one way to overcome this problem would be to sample items across pupils so that a single pupil answers only forty or fifty items (Cronbach, 1963). The second problem is perhaps more serious. How is the derived information aggregated? As we shall see presently, a single, total score approach is not helpful. Dealing with fifty or sixty separate scores is impractical; besides the use of fifty or sixty scores corresponding to objectives is so specific that generalization about programs could be difficult. Perhaps the performance on the fifty or sixty objectives could be reduced by rational and/or factor analytic procedures to a small number of subscores; however, at present there is no clear answer to this dilemma.

FORM OF MEASUREMENT

Lack of congruity between the form of measurement and the domain of tasks which the measurement instrument is designed to assess is always a serious problem. This was recognized by Rice (1897) when he found that the way in which words were pronounced by teachers on a spelling test could affect pupil performance. He subsequently devised two additional spelling tests. In the first, the words to be spelled were set in a sentence and care was taken to avoid words where pronunciation would give clues to the spelling. In the second test, pupils' spelling in essays was examined, thus avoiding clues from pronunciation.

Cronbach (1971) has pointed out that "the universe specification often gives attention exclusively to the selection of topics, ignoring the form of stimulus and the responses required. This can produce a bad test" (p. 453). It is easy to point to contrasts in the form of the stimuli and responses of tests as compared with those used in the everyday school context. For example, a recent assessment by the New Jersey Department of Education showed that pupils averaged 86 percent correct responses on vertical addition problems but only 46 percent on horizontal addition problems (Glass, 1977).

The multiple-choice format of standardized test requires the student to pick the correct or "best" response from a number of alternatives. This is rarely how teaching transpires in the classroom. Many of the school outcomes which educators regard as important cannot be directly measured using the multiple-choice format; these include speaking skills (including pronunciation) in a foreign language, the correct use of lab techniques in chemistry, the use of a microscope in biology. Often the items used to measure a skill bear little relation to the way that skill was taught, and in order to respond correctly, an additional set of skills not directly related to the content topic or area may be required. For example, when writing and spelling skills are measured, it is usually done by the indirect means of having a pupil recognize examples of poor writing or incorrect spelling. The demands of the test are thus different from those of producing a well-written essay or business letter, or of correctly spelling words dictated by the teacher or in the context of writing continuous passages. There is a need to validate an indirect measure of achievement (such as picking incorrectly spelled words from a list) against some direct assessment of the behavior of interest (spelling words correctly in written communication). Unfortunately, such validation has been neglected in constructing standardized achievement tests of the multiple-choice variety. Instead, the assumption is made that the behaviors measured by the multiple-choice items are an adequate measure of various school-related outcomes. In fact, correlations between standardized achievement tests and more direct measures of outcomes directly related to instruction are seldom high (Anderson et al., 1976; Ferris, 1962; Foley, 1971; Madaus & Rippey, 1966; Stake, 1972; Stodolsky, 1972). The low correlations would appear to be a function of differences in what is being measured by the two types of tests (one general ability, the other more specific skills) and of differences in measurement methods (direct versus indirect; supplying versus selecting).

Brimer (1976) points out that another serious consequence of using the multiple-choice format is to increase the within-school variance on achievement measures. The argument is based on a consideration of interaction between item format and item analysis techniques. The difficulty level of a test item can be varied by making the distractors (choices from which one has to select) in a multiple-choice format more or less homogeneous. Wrong answers may be inserted with the intention of tripping up the student who has only partial knowledge. Consequently, it is difficult for the less able student to demonstrate how much he or she knows, since the test is in fact designed to make the student appear ignorant. The real effect of this can be to make differences between children, particularly children in the same school, appear greater than they really are.

Much more research needs to be done on how the measurement method interacts with the skill or trait one is interested in measuring. At the very least, standardized-test publishers must begin to investigate the relation between their often indirect measures and more direct measures of the objectives in question. It is not enough to point to high correlations with teacher grades, which themselves may also be based, to a large degree, on general verbal abilities related to home background. Instead, the more costly and time-consuming approach of measuring various skills in the most direct and appropriate fashion and then correlating these results with more indirect measures must be carried out. In cases where the correlations are high, the indirect measure can be used (Furst, 1958; Smith & Tyler, 1942).

USE OF SUMMARY SCORES

The performance of an individual on a standardized achievement test is usually summarized into a single score or a small number of subscores, which serve to indicate performance in a number of content skill areas (e.g., reading comprehension, language usage, mathematical computation). That is individual items (or questions) are simply added to form total scores. Such summary scores are quite efficient in discriminating among individuals. However, they may also have the effect of obscuring differences among individuals or groups that may exist in subsets of the items comprising a test.

Samuels and Edwall (1975) have noted that reliance on a total score index of performance often results in the mixing of items which are generally related to the labeled score (e.g., reading achievement) but which may be based on a variety of different skills and abilities. Moreover, if the difficulty of the items within each of the skill or content areas being tested varies across areas, a distorted picture of pupils' achievement may be obtained. A total score may indicate how well the pupil can answer relatively easy items in one area and relatively difficult items in another, but not how well he or she can perform across all areas (Klein,

1971). Using a total test score may therefore lead to a loss of information about student performance, or provide a misleading impression when data are aggregated to the school level.

Airasian and Madaus (1976; 1978), used a variety of data sets in an attempt to determine whether subsets of items within standardized tests do in fact account for more between-school or between-class variance than does the total test score. Four test types were used in this investigation: typical elementary-school standardized norm-referenced achievement batteries; public examinations in England, constructed using normal psychometric procedures to examine performance in a variety of school subject areas at the high-school level; statewide objective-referenced tests, for which items were not psychometrically screened; and criterion-referenced tests developed for an early-childhood intervention program. All but the first type were designed to measure specific objectives, content areas, or topics. The public examinations and the criterion-referenced tests were closely related to a curriculum program or a prescribed syllabus; the objective-referenced tests were related to state-defined minimal competencies.

Four general findings emerged from the analysis of items in each of the data sets. First, it was shown that use of the total test score index in school comparisons hides unique and statistically significant school achievement differences at the test item or objective level. For all data sets studied and with samples of schools both matched and unmatched for total between-school variance, subtests consisting of items or objectives from within the total test were identified, grouped, and shown to evidence higher proportions of between-school variance than the total test score. Moreover, it was found that different groups of items from within the same test differentiated school performance in different directions. Some items and item subsets from within a test revealed highest achievement for a particular school, while other items and subsets from the same test indicated that different schools were superior. Thus, school-to-school differences were shown to exist on groups of items within the test. The use of a single total test score hid these more specific item- and item-subset-level differences in school performances.

Second, the nature of the subject matter tested, independent of the particular type of test used to measure achievement, appeared to affect the magnitude of observed school achievement differences. Thus tests in school-based subjects, such as mathematics and chemistry, evidenced larger school achievement differences than tests of a more home-based subject, such as reading.

Third, the psychometric nature of the items comprising a test did not appear to a be a central factor influencing the discovery of school achievement differences. For norm-referenced, objective-referenced, and criterion-referenced tests, embodying different content- and item-selection criteria, groups of items which differentiated school performance were identified. Psychometric screening on the basis of individual pupil differences does not seem necessarily to preclude an item from also differentiating at the school or program level.

Finally, as discussed in Chapter 3, the unit of analysis appeared to influence the amount of achievement variation observed. Analysis at the teacher-within-school and teacher-within-program levels indicated that a great deal of achievement variation at the individual teacher (class) level is ignored when analyses are performed at the school or program level across individual classes (Airasian & Madaus, 1976; Rakow, Airasian, & Madaus, 1978). With this overview, let us consider the findings regarding the use of the total test score in more detail.

The data sets analysed by Airasian and Madaus did not permit investigation of factors which might explain why subtests increased the percentages of between-school variation over that observed at the total-test level. However, a number of conjectures seem reasonable, if tentative. The subtest differences appeared to be school-, rather than home-related. This inference is based primarily upon the results obtained for matched school groups on the various tests analyzed. While home-background factors could not be controlled in most analyses, the fact that different subtests rank-ordered achievement in a group of schools differently suggests that home-background factors were not the primary cause of the observed achievement differences. Home factors would have been a much more plausible explanation for school achievement differences had the identified subtests rank-ordered schools identically. The argument that the differences were related to varying levels of home background or social class across schools would, in this case, be reasonable. However, when the schools evidenced no difference at the total-test level but significant differences at the subtest level—and when different subtests rank-ordered achievement in the schools differently—it was difficult to argue that either general or specific home-background factors were at the root of the differences.

The more likely explanation is that the subtests identified instructional differences across schools or teachers. Such differences may take a number of forms. They may be related to differences in the instructional emphasis accorded various topics across schools, or to the time testing took place. Or they may simply indicate different teaching quality across schools. Credence is lent to these more instructionally related explanations of observed school differences by the fact that, in mathematics and chemistry, subtests could be characterized according to the major topic of skill they tapped. In essence, the subtests appeared to be identifying specific instructional or learning differences in particular trait or skill areas within a more general content area.

In the light of this explanation, we may conceive of a general achievement test as tapping a series of more specific constructs. Performance measured at the total-test level indicates attainment of a general trait or achievement construct, defined as an aggregate performance over the specific constructs. Tests in different subject areas may contain few or many specific constructs. For example, mathematics items can usually be subdivided into a number of specific skill or topic areas, while reading comprehension tests tend to tap a more general, unitary verbal-ability construct. Differences in the number of specific skill or trait constructs tapped by tests in different subject areas may provide an explanation for the inability of Airasian and Madaus to identify unique content themes associated with the reading subtests found in various analyses.

On the basis of these arguments, and turning attention from the scores on tests and subtests to the constructs tapped by tests and subtests, we can postulate that school differences on specific skill areas or content topics are hidden when performance is judged at the general construct level. Just as the total test score hid score differences at the subtest level, so also do inferences made at the general construct level mask differences at the more specific skill level. The situation is somewhat analogous to scoring in the decathlon: two competitors may evidence very similar total scores over the ten events, but have performed very differently in each specific event.

If these propositions are in fact true, the construct validity of using a total test score to define differences in school performance is called into question. The Airasian and Madaus study has shown that schools which performed similarly at the total-test level evidence statistically significant differences at the subtest level. It appears inappropriate, in light of these findings, to infer equal performance across schools at the total-test or general construct level without also determining whether performance was similar on subtests or the more specific skill areas contained in the test. Overall, these latter, more specific components of general performance appear to have greater construct validity for assessing school or program effectiveness than the total test score. Further, this approach, though far less global than using a total score, avoids the problem of dealing with a great many scores on a number of individual objectives. It falls between the extremes of using one or two global scores and using a separate score for each instructional objective.

CONSTRUCT VALIDITY

At this stage we may ask: what is the construct validity of commercially developed standardized achievement tests? To what extent do the constructs tapped by standardized achievement tests match what is meant by achievement as taught in the schools? First, we will consider evidence that indicates that the tests do not behave in the way we would expect them to behave if they were valid measures of school-specific outcomes. And second, we will look at evidence which suggests that the tests really measure a general achievement factor, to which schooling undoubtedly contributes, but which is more closely related to general ability. The argument advanced is that the constructs measured by standardized achievement tests, like those measured by standardized ability tests, have their roots in and are fostered by factors largely external to schooling.

If achievement tests were valid measures of what goes on in schools, it should be possible to demonstrate that performance on such tests is related to school activities. For example, students who had received instruction in particular topics or skills over a given period of time should obtain higher scores than students who had not received such instruction (Burket, 1974). To our knowledge, however, this procedure has not been utilized in the validation of standardized achievement tests. In fact, the construct validity of achievement tests is generally ignored.

The results of the Coleman survey (1966) and of other studies may also be cited, of course, as evidence of the poor construct validity of standardized achievement tests. Such an interpretation, in the light of the other evidence we have been considering, is certainly as tenable as the conclusion that schools do not differentially affect achievement.

If standardized achievement tests do not adequately measure school learning, what do they measure? Before attempting to answer this question, a number of general points may be made. First, as we have seen, correlations between ability and achievement tests are high. Further, it is known that different intelligence tests correlate about as highly with achievement tests as they do among themselves (Anastasi, 1968; Bloom, 1976; Carroll, 1976; Coleman et al., 1966; Kelley, 1927). Second, the divergent validity (Campbell & Fiske, 1959) of achievement and ability measures is poor; that is, it is hard to distinguish between the constructs "achievement" and "ability" as measured by standardized tests. Even within an achievement area, it is difficult to distinguish some constructs from others. For example, Farr and Roelke (1971) examined three methods of measuring three reading skills: word analysis, vocabulary, and comprehension. They found a total lack of evidence to support a distinction between the three supposedly different subskills. As Cronbach (1971) points out, "if two tests are similar in what they measure, it complicates theory to retain two trait names for them" (p. 467).

Cooley and Lohnes (1976) claim that intelligence (or ability) and achievement tests are distinguishable from each other with respect to the domain of the items which are sampled; the former, they claim, samples a broader domain of school-related abilities than the latter. This may be so as far as content is concerned, but for the processes required to answer the test items, the distinction is less clear. Certainly, achievement tests which try to measure higher taxonomic cognitive skills—application, synthesis, and evaluation (Bloom, 1956)—seem to end up measuring general ability rather than specific knowledge or skills (Ebel, 1969; Madaus, Wood, & Nuttall, 1973). It is almost impossible to distinguish many aptitude (ability) items from many achievement items by inspection (Green, 1974). Cooley and Lohnes (1976) and T. Schwartz (1975) present a series of items, half of which come from an ability test and the other half from an achievement test, and the reader is challenged to categorize the items by test. Most readers who attempt this categorization would probably attain a low achievement (ability?) score on this test.

Evidence of this kind may be variously interpreted; Coleman (1966) and Cooley and Lohnes (1976) inferred that an ability measure is a measure of school achievement. We prefer to interpret the evidence as indicating that skills tapped by standardized achievement tests are basically the same as those tapped by ability tests, and that performance on neither type of test is indicative of school-specific learning.

Verbal ability plays a critical role in general achievement batteries. Bloom (1964), in his research into the stability of various traits, was struck by the largely verbal character of general achievement measures.

In order to read and understand the items on a standardized achievement test, it is necessary to possess skills commonly associated with tests of verbal ability. Thus, verbal ability is a crucial element for successful test taking in many subjects, particularly at the elementary level (Bloom, 1976).

An examination of specific test details also suggests strongly that achievement tests measure a general factor that does not seem to be too different from what ability tests measure. For example, Weaver and Bickley (1967) found that individuals who were not allowed to read the passages on which questions were based in standardized reading comprehension tests were still able to answer 67 percent of the number of items that individuals who had read the passages were able to answer. Samuels and Edwall (1975) make a similar point. Meier (1972) claims that items in reading often demand inferences unrelated to reading (e.g., the inference that a ball is round) and while many children are not able to focus on the specific relations involved in some items, this does not mean they cannot read. Meier further observes that some reading tests are probably more accurately regarded as synonym and antonym tests. Klein (1971) notes that on many reading tests, students have to store many separate bits of information, their sequence, and inferences from the information in order to answer the question correctly. He concludes, "At this point, one wonders whether the item belongs on a reading readiness test or a reasoning test or on a listening memory test . . ." (p. 4). He further notes that these problems are not confined to readiness tests but are also found in reading tests, where "getting the correct answer on an item seems to be as much a function of the pupil's ability to draw inferences as it is of his ability to read" (p. 5). All these problems raise questions concerning the amount of variance on elementary achievement batteries that may in fact be accounted for by a general ability factor rather than by any specific school learning.

The situation in which such factors as general ability, general reasoning, motivation, and test-taking skills come to play an important role in achievement testing can be attributed, at least in part, to the fact that many school systems lack agreed-upon or independent direct criteria against which to judge trial items. In the absence of such criteria, the nature of the distribution produced by the test becomes a powerful criterion for item selection. It is quite possible that the test created could be measuring variation in the ancillary factors required in answering the item, as much or more than it measures variation in the specific knowledge or skills directly related to instruction. If the population being tested varied more on the former factors than on the latter, of if the ancillary factors were normally distributed while the skills specific to instruction were not, the items chosen would tend to reflect the ancillary factors more heavily (Smith, 1975).

Likely candidates for such ancillary skills are the more general abilities of the type also measured by IQ tests, and factors which have to do with ease or speed of learning, reasoning, or thinking ability (to name them is not necessarily to understand them). These more general abilities and skills are built up over a lifetime of experience. In addition to verbal skills, such factors as temperament, ambition, attitudes toward test situations, ability or tendency to work quickly on a task with strict time requirements, carefulness about where to put marks, attitudes toward the examiner, toward competitiveness, toward risk taking—all deeply embedded in cultural and family background—can influence scores on more general achievement batteries, or for that matter, scores on any type of test (Kellaghan, 1972a). Familiarity with tests and item formats also helps. Some students make use of negative or partial information and eliminate distractors in attacking multiple-choice items. Many comprehension items require a good deal more of the test-taker than straightforward reading, reasoning and the ability to make inferences; in some cases, such items can be answered on the basis of simple recall of information acquired outside school.

The verbal abilities and short-term memory required to follow instruction on many achievement tests may result in general ability making a large contribution to variance in test performance (Klein, 1971). Similarly, when the method of testing a skill area is not related to the method of teaching that area, or when the area tested was never formally taught, pupils may be forced to rely upon general ability to answer items. Verbal ability and prior experience, both heavily loaded on home background and social class, are the tools most commonly used to attack new or unfamiliar problems. Whether or not a pupil or group of pupils solves the problem, then, can depend upon factors not necessarily related to school or program-specific instruction. The reason such home-based factors have appeared to be most powerful for explaining school achievement differences is that achievement had been defined at the general construct level, where such factors would be expected to be most powerful, rather than at the specific skill level, where school or program-instructional differences are most manifest.

WHAT KIND OF TEST MIGHT BE SENSITIVE TO SCHOOLING?

Given all the questions we have raised regarding the construct and content validity of standardized achievement measures, the question that must be asked is: what kinds of measures might be sensitive to school effects? While more general measures may not have a large independent school effect associated with them because of their dependence upon pupils' general ability, are there other kinds of measures which might exhibit a large independent school effect? The answer seems to be yes, though as yet such instruments are not generally available. We do, however, have evidence that speaks to the nature of such instruments as well as examples from a few countries which operate examination systems that appear to be sensitive to school practices.

The first general point that may be made about school-sensitive evaluation instruments is that they should attempt to measure specific skills and content rather than general achievement. We would agree with Cooley (1976) that "the challenge is to identify variations in school practices that will explain variance in end-of-year school performance not explained by initial abilities" (p. 59). What a pupil learns in school is to a large degree dependent on the teacher and the curriculum materials. Bloom (1976) sums it up this way: ". . . [the pupil] must learn what is contained in the instructional materials, what the teacher emphasizes in these instructional materials, and what else the teacher emphasizes in the instruction" (p.21). In order to measure what the pupil learns in school, we must therefore be sure that the test is relevant to his or her particular instructional experiences. If one uses a general achievement or ability test at the beginning of the year, and if the school treats all pupils in more or less the same way, then retesting with the same instrument at the end of the year will produce high correlation between the pre- and posttest scores (Bloom, 1976; Glaser, 1976). On the other hand, if the school accommodates instruction to different learning styles, or sets alternative terminal attainments, then the correlation between a general achievement test given at the outset of instruction and a measure specifically geared to the program of studies given at its conclusion will be low (cf. Bloom, 1976; Ferris, 1962; Glaser, 1976). However, as we have already noted, a general achievement test given at the end of the year under these alternative conditions might still have a high correlation with the more general test given initially.

This is so because schools do not directly teach at the general trait or construct level tapped by these tests, but rather at the level of specific skills or content topics. In most subject areas, a pupil progresses through instruction in the various component skills until he or she reaches some point, unpredictable and varying from pupil to pupil, when it can be said that he or she has obtained or can manifest the general trait or construct of interest. In schools, instructional variation seems to occur at the level of the component skills, which make up more general traits such as reading comprehension and mathematical computation. For example,virtually every elementary-school teacher in America would agree that one of his or her basic aims is to enable students to identify the main ideas in their reading. That this aim is so common and widely stressed is evidenced by the fact that virtually every reading comprehension test for the elementary grades includes it as a skill area tested. Yet if we look within the apparent mesh between this skill area and instruction, we find that there is room for variance in the interpretation of the skill. That is, "find main ideas" conveys different processes to different people. For some, finding the main idea means identifying the topic sentence; for others, it means selecting the best title for an untitled passage. For some, finding the main idea involves abstraction from the content of the passage; for others, it does not involve abstraction. For some, the main ideas sought are confined to prose passages; for others, the source may be plays, poems, or letters. Not only are there these differences between interpretations and implementations of the seemingly common and unanimously endorsed skill "finding the main idea," but there are also differences in the level of difficulty of passages which students are expected to deal with.

Farr (1970), after reviewing standardized tests of reading comprehension, concluded that at present there is no clear understanding of the nature of reading comprehension. He conjectures, however, that it is most likely composed of a variety of skills, dependent on conditions such as the content of the passage read, the length and difficulty of the passage, and the method used to measure comprehension.

Similarly, a simple first-grade mathematics skill such as "add one-digit numbers" can be interpreted and taught in a variety of ways. In some classrooms, adding one-digit numbers means demonstrating recall of basic number facts. In other classrooms, counting either aloud or on one's fingers is acceptable evidence that a student possesses the skill. In still other classes, a student is not certified as possessing this skill until he or she can relate the sum of two one-digit numbers to the number of objects in a corresponding set.

Further, there can be wide school-to-school variation in the emphasis accorded particular skill areas or content topics even when they are defined and taught in the same way. One school or teacher may devote large amounts of instructional time to finding the main idea and small amounts to defining words in context. Another school or teacher may evidence an entirely different emphasis on these two topics. As already noted, there may be real differences between schools or classes at the skills level because of variation in resources, time, or instructional emphasis, but these differences could wash out when the separate performances on the component skills are combined to form a total score, which then becomes the index of school effectiveness.

Pupils may perform differently on different skill areas comprising the total test in line with variance in instruction in these skill areas. This is true at all levels of education. R. Tyler (1936) has shown that the relation between recall of facts and ability to apply principles and draw inferences was quite low. At that time there was a belief that memorization of facts was closely related to the development of reflective thinking. Tyler demonstrated that if one wants to assess these separate abilities it is not enough to test for recall; one must specifically test for all three behaviors.

Different preschool programs may also differently affect behaviors associated with children's oral language achievement, and therefore achievement must be tested as specifically and directly as possible, dealing separately with behaviors such as pronunciation, vocabulary, and question-asking skills (Cazden, 1971). Some commentators have gone further, suggesting that tests of preschool achievement should avoid looking for the one correct answer and instead attempt to measure the child's thinking process (Hoffman, 1975; Kamii, 1971).

Describing school achievement at the general trait rather than the specific level on items which are frequently indirect measures of school instruction has its major impact on the construct validity of the inferences made on the basis of the tests. In studies of school or program effectiveness, the constructs tapped by the criterion instrument should coincide with outcomes associated with instruction, not with more general extraschool factors. In essence, school-specific achievement should be measured, and measured in a way that is congruent with how the material was taught and learned. When the specific skill areas most susceptible to instructional differences are measured in a mode that is different from how they taught or learned, or are ignored altogether in favor of performances on more general traits such as reading comprehension or mathematics concepts (traits which we still do not fully understand despite their seemingly straightforward label), validity of the inferences made is likely to be low.

We have already noted that scores on various standardized achievement tests are highly correlated (cf. Bloom, 1976; Jaeger, 1973). Further, we have noted that such tests are general in nature and become more general as the grade level for which they are intended gets higher. However, performance on tests designed to measure specific skills or objectives of particular programs are not as likely to be highly correlated with general measures of achievement, aptitude, or ability (Bloom, 1976; Ferris, 1962; Stake, 1972; Stodolsky, 1972).

For example, in Ferris's (1962) study of a new high-school science curriculum developed in the wake of Sputnik it was found that while correlations between scholastic aptitude measures and tests designed specifically to measure the objectives of these new curricula were initially high, they showed a marked decrease throughout the academic year. He attributed this finding to the fact that the curriculum materials were "teachable," so students at various ability and aptitude levels were able to learn the ideas presented. In essence, the nature of the materials and the instruction decreased the importance of general ability as a predictor of learning success.

Three points in Ferris's study should be noted. First, the achievement tests used were designed specifically for the course objectives. The measures did not tap general content common across all physics courses or all biology courses. Second, the sample of students studied was confined to those following the same science course. Third, pupils at the high-school level had already survived a weeding-out process prior to their enrollment in the science course studied. For this reason they tended to be more homogeneous in terms of background (home factors and educational histories), thereby diminishing the importance of these factors as achievement predictors.

Shaycofts's (1967) longitudinal (grades 9–12) study of achievement at the secondary level also points to the need to measure achievement in school-based rather than home-based subjects. She showed that schools were differentially effective in producing gains in achievement from grades 9 to 12. Further, the gains on school specific tests—literature, social studies, mathematics, accounting, mechanics, etc.—were greater than the gains on tests tapping more general areas.

Anderson, Scott, and Hutlock (1976) compared the differential effectiveness of a mastery learning program (Bloom, 1968) and a nonmastery program in elementary-school mathematics. Students in each group had been matched on the basis of intelligence and reading readiness. There were two groups at each grade level from 1 through 6. The Anderson study is of particular interest because the measures of student outcomes used were a standardized arithmetic test and an objective-referenced test built specifically for the program objectives. Care was taken to be sure that the objectives measured by the objective-referenced test were common to both the mastery and nonmastery classes. It was found that the mastery students scored as well as the nonmastery students on the standardized measures but significantly higher than the nonmastery students on the objective-referenced test at every grade level except grade 1. Anderson et al. points out the following implications of these results:

> . . . the different results obtained from the two cognitive instruments raise, once again, the usefulness of standardized versus objective-referenced instruments in assessing program effectiveness. The use of an appropriately constructed objective-referenced test, with care taken to insure relatively equal validity with respect to the two programs to be compared, seem to the authors to provide the most useful information with which to make decisions about the instuctional program. (p. 10)

Once again it should be pointed out that the pupils in the two programs were homogeneous with respect to aptitude and ability. This reemphasizes the fact that school- or program-effectiveness studies are best performed on homogeneous subpopulations rather than across the entire student population (Frederiksen et al., 1975; Stodolsky, 1972). When the entire school population is studied, aptitude, home, and educational variables differ among pupils in a school such that the achievement measure used must be general. This is particularly true at the secondary-school level.

Other studies have shown achievement differences directly associated with treatment when the criterion instrument used to measure achievement was closely matched to the actual objectives and instruction of the program. Reviews of evaluations of mastery learning, where students are periodically provided feedback and correctives where needed, have shown consistent student gains on objective-referenced criterion tests (cf. Block, 1971; Block 1974; Bloom, 1976; Bloom, Hastings, & Madaus, 1971). Further, Stodolsky's (1972) review of evaluations of preschool programs concluded that *"the programs that appear more successful on the basis of the data are those whose objectives or curricular emphases come closest to the measured objectives"* (p. 82, emphasis Stodolsky's). We know little or nothing about the psychometric properties of these tests; Anderson (1972) points out that tests built specifically for research or evaluation of programs are seldom adequately described in the literature.

Stodolsky further noted that programs which showed the greatest gains were those which were more structured, task- and cognitively oriented, and had a high degree of teacher control (cf. Smith, 1976). Shapiro (1973) interprets these results to mean that the programs are merely preparing the children for test taking. If by this Shapiro means "cramming" children with specific answers to test questions, then these achievement gains are meaningless. But if Shapiro means that the test adequately reflects what is taught and how it is taught, then inferences about "achievement" are valid. At some point pupils must be tested if we are really interested in determining whether or not a program is effective.

Perrone (1975), who is strongly opposed to using standardized achievement tests for program evaluation, feels that one reason these tests continue to be used is because

> teachers and school administrators are not sufficiently organized to describe either children's learning or school programs. Attempts at such description have been too random and not intensive enough. To engage in a systematic process of documentation . . . is to expend considerable energy but its potential usefulness is unlimited. (p. 98)

Very often those hired to perform an evaluation build criterion instruments solely on the basis of the objectives stated in curriculum guides. There is no independent check that these objectives are actually taught or on how they are taught. As in the case of standardized achievement tests, there is no independent check on the degree to which the common goals inferred from a review of textbooks are actually implemented in schools, or if they are, when and how they are implemented. Building a test which reflects not only stated objectives but what actually goes on in specific instructional situations has been labeled "criterion sampling" by McClelland (1973). The value of this approach is demonstrated in an evaluation of the career education program by Brickell (1976), who vainly attempted to show differences between treatment groups in career education programs in Ohio, using tests built to objectives stated in curriculum guides. Teachers and administrators strongly argued that the program was effective and that the tests were not picking up real achievement gains. Differences did emerge when criterion measures that reflected actual program activities in classrooms were constructed.

Brickell made an important distinction between tests that measure what teachers are teaching and those that measure what program designers planned for them to teach. One cannot assume congruence between a program designer's objectives and those of a teacher; nor can one assume congruence between a commercially developed standardized test's objectives and those of a teacher. In the Ohio program, it was necessary to observe the teachers in practice before building tests which reflected their behavior and implicit objectives; this may be a necessary procedure in the development of tests to assess schools and programs.

It is possible to gear tests to specific programs. It would be very difficult, however, to build a test to measure general school effectiveness in the teaching of a specific subject area. Part of the problem is that there is generally no commonly accepted nationwide syllabus that defines what is to be taught. The structure of American education, with its emphasis on local control, avoids agreement on a common curriculum for a given subject area. Historically, local school officials have strongly resisted any movement toward a national curriculum or toward the development of tests by the federal government which could be used to make interdistrict and interstate comparisons.

There are examples, however, of curricula which are defined by external examiners, which are regarded as extremely important by both students and teachers, and for which over a long period of time a tradition of what and how to teach has been built up (cf. Madaus & Macnamara, 1970a, 1970b). These are the public examination systems of Great Britain and Ireland. These examinations, taken at the secondary level, certify the successful completion of one level of education and are sometimes used to admit pupils to the next level or to certain occupations. Examinations for each subject area are set by an external agency (the Department of Education in Ireland; different examination boards in Great Britain). In Ireland there is a single syllabus for each secondary school subject; in Great Britain there are several, each associated with a particular examining board (e.g., London, Oxford, and Cambridge).

As noted, no comparable situation exists in the United States, although at one time the Regents examinations in New York State resembled the European situation. As we have also noted, American educators have generally been opposed to an external agency's setting up a syllabus and examinations based on the syllabus. However, this may not be true of the general public. In a recent Gallup poll, 65 percent of the respondents agreed that pupils should pass a standard national examination in order to graduate from high school (Gallup, 1976).

In fact, at present twenty-nine states, enrolling two-thirds of the nation's children, have initiated or are considering giving examinations to certify the mastery of a set of predefined minimal skills. These programs are generally referred to as competency-based graduation programs (Madaus & Airasian, 1977). The programs, often without realizing it, are moving toward a system similar in some important respects to the external examinations used in Europe. One of the arguments against such a system is that it had an adverse effect on the curriculum, on teaching practices, and on student learning (cf. Madaus & Macnamara, 1970a). Whether external examinations have adverse effects, depends very much on the character of the examination. If the examinations only measure recall of facts, as they did initially, then cramming is inevitable. Orwell (1968b), recounting his school days, provides an example of this type of cramming.

> They were the kind of stupid question that is answered by ripping out a name or a quotation. Who plundered the Begams? Who was beheaded in an open boat? Who caught the Whigs bathing and ran away with their clothes? Almost all our historical teachings was on this level. History was a series of unrelated, unintelligible but—in some way that was never explained to us—important facts with resounding phrases tied to them. Disraeli brought peace with honour. Clive was astonished at his moderation. Pitt called in the New World to redress the balance of the Old. And the dates, and the mnemonic devices! (Did you know, for example, that the initial letters of "A black Negress was my aunt: there's her house behind the barn" are also the initial letters of the battles in the Wars of the Roses?) (pp. 336–337)

If instead external examinations measure comprehension and application—the understanding and use of facts and principles—then cramming becomes extremely difficult. One can teach the test in the former situation; one can only teach *for* the test in the latter. This distinction goes to the heart of construct and content validity.

The experience at the University of Chicago during Hutchins's tenure as chancellor is a classic illustration of the beneficial aspects of certifying examinations on teacher practice (Bloom, 1950). Teachers decided upon the important objectives in their courses and communicated these to the university examiner, who constructed valid course examinations. Since teachers had initial input into the examination specifications, they did not end up coaching pupils for the examination but rather taught the topics they initially decided upon. Since the examinations reflected the teachers' instructional aims, the need to prepare pupils exclusively for certifying examinations did not interfere with the teachers' planned classroom emphases.

In the unlikely event the United States decides to move away from local control over curriculum to a state or national syllabus, we would do well to learn from the experience of the British system, with its weaknesses, faults, and strengths. We should also be careful to allow several prescribed syllabi and external examinations, rather than one, in each area of interest. Educators need to play an important part in deciding on the content and objectives of these syllabi and in constructing examinations related to them. Whether such a system could work at the elementary level is uncertain. However, the recent Quie amendment proposed allocating funds to elementary-school districts on the basis of an external test (cf. Madaus & Elmore, 1973).

What would happen in a school effectiveness study if tests geared to specific syllabi were used? Irish and English post-primary schools afford the opportunity of examining this question for several reasons. First, the public examinations are excellent criterion measures of specific achievement areas. Each test is geared to a separate prescribed syllabus. Tests are administered at the same time after a fixed period of study to all students in all schools, and they are perceived as extremely important by teachers, pupils, and parents; instruction is geared to preparing pupils for these examinations. Second, the groups sitting for the examinations are, because of the sorting function of the school, relatively homogeneous with regard to aptitude, educational history, and family background. Compare this population with Coleman's secondary-school population, where all pupils in the ninth and twelfth grades, regardless of type of school or curriculum traits, were tested with a general achievement measure. The tests in Ireland are of the essay variety; those in England include essay, short-answer, and multiple-choice tests. The short-answer and multiple-choice tests are built to a common prescribed syllabus following traditional psychometric criteria for item selection.

Given the relative homogeneity of the student body, it seems reasonable to suggest that differences between schools on the various achievement tests would be more readily found to be related to school or class (within school) factors than to background factors, as was the case in the United States. Two studies in which such conditions applied, and which we considered in Chapter 4 in the context of the explanatory power of process variables, present strong evidence of school effectiveness.

In the first of these studies, carried out in England (Brimer, et al., 1978), the London University Examination Board's "O" and "A" level examinations were used as criterion measures of achievement. The results confirmed the hypothesis that curriculum-sensitive achievement measures manifest larger between-school variance than that found in the Coleman survey. The amounts of between-school variance associated with the various "O" level achievement tests ranged from a low of 5 percent on the English literature examination (this was untypically low) to a high of 42 percent on the mathematics examination. The chemistry examination, for which 26 percent of the variance lay between schools, fell at the midpoint of the distribution. The results for the more advanced "A" level examinations were somewhat lower, ranging from 13 percent to 32 percent.

For a further sample of schools taking "O" level examinations, it was possible to compare results using total scores and part (sub-) scores on examinations. The use of part scores resulted in substantial increases in the amounts of variance found to lie between schools over the amounts found when total scores were used. Thus we have further evidence in support of our earlier argument of the value of part scores over total scores in assessing school differences.

In the second study, carried out in Ireland, evidence was also obtained that schools and classes within schools are differentially effective in preparing pupils for public examinations (Madaus, Kellaghan, & Rakow, 1975; Madaus, Kellaghan, Rakow, & King, 1979). This study differed from the British one in a number of ways. For one thing, it was possible to aggregate data at the class as well as at the school level. Further, the participating students, as well as sitting for public examinations, also took a number of standardized tests—ability, reading, mathematics, English, and Irish. Thus it was possible to compare the sensitivity of standardized tests with that of public examinations. With one exception, as much between-school variance was found to be associated with the standardized tests as with the various public examinations. However, when it came to explaining the observed variance that existed between classes in terms of school and home background, the amount that could be explained by school-based factors was considerably higher for the public examinations than for the standardized tests. For twenty-seven public examinations, across three different samples, the class-level factors *uniquely* explained over 50 percent of the between-class variance.

It was also found that commonality between blocks representing different spheres of influence (home, school) tended to be much higher for the standardized measures than for the public examinations. That is, school factors overlapped with individual, family, and IQ factors to explain variance in the standardized measures to a much greater degree than on the public examinations. The reason for this seems to be that despite the selectivity of Irish schools, which should increase commonality, the subjects examined in public examinations are still quite dependent on variations in classroom factors.

The findings of this study are not directly comparable with those of Coleman (1966), since the studies differed in their analytic methods, predictor variables, and choice of criterion variables. However, the trend of the findings does prompt us to raise the question: had Coleman used a more curriculum-sensitive outcome measure, would his analyses have revealed school factors to be more influential in explaining between-school variance? We feel the answer would be affirmative, since the verbal-ability measure used by Coleman was heavily dependent on background factors. In the Irish study, measures similar to those used by Coleman were used (standardized tests of ability and attainment) in addition to the more curriculum-sensitive public examinations. Thus it was possible to compare the sensitivity of both kinds of measure to school factors. Several analyses clearly indicate that what were called curriculum-sensitive measures were precisely that. Compared to the standardized tests, they clearly were more dependent on the characteristics of schools and what goes on in them.

CONCLUSION

We have suggested in this and in the preceding chapter that, to be considered valid, outcome measures in studies of school and program effectiveness must tap achievements, skills, processes, and learning that are, as far as possible, specific to school instruction. If the outcome measures used to assess school and program effectiveness are primarily surrogates for home background and general ability, rather than measures of school-specific achievement, inferences about the differential effectiveness of schools are invalid, since the measures tell us little about what is taught in schools. We have argued that standardized tests are relatively insensitive to detecting school-specific pupil achievements.

The reasons cited for this conclusion were varied, and related to the content and psychometric properties of standardized tests as well as to the manner in which student performance on these tests is summarized. Our conclusion is that the general constructs these tests actually measure are so heavily loaded on and confounded with home background and general ability as to render impossible a verdict about the differential effectiveness of different kinds of schools and school resources on pupil learning.

This should not be taken to imply that schools necessarily have an effect on pupil learning that is totally independent of pupils' home backgrounds and general abilities. Although we believe that different types of schools and school resources do have a unique impact, from an empirical point of view we must concur with the Scotch verdict "not proven," at least in the United States. For the most part, the studies we have cited which showed a large independent effect associated with different schools and resources have done so for groups of pupils whose general abilities were relatively homogeneous.

The United States is faced with two heretofore irreconcilable positions which influence the search for suitable outcome measures of school and program effectiveness. On the one hand is the mistrust of state and federal education bureaucracies and the strong desire to preserve local control and initiative over curriculum choices and schooling objectives. On the other hand is the desire of test publishers and many concerned laypeople to have tests with widespread applicability for assessing individual differences among pupils. The attempt to capture school objectives which vary across localities by means of a single, generalized test has led to most of the problems cited in this and the preceding chapter.

A resolution of the incompatability of local specificity of instructional emphases and nationally oriented tests is unlikely to be realized without compromise on both sides. It is unreasonable to expect that local school interests will ever totally give up the principle of local control of education, although federal funding and its attendant guidelines, as well as state-imposed mandates and guidelines, have begun to erode this principle. Neither is it likely that commercial test publishers will wish to begin designing specific tests for each local situation—and even if they did, questions about generalizing the results of such tests across local boundaries would inevitably arise. It would seem that one reasonable and more methodologically appropriate (see Chapters 3 and 4) solution to this dilemma could involve the examination of differential school effectiveness for subsets of schools and subgroups of pupils within these schools. For example, one might categorize schools according to which of the four or five leading introductory mathematics texts they use. A separate achievement test geared to each of the texts would be constructed, and comparative school effectiveness would be determined only among pupils in schools which used the same text. Thus there would be a number of effectiveness studies carried out simultaneously, each confined to a given mathematics curriculum.

Such an approach would do much to overcome, though not eliminate, the many problems associated with the use of a single generalized test across diverse curricula. By selecting a relatively homogeneous content domain to examine and by confining the pupils examined to those who have had direct experience with that content domain, the effects of home background and general ability on performance would be reduced. This is especially true at the secondary-school level, where pupils taking particular courses (algebra, chemistry, etc.) will already be relatively homogeneous in ability. To a large extent, this approach mirrors the strategy followed in the external examination systems of various European countries, studies of which have produced some of the clearest evidence for the existence of an independent differential school effect on pupil learning.

However, whatever the strategy adopted in future examinations of differential school effectiveness, it is clear that a conscious effort must be undertaken to disentangle school-related differences in pupil performance from differences associated with extra-school influences, such as home background. Until this separation or some close approximation to it is effected, differential school effectiveness as a meaningful and measurable construct will be elusive.

chapter 7

School Effectiveness: What Can We Say?

INTRODUCTION

If the 1960s was a period for the critique of social myths and beliefs in American national life (Mosteller & Moynihan, 1972), it was perhaps also a period for the creation of new ones. Thus for some people, the long-held belief in schooling as an institution which acted as a social equalizer gave way to the belief that schooling did little to foster the cognitive abilities of students.

At the beginning of this book, we argued that the position which one adopts on school effectiveness is far from academic. Some of its practical consequences have been spelled out by Guthrie (1970).

> The belief has become increasingly pervasive that patterns of academic performance are immutably molded by social and economic conditions outside the school. If incorrect, and if allowed to persist unexamined and unchallenged, this belief could have wildly disabling consequences. It is not at all difficult to foresee how it could become self-fulfilling: administrators and teachers believing that their school and schoolroom actions make no difference might begin to behave accordingly. Conversely, if the assertion is correct but allowed to pass unheeded, the prospect of pouring even more billions of local, state, and federal dollars down an ineffective rathole labelled "schools" is equally unsettling. (p. 25)

Given implications of this order, we examined in earlier chapters the evidence on which beliefs about the effectiveness of schools are based and concluded that the pessimism inherent in the statement that "schools bring little influence to bear upon a child's achievement that is

173

independent of his background and general social context" (Coleman, et al., 1966, p. 325) is basically unwarranted. This negative inference about the influence of schools is a function of the unit (the school) selected for study, the methodology employed (stepwise regression), the input variables chosen (static or status variables) and most importantly the procedures employed to measure "achievement" (standardized, norm-referenced, verbal ability and reading and arithmetic tests). We have examined considerable evidence in the previous chapters that cast serious doubt on such a pessimistic conclusion about schools' effectiveness; rather, we were led to the conclusion that schools differentially affect student achievement and, further, that differences between schools in achievement can be explained by factors related to school and classroom characteristics. When one or more of the following components of a study of school effectiveness is changed, pessimistic conclusions give way to more optimistic inferences about the differential effects of schooling: (1) the method of data analysis, (2) the unit of schooling studied, (3) the input variables selected, and (4) the output or achievement measures employed.

Thus we saw that when Mayeske et al. (1972) reexamined the Coleman data using commonality analysis, they concluded that the family influence was not preeminent but that the school and family have a strong collusive effect on achievement measured by scores on a composite measure derived from all the Coleman measures.

When the achievement measures used are syllabus-specific and important in the minds of the teachers and the pupils, then there are substantial differences in the achievement level between schools and classes within schools following the prescribed syllabus. Some schools and/or classes simply do a better job than others in helping pupils learn the syllabus material, or in preparing pupils to take the tests, or both. Further, a substantial part of these differences can be explained by differences in the academic press of the school or classroom rather than by home-background factors. Schools or classes that have strong press for academic excellence, value discipline, provide structure, emphasize homework and study, and where pupils expect—and are expected—to do well achieve at higher levels than pupils in classes that do not subscribe to these more "traditional" values of teaching and learning. In short, we feel that schools, particularly at the secondary level, make a difference in subject-specific instruction. Further, this difference is to a large extent independent of home background, and is related to structure, discipline, homework, and general press to achieve in the school.

Given these general positive conclusions, in this concluding chapter we shall consider what studies of school effectiveness do and do not tell us and where we stand in terms of our knowledge of school effectiveness.

WHAT STUDIES OF SCHOOL EFFECTIVENESS DO AND DO NOT TELL

We saw in Chapters 1 and 2 that the major empirical basis for beliefs about the ineffectiveness of schools was the findings of the Coleman survey and several reanalyses of the data collected. The findings carried considerable weight, perhaps because of the sheer magnitude of the study, and perhaps also because it had been carried out to investigate the topical and politically sensitive issue of equality of educational opportunity. It was hoped that the findings would contribute to a greater understanding of "the critical factors relating to the education of minority children," thus providing "a sound basis for recommendations" for improving these children's education (Coleman et al., 1966, p. 1). It is not surprising that a study which set out to examine equality of opportunity, particularly in the context of minority children, would frequently be cited in the debates over this issue. However, the inferences made from the study were not limited to minority group children but were applied to schools and achievement in general.

When we examined critically the findings of the report in succeeding chapters we found that the pessimistic conclusions go far beyond the available evidence. Actually, the findings of the Coleman study and of the reanalyses tell relatively little about schooling. A few general conclusions seem to stand. First, data from these studies indicate that minority students—with the exception of Oriental Americans—score lower than majority (white) students on standardized tests of verbal and nonverbal ability and of attainment in reading, mathematics, and general information. These findings could hardly be regarded as unexpected; similar ones have appeared in the literature over a long period of time (cf. Garth, 1931), and indeed it was the awareness of such differences that prompted much of the legislative and innovative action in education in the United States in the 1960s. The Great Cities School Improvement Project (cf. E. Gordon, 1971; Marburger, 1963) and Head Start did not have the results of the Coleman survey to decide that action was needed to deal with the problems of educating minority children.

More surprising was Coleman's finding that variance between schools in students' performance on standardized tests was small, on average something of the order of 10 percent. In the light of reports about differences in mean achievement between school systems, one might have expected that figure to have been larger. Furthermore, a close linear relation was not found between between-school variance in mean student test performance and variation in school-based resources, such as library facilities, laboratories, and teacher characteristics. To the extent that any relation between test performance and school resources existed, it was stronger for minority students than for white students. If, in fact, it is shown that resources which can be relatively easily manipulated by policymakers are not very important in accounting for what students learn in school, then the task of the policymaker becomes more complex and demanding. However, what the Coleman study showed was that school resources are not strongly related to performance on conventional standardized norm-referenced tests.

What has not been learned from school effectiveness studies, even from ones which, unlike Coleman, demonstrated the relevance of school characteristics, is perhaps more revealing than what has been learned. We have learned nothing about the absolute effects of schooling. We cannot say to what extent schools affect student behavior; we do not know if students are different for having gone to school. Recent research has not addressed this issue. To obtain conclusive evidence, it would be necessary to observe the behavior of two comparable groups of children, one of which had attended school, the other of which had not. The nearest we have come to this situation in recent years has been the investigation of the effects of compensatory education for disadvantaged children. In some investigations, it was possible to compare performance of a group of children which had taken part in a compensatory program with the performance of a group which had not. This comparison raises many methodological problems. Apart from these, there are also serious problems if one attempts to make general statements about the effects of schooling on the basis of the findings of studies carried out with highly selected and atypical populations. Furthermore, compensatory programs focused on the early childhood period and so can provide no information on the effects of schooling in later childhood.

One of the most frequently cited conclusions of studies of school effectiveness, whether carried out in the United States or in Europe, is that students' home background bears a strong relation to students' mean test performance. The Coleman report concludes that "schools bring little influence to bear upon a child's achievement that is independent of his background and general social context" (p. 325). There is ample evidence apart from that contained in the report that home factors are related to performance on standardized ability and attainment tests and indeed to other indexes of school achievement. However, the unique character of the home's contribution is less clear than the findings of several studies of school effectiveness might seem to indicate. By assuming in their method of analysis that home factors operate prior to and independently of school influences, they probably overestimated the unique contribution of home factors to school achievement, even as measured by standardized tests. An alternative method of analysis, in which common as well as unique contributions of groups of variables are examined, suggests strongly that achievement is the result of a collusion between home and school factors (Brimer et al., 1978; Mayeske et al., 1972). Further, when groups of students following a prescribed syllabus at the secondary level are studied, differences in achievement levels between them are largely unrelated to variations on measures of traditional home background factors. For such students, the sorting function of the school and self-selection have ensured that most come from homes which value and support educational achievement.

Findings that variation in school resources, such as expenditure and physical amenities, bears little relation to standardized test performance has also received considerable prominence, and this too deserves careful scrutiny. First, it is important to bear in mind that for many characteristics, the comparison is not between the effects of a characteristic's presence and its absence. All schools have certain facilities, such as buildings and teachers. The Coleman findings cannot speak to the effect of having a teacher as against not having one; they can say nothing about the absolute effect of teachers. What they speak of is variations in training, ability, or background of the teachers who exist in every school. Second, instances where characteristics were present in some schools and absent in others, were not very common. For example, in the Coleman study most students were in schools which had chemistry laboratories (from a low of 94 percent for Puerto Ricans and blacks to a high of 99 percent for Indians and Orientals). For biology laboratories, the range was somewhat greater (from 84 percent for Puerto Ricans to 96 percent for Indians and Orientals), and for physics laboratories slightly greater again (80 percent for blacks to 96 percent for Orientals) (Coleman et al., 1966, Table 2). Given this limited variation, it is not too surprising that the absence or presence of a laboratory did not turn out to be significantly related to other variables.

Overall, then, the findings of the Coleman study do not reveal a great deal that is new, and what they do reveal seems very peripheral to the area of school effectiveness. Why this is so may become clearer when we compare the conceptual framework of the study with an alternative framework derived from an examination of the working of schools.

THE CONCEPTUAL FRAMEWORK OF STUDIES OF SCHOOL EFFECTIVENESS

To examine school effectiveness one would first need to identify some school objectives; one could then proceed to investigate the extent to which schools achieved those objectives. If one suspected that schools were differentially effective in achieving the objectives they set themselves, one might go further and attempt to identify the variables which seemed likely to contribute to the realization of the objectives. All this would be much easier if an adequate theory of schooling were available to investigators. However, no such theory existed to guide the efforts of Coleman and his collaborators and so, like other investigators, they had to construct typologies of ordered school service components and then pick from existing instruments what they regarded as the most appropriate ones to represent their typological categories (cf. Guthrie et al., 1971).

The Coleman survey did not attempt to describe the school objectives, either as perceived by school personnel or as inferred from observing what goes on in schools. Rather, it set about finding out to what extent schools achieve equality of opportunity, and at the same time looked at the kinds of resources which were traditionally regarded as contributing to the effective working of schools in general and student achievement in particular. This, of course, is legitimate; one may ask to what extent schools achieve any objective—students' emotional, religious, or moral development, or even the development of students' extrasensory perceptual abilities. Given the historical image of American schools as social equalizers and as vehicles of social mobility, it was perhaps not unreasonable to ask to what extent they contributed to equality of opportunity, though one might have serious reservations about operationalizing this objective through the use of a standardized test of verbal ability. What is unreasonable is to generalize findings about schools based on the one objective, which may be rather peripheral to the work of the school, to general statements about school effectiveness and student achievement.

When one recalls the political context in which the Coleman study was carried out, it is not surprising that its findings contribute little to our understanding of schooling. In retrospect, the input and output variables chosen seem rather remote from the everyday business of the school.

The Coleman survey—and indeed, with less reason, most other school effectiveness studies—was carried out in what Kerlinger and Pedhazur (1973) term a predictive rather than an explanatory framework. Concerned primarily as it was with practical application, the Coleman study attempted to document differences between schools and then, in the light of those differences, to identify policy-manipulable characteristics of the schools which contributed to such differences. Were such factors as expenditure or resources found to predict between-school variance in achievement, the way would have been open to the policymaker to provide for changes where appropriate. The study's concern was not explanatory; it was not based on theoretical formulations or considerations, and its objective, despite the hope that it would contribute to a greater understanding of the education of minority children (Coleman et al., 1966, p. 1), was not really to increase understanding of the working of schools.

Concern with prediction had a number of consequences which make attempts to use findings of school-effectiveness studies to further our understanding of schooling hazardous. The very choice of their predictor variables was limited to policy-manipulable ones which might be of little value in understanding what goes on in schools. Indeed, our discussion of the ambiguity of many of the input variables used in school-effectiveness studies should make it very clear that the use of such variables is not likely to promote our knowledge of schooling, since what the variables represent is often not at all clear. Coleman's concern with prediction is further evidenced in the screening of variables for inclusion in the blocks of variables used to represent home-background and school factors. Variables were selected to maximize prediction, not because they seemed to fit a conceptual representation of schooling. Given the strong relations that existed among the predictor variables themselves, this procedure could well have resulted in the screening out of variables which might have been of potential value in promoting understanding of schooling.

We feel that by paying too little attention to what goes on in schools, the Coleman survey actually misrepresented the work of schools and what they try to achieve. As a consequence of this misrepresentation, which is also a feature of studies based on reanalyses of the Coleman data, a distorted picture of what schools do has achieved a certain notoriety.

There are several points on which we can raise doubts about the validity of the view of schooling implicit in the Coleman study. In this context, the question of the schools' objectives is primary. This may be considered at two levels: at a general level, we may ask whether schools strive to achieve equality of output; and at a more specific level, we may ask whether schools set out to teach the skills measured by standardized tests of ability and attainment. Three further questions arise in considering Coleman's implicit model of schooling. Do schools strive to work independently of the student's home background? Do all students share equally the resources of the school? And are physical resources, such as library and laboratory facilities, regarded as important determinants of student achievement? In considering each issue, we suggest alternative hypotheses to those implied in many school effectiveness studies.

Do Schools Strive to Achieve Equality of Educational Output?

A school or school system may decide, implicitly if not explicitly, what its desired distribution of student outputs should be; it would then presumably allocate its resources in a way that would contribute to the achievement of such a distribution. A number of options are open to the school or school system (Brown & Saks, 1975). It may strive to achieve a small dispersion in student outcomes (for example, in reading ability or in knowledge of history); such a school or system could be termed a "leveler," one which stresses equality of educational attainment. A school might attempt to achieve a wide dispersion in outcomes; this school could be termed "elitist." And a school may have no policy relating to the dispersion of student outcomes. Note that all policies might result in a similar mean level of attainment for students. Implementing the first policy, however, should result in little variation around the mean, while following the second would result in great variation.

While many governments subscribe in general to the concept of equality of educational opportunity, precisely what is implied by the term is not always clear. Some, no doubt, mean equality of access for members of both genders and all races, ethnic groups, and religions. Others may mean equality of participation. It may be that some mean equality of attainment. Coleman's findings that mean level of performance was not the same for all racial and ethnic groups can be interpreted to mean that equality of opportunity, in the sense of equality of performance as measured by a range of standardized tests, does not exist in the United States.

We may note that it is more difficult to interpret Coleman's discovery of the low amount of variance in achievement found to lie between schools. This finding could represent schools with low levels of achievement variance or schools with high levels of achievement variance; in other words, both "levelers" and "elitists," provided all schools were of the same type, would exhibit the same pattern of between-school variance.

The implications of interpreting the concept of equality to indicate equality of output and of expecting schools to achieve such equality requires serious consideration. For the underlying issues are ideological as well as practical.

One of the basic ideological issues relates to the emphasis which is placed on equality versus liberty in the social system. For liberty and equality in their extreme forms cannot be pursued simultaneously. If equality is emphasized, a loss of individual liberty will result, since the imposition of equality implies that feedom of choice will be curtailed (Nozick, 1974). Thus, when the principle is applied to educational practice, schools would not be free to build on and enhance the individual strengths which students exhibit even at the time they enter the school system. It has been a widely accepted view in education, however, that the development of individual students' potential should receive a high priority. This view also regards the individual as entitled to the use and disposal of his or her talents and resources (Nozick, 1974). Complete freedom or liberty, however, to foster and exploit individual differences in ability, motivation, effort, and privilege will almost inevitably conspire to create a situation in which inequality is maximized (cf. Brookover et al., 1974).

There are also practical problems raised if an objective of equality of educational output is posited for schools. For such a policy may conflict with what actually goes on in the schools. Changes in the structure of the educational system—for example, making a selective system comprehensive—may go some way toward providing conditions which facilitate the implementation of a particular policy, though structural changes may be more limited in their effects than their initiators may believe. It may well be impossible to achieve the objectives of a new policy unless radical changes in the values and objectives of those who are expected to implement it take place. Thus, even if a policy were to dictate a "leveling" of students' achievements, the structure, value, and practices of schools might be so geared to increasing differentiation among students that the policy would be of no avail (Brown & Saks, 1975). While American public education traditionally has had egalitarian overtones, particularly in terms of control, the liberal tradition has also been strong. One can go back as far as 1776 to the Declaration of Independence, if not to the intentions of the earliest emigrants to the United States, to find a recognition of the equality of men combined with a belief in liberty as "an unalienable right" of the individual.

In their writings, the Founding Fathers—particularly John Adams—point to the need to protect equality, while at the same time recognizing problems which arise from the "natural" differences which they observed to exist between men and which they felt should be developed in the interests of society.

While most school personnel would probably subscribe to the idea that they should be equally concerned about the well-being and achievement of each student, this does not mean that students are not treated differently. In many schools, students are divided into groups within classes and, particularly at the high-school level, into tracks or streams. Categorizations of this sort are usually based on a consideration of a student's present levels of achievement and on postgraduation plans or expectations. Once students are divided into groups, the resources made available to them—textbooks, teachers, and facilities—will vary according to the group the student belongs to. Behind such categorization and differential treatment is the idea that the school responds to children's individual characteristics, their ability, "readiness," or motivation to learn, in such a way as to enhance those characteristics. The effect is usually that students, on the whole, maintain their positions relative to one another in achievement throughout their schooling and, indeed, variance between them may well increase with length of schooling.

Our task here has not been to attempt to explicate a philosophy for American schools or even to attempt to determine what the balance between equality and liberty as objectives should be. Rather, we wish to suggest that there may be a serious lack of congruence between the objective of equality as implied in the Coleman study and the objectives of schools as one may infer them from everyday practice. There is obviously a need for empirical information about what in fact American schools strive to achieve. In the absence of such information, attempted assessments of their effectiveness can tell us little.

Do Schools Teach Skills Measured by Standardized Tests of Ability and Attainment?

The objectives which have been posited for schools are many and cover a wide range of personal and institutional goals. In our discussions, we have confined our attention largely to objectives in the cognitive sphere, as indeed have most school effectiveness studies. The most usual measures of school outcome employed in such studies have been standardized cognitive tests of ability and achievement. In the case of the Coleman study, a measure of verbal ability was the main measure of school outcome.

We are extremely doubtful that many teachers would perceive their function as teaching verbal ability. Perhaps schools would hope to influence the development of such ability, but not many would place such development among their immediate goals. The constructs represented in reading and mathematics tests might seem more appropriate to the tasks that schools set themselves. However, the appropriateness of norm-referenced standardized tests to represent school achievements, even in such basic areas as reading and mathematics, can be seriously challenged, as we saw in Chapters 5 and 6. Such measures, because of the emphasis on local control of curriculum, abhorrence of government controlled tests, the commercial nature of the tests and the manner in which they are constructed, do not seem to be appropriate measures of school outcomes. The construction of norm-referenced achievement tests follows the same psychometric procedures as are followed in the construction of norm-referenced ability tests: indexes of difficulty and discrimination are employed on the assumption that the traits being measured are normally distributed within populations and with the purpose of providing maximum discrimination between students. Further, in the United States, such tests are not referenced to a common prescribed syllabus, but instead must represent a number of curricula. The final test product is, not surprisingly, largely homogeneous with respect to the construct being measured. Furthermore, we believe that the construct of achievement based on this kind of measure is very similar to the construct measured by ability tests, particularly verbal ones. The high correlations that are frequently reported between ability and achievement tests may be interpreted as supporting this view.

When students are called upon in a test to answer questions based on material they have not been exposed to in class, or when the questions are phrased in ways that differ from those used in normal instruction, we may hypothesize that students will rely heavily on skills and knowledge other than those which they acquired in school. In this situation, we would expect home and background factors to play an important role in students' performance.

This is not to suggest that performance on standardized tests bears no relation to the student's school-based experience. If we could compare the test performance of children who had attended school with that of children who had not attended school, we would expect a strong relation between test performance and school attendance. However, if we are looking at the performances of children who have all had some kind of school experience, then we feel more sensitive measures, ones more directly tied to the school's instructional content, are required to demonstrate schools' differential effectiveness.

Some investigators who have examined schools' and programs' differential effectiveness have used measures of this kind. When outcome measures have been specifically constructed to assess the instructional emphases of a particular school or program, large differences in achievement have been found between pupils exposed to the instruction in question and pupils not exposed (Block, 1971, 1974; Bloom, 1976; Brickell, 1976; Stodolsky, 1972).

The case of European public examinations is rather different. Instead of constructing tests following the investigation of the curricular emphases of schools, educators define syllabi of instruction for schools in advance. Examinations are then based on the syllabi; since these exams have crucial consequences for students' career prospects, schools, teachers, and students focus their work upon the topics and skills defined by the syllabus. When students' performance on these examinations in different schools is compared, strong evidence of the differential effectiveness of the schools is found (Brimer et al., 1978; Madaus, Kellaghan, & Rakow, 1975).

From an examination of the kinds of criterion measures that exhibit school effectiveness, we can infer what schools attempt to achieve. For the most part, schools seem to be concerned with the acquisition of fairly specific knowledge and skills. This is best exemplified at the high-school level, where instruction is organized into traditional subject areas, such as history, chemistry, physics, mathematics, and foreign languages. In any of these subject areas, it is relatively easy to specify a range of knowledge and skills that students are expected to acquire. For example, in history, a particular period and the major characters and events of the period may be prescribed for study. Likewise in chemistry, one may specify such topics as the structure of the atom, electrons, protons, neutrons, and isotopes, the structure and valence of elements, and so on.

Few schools would deny that it is their business to see that students acquire knowledge related to such topics. Some schools might also claim to be concerned that students, as a result of the acquisition of such knowledge, develop more generalized traits relating to thinking, reasoning, and analysis. But the latter is a more remote objective than the former, and whether or not a test of verbal ability would be sensitive to differences in its achievement is open to question.

Do Schools Strive to Work Independently of Students' Home Background?

Since longitudinal information was not available for most studies of school effectiveness, information on students' home background was used as proxy data for students' initial status. This is not an unusual response to the perceived need to exercise some kind of control over student characteristics in analyzing school effectiveness. However, since this control is achieved by entering home variables first in regression analyses, it involves assumptions that home influences on achievement operate only prior to, and independently of, school influences. Either assumption is difficult to sustain. It seems reasonable to suppose that home influences continue to affect a student's scholastic progress during his or her entire school career. After all, students move from home to school and back every day; it would be unreasonable to assume their behaviors are tightly compartmentalized according to the institution in which they happen to find themselves.

Furthermore, one would expect an interaction between the values, attitudes, and expectations of the home and those of the school. It is easy to imagine a situation in which positive attitudes toward achievement in the home contribute to the initial success of the child in school, which in turn may elicit increased interest and stimulation in the home. One could also imagine a situation in which failure at school evokes negative reactions to schooling in the home.

In the educational literature, home and school are viewed as the two major agencies of the child's socialization, and their influences on achievement are generally regarded as collusive. Most programs for disadvantaged children over the past two decades have emphasized the need for parental, and often community, involvement in the educational process—a concept with firm antecedents in John Dewey's educational policy.

While teachers are frequently exhorted to get to know the home circumstances of their pupils and to enlist the support of the home in the educational enterprise, their efforts at establishing links between school and home may not always be successful. At times, they may see the school-home interaction in rather simplistic terms (Goodacre, 1968; Jackson & Marsden, 1962), or they may devote too much of their attention to "problems" they perceive as arising in the home (Mays, 1962). Nevertheless, few would not believe that the continuing support (or lack of support) of a student's home is not an important determinant of scholastic progress.

Reanalyses of the Coleman data by Mayeske et al. (1972) employed a method which permitted the demonstration of common as well as unique contributions of home and school variables to the explanation of achievement variance. The common contribution of the school and of the students' backgrounds was found to exceed either of their distinguishable influences. The size of the commonality should not mislead one into supposing that partitioning has not been useful, that the "right" partitioning to represent factors was not made or that there are no "pure" indicators of the factors (Tatsuoka, 1973). Rather, it indicates the importance of the dynamic interaction between home and school in the educational process. We as yet have little knowledge of the nature of the functioning of that interaction; herein lies a crucial area in the future investigation of school effectiveness.

Do All Students Share Equally the School's Resources?

In investigating the relation between input variables and achievement in both studies of school and compensatory-program effectiveness, input variables have generally been aggregated to the school level. However, students are grouped within schools, very often on the basis of ability or achievement (cf. Finley & Brian, 1971), and these groups do not have similar access to school resources. To take an obvious example, classes are taught by different teachers; aggregating teacher characteristics to the school level obscures the characteristics of individual teachers and prevents the matching of individual teachers to groups of students.

Studies which have differentiated between groups within schools have found considerable within-school variance in achievement to be related to classes within schools (Kellaghan, Madaus, & Rakow, 1979; Madaus, Kellaghan, & Rakow, 1976; Martin & Kellaghan, 1977; Rakow, Airasian, & Madaus, 1978). This is what one would expect, given that schools group students and then, in many cases proceed to treat those groups differently.

Not only is one group of students treated differently from other groups in a school, but individual students within a group may receive differential treatment from a teacher. Such differential treatment within a group (class) could conceivably have an adverse effect on achievement if a teacher formed a low expectation of a pupil's performance and then treated the pupil as if his or her "evident or probable" destiny were fixed (cf. Perkinson, 1968). Or differential treatment of pupils may be geared to the different kinds and levels of aptitude with which pupils enter a program, with the objective of reducing the initial relation found between aptitude and attainment and thus producing a generally more uniform level of attainment among students (Bloom, Hastings, & Madaus, 1971). Policies of discrimination which favor more needy students (Great Britain: Department of Education and Science, 1967) are based on this assumption. We may note that if one accepts this line of reasoning, equality of educational output—the objective investigated in the Coleman survey—would not be likely to occur if all students had similar access to school resources, an assumption that the same report made when it chose the school as its unit of analysis.

Are Physical Resources Important Determinants of Student Achievement?

There can be little doubt that most people, whether directly involved in education or not, would have agreed at the time of the Coleman survey that physical resources are important features of a school. What is less clear is whether school features have been regarded as important determinants of achievement or simply as important in terms of the comfort and working conditions of students and teachers. Insofar as facilities might have been regarded as important for achievement, it is however doubtful if their effect would have been regarded as simply additive, as is implied by the use of a linear additive model of analysis in school-effectiveness studies.

Research to date does not indicate clearly the precise contribution of physical facilities to student achievement. It seems reasonable to say, however, that expenditure, books, and laboratories are prerequisites for learning in schools as they are presently constituted. Teachers and students may, of course, use resources in different ways. Furthermore, teachers and students interact among themselves as well as with physical facilities, thus creating social-psychological resources in the school, which seem to be more important than physical resources. There is evidence that a school climate characterized by social rewards for academic excellence, where discipline and scholastic achievement are valued by teachers and students, and teaching and learning are structured and focused on scholastic goals, contributes to high student achievement (Bloom, 1976; Brimer et al., 1978; Madaus, Kellaghan, & Rakow, 1975; Madaus, Kellaghan, Rakow, & King, 1979; Smith, 1976; Walberg & Rasher, 1974).

CONCLUSION

A good deal of this book has been devoted to a consideration of the limitations of research on school effectiveness. We have noted that available research does not speak to the absolute effects of schooling on achievement, and that there are many limitations in what it can tell us about the differential effects of schooling. These limitations were discussed in the context of methodological problems relating to the specification and measurement of school input and output variables, and to the way in which input variables are related to measures of output. Despite these limitations, evidence from some studies indicates that what goes on in schools is clearly related to student achievement.

In the final chapter, the extent to which the methodological approaches employed in most recent large-scale studies of school effectiveness can be taken to provide fair representation of what actually goes on in American schools was raised. On a number of counts, we felt that the representation in such studies does not reflect what American schools try to achieve or the manner in which they pursue their objectives.

It could be argued that Coleman and other investigators were not so much concerned with what American schools actually do as with what they should do: that is, provide equality of opportunity, however that term might be defined, for all students. This is not an unreasonable position, though it is open to abuse, as is clear when one considers the school-effectiveness controversy, in which generalizations about school effectiveness were made which went far beyond Coleman's quite limited findings. Furthermore, unless we have a greater understanding of what it is schools actually accomplish and the manner in which they achieve their objectives, our prescriptions for reform are likely to be very weak indeed.

There have been many attempts at educational reform through the 1960s. At the federal level alone, there was the Vocational Education Act of 1963, the Civil Rights Act of 1964, the Economic Opportunity Act of 1964, the National Defense Education Act of 1965, the Higher Education Act of 1965, and the Elementary and Secondary Education Act of 1965. The history of such intervention has not, unfortunately, been very distinguished as far as raising pupils' achievement was concerned.

The problems facing schools today cannot be regarded as inconsequential; this is clear when we consider the social ferment of the last fifteen years and the increasing disillusionment that the school can solve many pressing problems (Passow, 1977). However successful schools may have been in achieving some objectives—and we believe they have been for a large proportion of the population—they have not been very successful in coming to grips with the changing values and needs of at least some of their students. In particular, their record has been weak in providing students from disadvantaged backgrounds with the skills, both cognitive and social, traditionally acquired in school.

If schools are to continue to have an important role to play in the social system in the face of competing demands for finance for other services, such as health and welfare, educators must be in a position to demonstrate what it is schools can and cannot do. In the 1960s and into the 1970s, for a variety of reasons, schools became a primary institution for the solution of America's perceived social problems. Schools and school programs were to be the vehicles through which pupils would attain not only basic cognitive skills such as reading and mathematics, but also, through the attainment of such skills, greater social, economic, and occupational independence.

It seems crucial that citizens, educators, politicians, and social planners think more carefully and dispassionately about the goals of schools and schooling. They must decide what are realistic expectations for schools: what effects they *can* and should have upon pupils and society. The place of schools as institutions in the context of society and its other institutions must be reconsidered, instead of automatically making the school and its mission the focal point for social and economic reform. The school may have a role to play in such reform, but whether that role is primary for all goals or incidental for many should be looked at in the light of the evidence we have considered. Perhaps the single most important lesson to be learned from recent school-effectiveness studies is the inadequacy of knowledge in this regard. It may be that the school will have to alter its objectives and approaches if it is to make a contribution to the solution of today's social problems. However, until we have a better understanding of the phenomenon of schooling, we will have little to guide us in deciding what should be changed or how it should be changed.

At this stage in the investigation of school effectiveness, it seems clear that the primary need is not for more studies which will attempt to predict certain outputs on the basis of knowing certain inputs, but rather for investigations which will promote a clearer understanding and explanation of the process of schooling. In designing research studies, more attention than has been given in the past will have to be paid to the conversion of basic questions into research procedures which will ensure that the data obtained will be adequate to answer the questions. It is clear that the identification of the objectives of schooling and the design of measures congruent with those objectives and with the instructional processes of schools are in need of particular attention. As yet, we know relatively little about school environments, their nature, antecedents, and consequences. In the identification of variables to represent such environments, the lack of clarity which prevailed in the past must be avoided. Cross-sectional correlational data will also have to give way to other data if we are to begin, with any confidence, to trace causal relations in the schooling process.

A dramatic increase in our understanding of schooling is not something which will occur overnight. Hearing physical scientists say that a cure for cancer may require twenty years of research at a cost of $30 billion strikes few of us as unreasonable. Why then should a similar statement about the problem of identifying manipulable school and program variables which will raise pupils' achievement—an exceedingly complex problem—not be received likewise? Scientific research, whether concerned with the search for a cancer cure or the dimensions of school effectiveness, develops knowledge by creating models and theories which are then tested and improved in the light of empirical evidence. This process tends to proceed slowly. However, the experience of the first ten years of intensive research on schooling should clearly indicate that there is no other alternative.

References

Acland, H. People love school? Los Angeles, Calif.: University of Southern California, 1975 (mimeo).

Airasian, P. W. Designing summative evaluation studies at the local level. In W. J. Popham (Ed.), *Evaluation in education. Current applications.* Berkeley, California: McCutchan, 1974.

Airasian, P. W. Societal experimentation. Paper presented at Annual Conference of the British Psychological Society, University of Exeter, April 1977.

Airasian, P. W. & Madaus, G. F. Criterion referenced testing in the classroom. *NCME Measurement in Education,* 1972, 3 (4), 1-7.

Airasian, P. W. & Madaus, G. F. A study of the sensitivity of school and program effectiveness measures. Report submitted to the Carnegie Corporation, New York, July 1976. Chestnut Hill, Mass.: Boston College, 1976.

Airasian, P. W. & Madaus, G. F. A post hoc technique for identifying between program differences in achievement. *Studies in Educational Evaluation,* 1978, 4, 1-8.

American Psychological Association. *Standards for educational and psychological tests.* Washington, D. C.: Author, 1974.

Anastasi, A. *Psychological testing* (3rd ed.) New York: Macmillan, 1968.

Anderson, L. W., Scott, C. C., & Hutlock, N. The effects of a mastery learning program of selected cognitive, affective and interpersonal variables in grades 1 through 6. Paper read at Annual Meeting of the American Educational Research Association, San Francisco, April 1976.

Anderson, R. C. How to construct achievement tests to assess comprehension. *Review of Educational Research,* 1972, 42, 145-170.

Armor, D. J. School and family effects on black and white achievement. A re-examination of the USOE data. In F. Mosteller & D. P. Moynihan (Eds.), *On equality of educational opportunity.* New York: Vintage Books, 1972.

Averch, H. A., Carroll, S. J., Donaldson, T. S., Kiesling, H. J., & Pincus, J. *How effective is schooling? A critical review and synthesis of research findings.* Santa Monica, California: Rand Corporation, 1972.

191

Ayres, L. P. *Laggards in our schools.* New York: Russell Sage Foundation, 1909.

Beaton, A. E. Commonality. Unpublished manuscript, March 1973.

Beaton, A. E. Multivariate commonality analysis. In G. W. Mayeske, A. E. Beaton, C. E. Wisler, T. Okado & W. M. Cohen. *Technical supplement to "A study of the achievement of our nation's students".* Washington, D. C.: U.S. Department of Health, Education, and Welfare, 1974.

Beaton, A. E., Hilton, T. L., & Schrader, W. B. *Changes in the verbal abilities of high school seniors, college entrants, and SAT candidates between 1960 and 1972.* Princeton, N. J.: Educational Testing Service, 1977.

Bell, D. Meritocracy and equality. *Public Interest,* Fall 1972, No. 29, 24–68.

Benson, C. et al. *State and local fiscal relationships in public education in California.* Report of the Senate Fact Finding Committee on Revenue and Taxation, Senate of the State of California, Sacramento, March 1965.

Biddle, B. J. & Ellena, W. J. (Eds.) *Contemporary research on teacher effectiveness.* New York: Holt, Rinehart & Winston, 1964.

Bidwell, C. E. Nations, school districts and schools: Are there schooling effects anywhere? Paper read at Annual Meeting of the American Educational Research Association, Washington, D. C., April 1975.

Bidwell, C. E. & Kasarda, J. D. School district organization and student achievement. *American Sociological Review,* 1975, *40,* 55–70.

Biemiller, A. J. Aid to elementary and secondary education. Hearings before the General Subcommittee on Education of the Committe of Education and Labor, House of Representatives, 89th Congress, 1st Session, on H.R. 2361 and H.R. 2362, Jan. 29, 1966, Vol. I.

Bissell, J. S. The cognitive effects of pre-school programs for disadvantaged children. Unpublished doctoral dissertation, Harvard University, 1970.

Bissell, J. S. Planned variation in Head Start and Follow Through. In J. C. Stanley (Ed.), *Compensatory education for children, ages 2 to 8. Recent studies of educational intervention.* Baltimore: Johns Hopkins University Press, 1973.

Blau, P. M. & Duncan, O. D. *American occupational structure.* New York: Wiley, 1967.

Block, J. H. (Ed.) *Mastery learning: Theory and practice.* New York: Holt, Rinehart & Winston, 1971.

Block, J. H. (Ed.) *School, society and mastery learning.* New York: Holt, Rinehart & Winston, 1974.

Bloom, B. S. *The idea and practice of general education.* Chicago: University of Chicago Press, 1950.

Bloom, B. S. (Ed.) *Taxonomy of educational objectives: The classification of educational goals. Handbook I: The cognitive domain.* New York: McKay, 1956.

Bloom, B. S. *Stability and change in human characteristics.* New York: Wiley, 1964.

Bloom, B. S. Learning for mastery. *University of California Evaluation Comment*, 1968, *1*, 1-12.

Bloom, B. S. Implications of the IEA studies for curriculum and instruction. In A. C. Purves & D. U. Levine (Eds.), *Educational policy and international assessment. Implications of the IEA surveys of achievement.* Berkeley, California: McCutchan, 1975.

Bloom, B. S. *Human characteristics and school learning.* New York: McGraw-Hill, 1976.

Bloom, B. S. Hastings, J. T. & Madaus, G. F. *Handbook on formative and summative evaluation of student learning.* New York: McGraw-Hill, 1971.

Bobbit, F. *The supervision of city schools: Some general principles of management applied to the problems of city school systems. Twelfth Yearbook of the National Society for the Study of Education, Part I.* Bloomington, Ill.: Public School Publishing Co., 1913.

Bollenbacher, J. The testing scene: Chaos and controversy. In *Testing and the public interest, Proceedings of the 1976 ETS Invitational Conference.* Princeton, N. J.: Educational Testing Service, 1976.

Boulding, K. *The impact of the social sciences.* New Brunswick, N. J.: Rutgers University Press, 1966.

Bowles, S. & Levin, H. M. More on multicollinearity and the effectiveness of schools. *Journal of Human Resources*, 1968a, *3*, 393-400.

Bowles, S. & Levin, H. M. The determinants of scholastic achievement: An appraisal of some recent evidence. *Journal of Human Resources*, 1968b, *3*, 3-24.

Bradley, L. A. & Bradley, G. W. The academic achievement of black students in desegregated schools: A critical review. *Review of Educational Research*, 1977, *47*, 399-449.

Brickell, H. M. Needed: Instruments as good as our eyes. *Evaluation Center Occasional Paper Series No. 7.* Kalamazoo, Michigan: Western Michigan University, 1976.

Brimer, A. Whosoever hath . . . ? An inaugural lecture from the Chair of Education delivered on January 27, 1976. *Supplement to the Gazette of the University of Hong Kong*, 1976, *23* (3), 1-8.

Brimer, A., Madaus, G. F., Chapman, B., Kellaghan, T., & Wood, R. *Sources of difference in school achievement.* Slough: NFER Publishing Co., 1978.

Bronfenbrenner, U. Is early intervention effective? In M. Guttentag & E. L. Struening (Eds.), *Handbook of evaluation research, Volume 2.* Beverly Hills, California: Sage, 1975.

Brookover, W. B., Gigliatti, R. J., Henderson, R. D., Niles, B. E. & Schneider, J. M. Quality of educational attainment, standardized testing, assessment, and accountability. In C. W. Gordon (Ed.), *Uses of the sociology of education. Seventy-third Yearbook of the NSEE. Part II.* Chicago: National Society for the Study of Education, 1974.

Brookover, W. B., Schweitzer, J. H., Schneider, J. M., Beady, C. H., Flood, P. K., & Wisenbaker, J. M. Elementary school social climate and school achievement. *American Educational Research Journal*, 1978, *15*, 301–318.

Brown, B. W., & Saks, D. H. The production and distribution of cognitive skills within schools. *Journal of Political Economy*, 1975, *83*, 571–593.

Burket, G. R. Empirical criteria for distinguishing and validating aptitude and achievement measures. In D. R. Green (Ed.), *The aptitude-achievement distinction*. Monterey, California: CTB/McGraw-Hill, 1974.

Burkhead, J., Fox, T. G. & Holland, J. W. *Input and output in large city high schools*. Syracuse, N.Y.: Syracuse University Press, 1967.

Burstein, L. The choice of unit of analysis in the investigation of school effects: IEA in New Zealand. *New Zealand Journal of Educational Studies*, 1976, *11*, 11–24.

Burt, C. Intelligence and heredity: Some common misconceptions. *Irish Journal of Education*, 1969, *3*, 75–94.

Callahan, R. E. *Education and the cult of efficiency*. Chicago: University of Chicago Press, 1962.

Campbell, D. T. Reforms as experiments. *American Psychologist*, 1969, *4*, 409–429.

Campbell, D. T. Assessing the impact of planned social change. *Evaluation Center Occasional Paper Series No. 8*. Kalamazoo, Michigan: Western Michigan University, 1976.

Campbell, D. T. & Erlebacher, A. How regression artifacts in quasi-experimental evaluations can mistakenly make compensatory education look harmful. In J. Hellmuth (Ed.), *Disavantaged child. Volume 3. Compensatory education: A national debate*. New York: Brunner/Mazel, 1970.

Campbell, D. T. & Fiske, D. W. Convergent and discriminant validation by the multi-trait-multimethod matrix. *Psychological Bulletin*, 1959, *56*, 81–105.

Campbell, D. T. & Stanley, J. C. Experimental and quasi-experimental designs for research on teaching. In N. L. Gage (Ed.), *Handbook of research on teaching*. Chicago: Rand McNally, 1963.

Caro, F. G. Issues in the evaluation of social programs. *Review of Educational Research*, 1971, *41*, 87–114.

Carroll, J. B. A model of school learning. *Teachers College Record*, 1963, *64*, 723–733.

Carroll, J. B. Psychometric tests as cognitive tasks: A new "structure of intellect." In L. B. Resnick (Ed.), *The nature of intelligence*. New York: Wiley, 1976.

Carver, R. P. The Coleman report: Using inappropriately designed achievement tests. *American Educational Research Journal*, 1975, *12*, 77–86.

Cazden, C. B. Evaluation of learning in preschool education. In B. S. Bloom, J. T. Hastings & G. F. Madaus (Eds.), *Handbook on formative and summative evaluation of student learning*. New York: McGraw-Hill, 1971.

Celebrezze, A. Hearings before the Committee of Education and Labor, House of Representatives, *Education Act of 1965*.

Cicirelli, V. G. The relevance of the regression artifact problem to the Westing-house-Ohio Evaluation of Head Start: Reply to Campbell and Erlebacher. In J. Hellmuth (Ed.), *Disadvantaged child, Vol. 3.* New York: Brunner/Mazel, 1970.

Cicirelli, V. G., et al. *The impact of Head Start. An evaluation of the effects of Head Start on children's cognitive and affective development.* Study by Westinghouse Learning Corporation and Ohio University. Washington, D. C.: Office of Economic Opportunity, 1969.

Cicirelli, V. G., Evans, J. W. & Schiller, J. S. The impact of Head Start: A reply to the report analysis. *Havard Educational Review,* 1970, *40,* 105–129.

Coffman, W. E., A moratorium. What kind? *NCME Measurement in Education,* 1974, *5*(2), 1–7.

Cohen, D. K. Politics and research: Evaluation of social action programs in education. *Review of Educational Research,* 1970, *40,* 213–238.

Cohen, J. & Cohen, P. *Applied multiple regression/correlation analysis for the behavioral sciences.* New York: Wiley, 1975.

Coleman, J. S. *The adolescent society. The social life of the teenager and its impact on education.* New York: Free Press, 1961.

Coleman, J. S. The concept of equality of educational opportunity. *Harvard Educational Review,* 1968, *38,* 7–22.

Coleman, J. S. The evaluation of Equality of Educational Opportunity. In F. Mosteller & D. P. Moynihan (Eds.), *On equality of educational opportunity.* New York: Vintage Books, 1972.

Coleman, J. S. Methods and results in the IEA studies of effects of school on learning. *Review of Educational Research,* 1975a, *45,* 335–386.

Coleman, J. S. What is meant by an "equal educational opportunity?" *Oxford Review of Education,* 1975b, *1,* 27–29.

Coleman, J. S. Court ordered school bussing. Remarks on Senate Bill 1364 of 1976. *Boston Globe,* March 20, 1976.

Coleman, J. S., Campbell, E. Q., Hobson, C. J., McPartland, J., Mood, A. M. Weinfeld, F. D. & York, R. L. *Equality of educational opportunity.* Washington, D.C.: Office of Education, U.S. Department of Health, Education, and Welfare, 1966.

Coleman, J. S. & Karweit, N. L. *Information systems and performance measures in schools.* Englewood Cliffs, N. J.: Educational Technology Publications, 1972.

Comber, L. C. & Keeves, J. P. *Science education in nineteen countries. An empirical study.* New York: Wiley, 1973.

Convey, J. J. Determining school effectiveness following a regression analysis. *Journal of Educational Statistics,* 1977, *2,* 27–39.

Cook, T. D. & Campbell, D. T. The design and conduct of quasi-experiments and true experiments in field settings. In M. D. Dunnette, and J. P. Campbell (Eds.) *Handbook of industrial and organizational research.* Chicago: Rand McNally, 1975.

Cooley, W. W. Assessment of educational effects. *Educational Psychologist*, 1974, *11*, 29-35.

Cooley, W. W. Who needs general intelligence? In L. B. Resnick (Ed.), *The nature of intelligence*. New York: Wiley, 1976.

Cooley, W. W. & Lohnes, P. R. *Evaluation research in education*. New York: Wiley, 1976.

Crano, W. D. Causal analyses of the effects of socio-economic status and initial intellectual endowment on patterns of cognitive development and academic achievement. In D. R. Green (Ed.), *The aptitude-achievement distinction*. Monterey, California: CTB/McGraw-Hill, 1974.

Crano, W. D., Kenny, D. A. & Campbell, D. T. Does intelligence cause achievement? A cross-lagged panel analysis. *Journal of Educational Psychology*, 1972, *63*, 258-275.

Crawford, J., Brophy, J. E., Evertson, C. M. & Coulter, C. L. Classroom dyadic interaction: Factor structure of process variables and achievement correlates. *Journal of Educational Psychology*, 1977, *69*, 761-772.

Cremin, L. A. *The transformation of the school*. New York: Knopf, 1962.

Cronbach, L. J. Course improvement through evaluation. *Teachers College Record*, 1963, *64*, 672-683.

Cronbach, L. J. Test validation. In R. L. Thorndike (Ed.), *Educational measurement* (2nd ed.). Washington, D. C.: American Council on Education, 1971.

Cronbach, L. J. Five decades of public controversy over mental testing. *American Psychologist*, 1975, *30*, 1-14.

Cronbach, L. J. & Furby, L. How should we measure "change"—or should we? *Psychological Bulletin*, 1970, *74*, 68-80.

Dacey, J., Madaus, G. F. & Allen, A. The relationship of creativity and intelligence in Irish adolescents. *British Journal of Educational Psychology*, 1969, *39*, 261-266.

Datta, L. E. The impact of the Westinghouse/Ohio evaluation on the development of Project Head Start: An examination of the immediate and longer-term effects and how they came about. In C. Abt (Ed.), *The evaluation of social programs*. Beverly Hills, Calif.: Sage Publications, 1976.

Dave, R. H. The identification and measurement of environmental process variables related to educational achievement. Unpublished doctoral dissertation. University of Chicago, 1963.

Dunkin, M. J. & Biddle, B. J. *The study of teaching*. New York: Holt, Rinehart & Winston, 1974.

Dyer, H. S. School factors and equal educational opportunity. *Harvard Educational Review*, 1968, *38*, 38-56.

Dyer, H. S. Some thoughts about future studies. In F. Mosteller and D. P. Moynihan (Eds.), *On equality of educational opportunity*. New York: Vintage Books, 1972.

Dyer, H. S., Linn, R. L., & Patton, M. J. A comparison of four methods of obtaining discrepancy measures based on observed and predicted school system means on achievement tests. *American Educational Research Journal*, 1969, *6*, 591–605.

Ebel, R. L. Knowledge vs. ability in achievement testing. In *Toward a theory of achievement measurement. Proceedings of the 1969 Invitational Conference on Testing Problems.* Princeton, N. J.: Educational Testing Service, 1969.

Elmore, R. F. Design of the Follow Through experiment. In A. M. Rivlin & P. M. Timpane (Eds.), *Planned variation in education: Should we give up or try harder?* Washington, D. C.: The Brookings Institution, 1975.

Evans, J. W. Evaluating social action programs. *Social Science Quarterly*, 1969, *50*, 568–581.

Evans, J. W. & Schiller, J. How preoccupation with possible regression artifacts can lead to a faulty strategy for the evaluation of social action programs: A reply to Campbell and Erlebacher. In J. Hellmuth (Ed.), *Disadvantaged child, Volume 3: Compensatory education: A national debate.* New York: Brunner/Mazel, 1970.

Farr, R. *Reading: What can be measured?* Newark, Delaware: International Reading Association, 1970.

Farr, R. & Roelke, P. Measuring subskills of reading: Inter-correlations between standardized reading tests, teachers' ratings, and reading specialists' ratings. *Journal of Educational Measurement*, 1971, *8*, 27–32.

Fennessy, J. *Using achievement growth to analyze educational programs. Report No. 151.* Baltimore, Maryland: Center for Social Organization of Schools, The Johns Hopkins University, 1973.

Ferris, F. L., Jr. Testing in the new curriculum: Numerology, "tyranny", or common sense? *School Review*, 1962, *70*, 112–131.

Finley, W. G. & Brian, M. M. *Ability grouping 1970: Status impact and alternatives.* Athens, Ga.: Center for Educational Improvement, University of Georgia, 1971.

Fitzgibbon, T. Dear Mama: Why don't they love me anymore? *NCME Measurement in Education*, 1975a, *6* (4), 1–8.

Fitzgibbon, T. *The use of standardized instruments with urban and minority group pupils.* New York: Harcourt Brace & Jovanovich, 1975b.

Flanagan, J. C. & Cooley, W. W. *Project Talent: One-year follow-up studies.* Pittsburgh, Pa.: School of Education, University of Pittsburgh, 1966.

Foley, J. J. Evaluation of learning in writing. In B. S. Bloom, J. T. Hastings and G. F. Madaus (Eds.) *Handbook on formative and summative evaluation of student learning.* New York: McGraw-Hill, 1971.

Fraser, E. *Home environment and the school.* London: University of London Press, 1959.

Frederiksen, J. R. & Bolt, Beranek & Newman Inc. *School effectiveness and equality of educational opportunity.* Report submitted to the Carnegie Corporation of New York, 1975.

Fullan, M. & Pomfret, A. Research on curriculum and instruction implementation. *Review of Educational Research,* 1977, 47, 335-397.

Furst, E. J. *Constructing evaluation instruments.* New York: McKay, 1958.

Gallup, G. H. *How the nation views the public schools: A study of the public schools of the United States.* Princeton, N.J.: Gallup International, 1969.

Gallup, G. H. Eighth annual Gallup poll of the public's attitudes toward the public schools. *Phi Delta Kappan,* 1976, 58, 187-200.

Gallup, G. H. Ninth annual Gallup Poll of the public's attitudes toward the public schools. *Phi Delta Kappan,* 1977, 59, 33-48.

Garth, T. R. *Race psychology: A study of racial mental differences.* New York: McGraw-Hill, 1931.

Gerard, H. B. & Miller, N. (Eds.) *School desegregation.* New York: Plenum Press, 1975.

Getzels, J. W. A social psychology of education. In G. Lindzey & E. Aronson (Eds.), *The handbook of social psychology* (2nd ed.), Volume 5. Reading, Mass.: Addison-Wesley, 1969.

Getzels, J. W. & Madaus, G. F. Creativity. In R. Ebel (Ed.), *Encyclopedia of educational research* (4th ed.). London: Collier-Macmillan, 1969.

Glaser, R. The processes of intelligence and education. In L. B. Resnick (Ed.), *The nature of intelligence.* New York: Wiley, 1976.

Glass, G. V. Education of the disadvantaged: An Evaluation Report, Title I, Elementary and Secondary Education Act of 1965, Fiscal Year 1969. University of Colorado, Boulder, Colorado, 1970 (Mimeo).

Glass, G. V. *Standards and criteria.* Boulder, Colorado: University of Colorado, 1977.

Glass, G. V., et al. *Data analysis of the 1968-69 survey of compensatory education, Title I, Final Report on Grant No. OEG8-8-961860 4003-(058).* Washington, D. C.: U.S. Office of Education, 1970.

Good, T. L., Biddle, J. E. & Brophy, J. E. *Teachers make a difference.* New York: Holt, Rinehart & Winston, 1975.

Good, T. L. & Brophy, J. E. *Looking in classrooms.* New York: Harper & Row, 1973.

Goodacre, E. J. *Teachers and their pupils' home background.* Slough: NFER Publishing Co., 1968.

Goodman, S. M. *The assessment of school quality.* Albany, N.Y.: The State Education Department of New York, 1959.

Gordon, E. W. *Utilizing available information from compensatory education and surveys. Final Report.* Washington, D. C.: Office of Education, 1971.

Gordon, H. *Mental and scholastic tests among retarded children.* Education Pamphlet No. 44. London: Board of Education, 1923.

Grant, G. Shaping social policy: The politics of the Coleman Report. *Teachers College Record*, 1973, 75, 17–54.

Great Britain: Department of Education and Science. *Children and their primary schools*. A report of the Central Advisory Council for Education (England). London: Her Majesty's Stationery Office, 1967.

Great Britain: Department of Education and Science. *A language for life*. London: Her Majesty's Stationery Office, 1975.

Green, D. R. *The aptitude-achievement distinction*. Monterey, California: CTB/ McGraw-Hill, 1974.

Green, R. L., Hofman, L. T., Morse, R. J., Hayes, M. E. & Morgan, R. F. *The educational status of children in a district without public schools*. Co-operative Research Project No. 2321, Office of Education, U. S. Department of Health, Education, and Welfare. Lansing, Michigan: Michigan State University, College of Education, 1964.

Greenfield, P. M. On culture and conservation. In J. S. Bruner, R. R. Olver, P. M. Greenfield et al., *Studies in cognitive growth*. New York: Wiley, 1966.

Greenfield, P. M., Reich, L. C. & Olver, R. R. On culture and equivalence: II. In J. S. Bruner, R. R. Olver, P. M. Greenfield et al., *Studies in cognitive growth*. New York: Wiley, 1966.

Greenough, J. B. & Kittredge, G. L. *Words and their ways in English speech*. New York: Macmillan, 1961.

Guthrie, J. Q. A survey of school effectiveness studies. In *Do teachers make a difference?* Washington, D. C.: U. S. Government Printing Office, 1970.

Guthrie, J. W., Kleindorfer, G. B., Levin, H. M. & Stout, R. T. *Schools and inequality*. Cambridge, Mass.: Massachusetts Institute of Technology Press, 1971.

Guttman, L. Integration of test design and analysis. In *Toward a theory of achievement measurement. Proceedings of the 1969 Invitational Conference on testing problems*. Princeton, N. J.: Educational Testing Service, 1969.

Haggard, E. *Interclass correlation and the analysis of variance*. New York: Dryden Press, 1958.

Haney, W. *The Follow Through planned variation experiment: Vol. 5 of the Follow Through evaluation: A technical history*. Prepared for the Office of Planning, Budgeting and Evaluation. Washington, D. C.: Office of Education, Department of Health, Education, and Welfare, Contract No. OEC-0-74-0394, August, 1977.

Hanushek, E. *The value of teachers in teaching*. Santa Monica, California: Rand Corporation, 1970.

Hanushek, E. A. & Kain, J. F. On the value of Equality of Educational Opportunity as a guide to public policy. In F. Mosteller & D. P. Moynihan (Eds.), *On equality of educational opportunity*. New York: Vintage Books, 1972.

Harnischfeger, A. & Wiley, D. E. *Achievement test score decline: Do we need to worry?* Chicago: CEMREL, Inc., 1975.

Haskew, L. D. As I see it . . . . In *Christopher Jencks in perspective*. Arlington, Virginia: American Association of School Administrators, 1973.

Hawkes, H. E., Lindquist, E. F. & Mann, C. R. *The construction and use of achievement examinations.* Boston: Houghton Mifflin, 1936.

Hawkridge, D. G., Chalupsky, A. B. & Roberts, A. O. H. *A study of selected exemplary programs for the education of disadvantaged children.* Washington, D.C.: U.S. Department of Health, Education, and Welfare, 1968.

Hawkridge, D. G., Tallmadge, G. K. & Larsen, J. K. *Foundations for success in educating disadvantaged children.* Washington, D. C.: U.S. Department of Health, Education, and Welfare, 1968.

Henrysson, S. Gathering, analyzing and using data on test items. In R. L. Thorndike (Ed.), *Educational measurement* (2nd ed.) Washington, D. C.: American Council on Education, 1971.

Heyneman, S. P. Influences on academic achievement: A comparison of results from Uganda and more industrialized societies. Paper read at Annual Meeting of the American Educational Research Association, Washington, D. C., April 1975.

Hilton, T. L. & Patrick, C. Cross-sectional versus longitudinal data: An empirical comparison of mean differences in academic growth. *Journal of Educational Measurement,* 1970, *7,* 15–24.

Hodgson, G. Do schools make a difference? In D. M. Levine & M. J. Bane (Eds.), *The "inequality" controversy: Schooling and distributive justice.* New York: Basic Books, 1975.

Hoffman, R. J. The concept of efficiency in item analysis. *Educational and Psychological Measurement,* 1975, *35,* 621–640.

Holmes, E. G. A. *What is and what might be: A study of education in general, and elementary in particular.* London: Constable, 1911.

Hopkins, K. P. & Bracht, G. H. Ten-year stability of verbal and non-verbal IQ scores. *American Educational Research Journal,* 1975, *12,* 469–477.

House, E. R. (Ed.) *School evaluation, the politics and process.* Berkeley, California: McCutchan, 1973a.

House, E. R. Validating a goal-priority instrument. Paper read at Annual Meeting of the American Educational Research Association, New Orleans, March 1973b.

Hunt, J. McV. *Intelligence and experience.* New York: Ronald Press, 1961.

Husek, T. R. Different kinds of evaluation and their implications for test development. Paper read at Annual Meeting of the American Educational Research Association, Chicago, April 1966.

Husen, T. (Ed.) *International study of achievement in mathematics. A comparison of twelve countries. Volume II.* New York: Wiley, 1967.

Illich, I. *Deschooling society.* New York: Harper & Row, 1971.

Iwanicki, E. F. A school practitioner's guide to design for the evaluation of compensatory educational programs. Paper presented at Annual Meeting of American Educational Research Association, Chicago, April 1974.

Iwanicki, E. F. The use of grade equivalent scores in the assessment of basic skills growth: A cautionary note. Paper presented at Annual Meeting of the American Educational Research Association, New York, April 1977.

Jackson, B. & Marsden, D. *Education and the working class.* London: Routledge & Kegan Paul, 1962.

Jackson, P. *Life in classrooms.* New York: Holt, Rinehart & Winston, 1968.

Jaeger, R. M. The national test-equating study in reading, (The Anchor Test Study). *NCME Measurement in Education,* 1973, 4(4), 1-8.

Jencks, C. S. Education: The racial gap. *New Republic,* Oct. 1966, 21-26.

Jencks, C. S. The Coleman report and the conventional wisdom. In F. Mosteller & D. P. Moynihan (Eds.), *On equality of educational opportunity.* New York: Vintage Books, 1972a.

Jencks, C. S. The quality of the data collected by the Equality of Educational Opportunity Survey. In F. Mosteller & D. P. Moynihan (Eds.), *On equality of educational opportunity.* New York: Vintage Books, 1972b.

Jencks, C. S. Brown, M. D. Effects of high schools on their students. *Harvard Educational Review,* 1975, 45, 273-324.

Jencks, C. S., Smith, M., Acland, H., Bane, M. J., Cohen, D., Gintis, H., Hyns, B. & Michelson, S. *Inequality: A reassessment of the effect of family and schooling in America.* New York: Basic Books, 1972.

Jensen, A. R. How much can we boost IQ and scholastic achievement? *Harvard Educational Review,* 1969, 39, 1-123.

Kamii, C. K. Evaluation of learning in preschool education: Socio-emotional, perceptual motor, cognitive development. In B. S. Bloom, J. T. Hastings, & G. F. Madaus (Eds.), *Handbook of formative and summative evaluation of student learning.* New York: McGraw-Hill, 1971.

Katzman, M. Distribution and production in a big city elementary school system. *Yale Economic Essays,* 1968, 8, 201-256.

Kellaghan, T. Abstraction and categorization in African children. *International Journal of Psychology,* 1968, 3, 115-120.

Kellaghan, T. Evaluation in Irish schools. Paper presented at Invitational International Symposium on Testing and Cross-national Studies. National Council for Measurement in Education Annual Meeting, Chicago, April 1972a.

Kellaghan, T. Preschool intervention for the educationally disadvantaged. *Irish Journal of Psychology,* 1972b, 6, 160-176.

Kellaghan, T. Intelligence and achievement in a disadvantaged population: A cross-lagged panel analysis. *Irish Journal of Education,* 1973, 7, 23-28.

Kellaghan, T. Measuring school effectiveness. In R. Sumner (Ed.), *Monitoring national standards of attainment in schools.* Slough: NFER Publishing Co., 1977a.

Kellaghan, T. Relationships between home environment and scholastic behavior in a disadvantaged population. *Journal of Educational Psychology,* 1977b, 69, 754-760.

Kellaghan, T. *The evaluation of an intervention programme for disadvantaged children.* Slough: NFER Publishing Co., 1977c.

Kellaghan, T., Madaus, G. F. & Rakow, E. A Within-school variance in achievement: School effects or error? *Studies in Educational Evaluation,* 1979, *5,* 101–107.

Kelley, T. L. *The interpretation of educational measurement.* Yonkers-on-Hudson, N. Y.: World Book Company, 1927.

Kendall, C. N. Efficiency of schools and school systems. *NEA Journal of the Proceedings and Addresses of the 53rd Annual Meeting,* 1915, 389–395.

Kennedy, R. *Elementary and Secondary Education Act of 1965.* Hearings before the Subcommittee of Education of the Committee on Labor and Public Welfare, U.S. Senate, 89th Congress, 1st Session on S. 370. Jan. 26, 1965, Vol. I, Part 1.

Kerlinger, F. N. & Pedhazur, E. J. *Multiple regression in behavioral research.* New York: Holt, Rinehart & Winston, 1973.

Kiesling, H. J. *The relationship of school inputs to public school performance in New York State.* Santa Monica, California: Rand Corporation, 1969.

Klein, S. P. The uses and limitations of standardized tests in meeting the demands of accountability. *University of California Evaluation Comment,* 1971, 4(2), 1–7.

Klein, S. P. Cost-quality research limitations: The problem of poor indices. In J. E. McDermott (Ed.), *Indeterminacy in education.* Berkeley, Calif.: McCutchan, 1976.

Klineberg, O. *Negro intelligence and selective migration.* New York: Columbia University Press, 1935.

Knapp, T. R. The unit-of-analysis problem in application of simple correlation analysis to educational research. *Journal of Educational Statistics,* 1977, *2,* 171–186.

Kwansa, K. B. Content validity and reliablility of domain referenced tests. *African Journal of Educational Research,* 1974, *1,* 73–79.

Lavin, D. E. *The prediction of academic performance.* New York: Russell Sage Foundation, 1965.

Lee, E. S. Negro intelligence and selective migration: A Philadelphia test of the Klineberg hypothesis. *American Sociological Review,* 1951, *16,* 227–232.

Levin, H. M. A new model of school effectiveness. In *Do teachers make a difference.* Washington, D. C.: U. S. Department of Health, Education, and Welfare, 1970.

Levine, D. M. & Bane, M. J. Introduction. In D. M. Levine & M. J. Bane (Eds.), *The "inequality" controversy: Schooling and distributive justice.* New York: Basic Books, 1975.

Levine, M. The academic achievement test: Its historical context and social functions. *American Psychologist,* 1976, *31,* 228–238.

Lewy, A. Discrimination among individuals vs. discrimination among groups. *Journal of Educational Measurement*, 1973, *10*, 19-24.

Lindquist, E. F. Norms of achievement by schools. In A. Anastasi (Ed.), *Testing problems in perspective*. Washington, D. C.: American Council on Education, 1966.

Linnan, R. & Airasian, P. W. Ethnic comparisons of environmental predictors of three cognitive abilities. Paper presented at Annual Meeting of the American Educational Research Association, Chicago, April 1974.

Lourie, S. Policy, research and decision making in education. In C. C. Abt (Ed.), *The evaluation of social programs*. Beverly Hills, Calif.: Sage Publications, 1976.

Luecke, D. F. & McGinn, N. F. Regression analyses and education production functions: Can they be trusted? *Harvard Educational Review*, 1975, *45*, 325-350.

Lukas, C. V. Problems in implementing Head Start Planned Variation models. In A. M. Rivlin & P. M. Timpane (Eds.), *Planned variation in education: Should we give up or try harder?* Washington, D. C.: Brookings Institution, 1975.

Madaus, G. F. A cross-cultural comparison of the factor structure of selected tests of divergent thinking. *Journal of Social Psychology*, 1967b, *73*, 13-21.

Madaus, G. F. Divergent thinking and intelligence: Another look at a controversial question. *Journal of Educational Measurement*, 1967a, *4*, 227-235.

Madaus, G. F. Memorandum to the joint committee on Test Standards revision on the need for a companion volume dealing with standards for the use of tests in program evaluation, 1973.

Madaus, G. F. & Airasian, P. W. Issues in evaluating student outcomes in competency based graduation programs. *Journal of Research and Development in Education*, 1977, *10*(3), 79-91.

Madaus, G. F., Airasian, P. W. & Kellaghan, T. The effects of standardized testing. *Irish Journal of Education*, 1971, *5*, 70-85.

Madaus, G. F. & Elmore, R. F. Allocation of federal compensatory education funds on the basis of pupil achievement test performance. Hearings before the General Subcommittee on Education of the Committee on Education and Labor, House of Representatives, 93rd Congress, First session, on H.R. 16, H.R. 69, H.R. 5163, H.R. 5823. Washington, D. C.: U.S. Government Printing Office, 1973, 3014-3028.

Madaus, G. F., Kellaghan, T. & Rakow, E. A. A study of the sensitivity of measures of school effectiveness. Report submitted to the Carnegie Corporation of New York. Dublin: Educational Research Centre, St. Patrick's College, and Chestnut Hill, Mass.: Boston College, 1975.

Madaus, G. F., Kellaghan, T. & Rakow, E. A. School and class differences in performance on the Leaving Certificate examination. *Irish Journal of Education*, 1976, *10*, 41-50.

Madaus, G. F., Kellaghan, T. Rakow, E. A., & King, D. The sensitivity of measures of school effectiveness. *Harvard Educational Review*, 1979, *49*, 207-230.

Madaus, G. F. & Linnan, R. The outcome of Catholic education? *School Review*, 1973, *8*, 207-232.

Madaus, G. F. & Macnamara, J. *Public examinations: A study of the Irish Leaving Certificate*. Dublin: Educational Research Centre, St. Patrick's College, Dublin, 1970a.

Madaus, G. F. & Macnamara, J. The quality of the Irish Leaving Certificate examination. *Irish Journal of Education*, 1970b, *4*, 5-18.

Madaus, G. F. & Rippey, R. M. Zeroing in on the STEP writing test: What does it tell a teacher? *Journal of Educational Measurement*, 1966, *3*, 19-25.

Madaus, G. F., Wood, E. M. & Nuttall, R. L. A causal model analysis of Bloom's taxonomy. *American Educational Research Journal*, 1973, *10*, 253-262.

Madow, W. G. Project Head Start, a national evaluation: A methodological critique. In D. G. Hays (Ed.), *Britannica Review of American Education, Vol. 1*. Chicago: Encyclopedia Britannica, 1969, 245-252.

Mann, H. Horace Mann to Samuel Gridley Howe, May 1845, *Mann Papers*. Boston, Mass: Massachusetts Historical Society.

Marburger, C. L. Considerations for educational planning. In A. H. Passow (Ed.), *Education in depressed areas*. New York: Teachers College, Columbia University, 1963.

Marco, G. L. A comparison of selected school effectiveness measures based on longitudinal data. *Journal of Educational Measurement*, 1974, *11*, 225-234.

Marco, G. L., Murphy, R. T. & Quirk, T. A classification of methods of using student data to assess school effectiveness. *Journal of Educational Measurement*, 1976, *13*, 243-252.

Marjoribanks, K. Environment, social class, and mental abilities. *Journal of Educational Psychology*, 1972, *63*, 103-109.

Marjoribanks, K. (Ed.) *Environments for learning*. Slough: NFER Publishing Co., 1974.

Marland, S. Hearings before the Committee on Education and Labor, House of Representatives, Education Act of 1965, H. R. 2361 and H. R. 2362. 89th Congress. Washington, D. C.: U. S. Government Printing Office, 1965.

Martin, M. & Kellaghan, T. Factors affecting reading attainment in Irish primary schools. In V. Greaney (Ed.), *Studies in reading*. Dublin: Educational Company of Ireland, 1977.

May, P. Standardized testing in Philadelphia, 1916 to 1938. Unpublished manuscript, July 7, 1971.

Mayeske, G. W. & Beaton, A. E. *Special studies of our nation's students*. Washington, D. C.: U. S. Department of Health, Education, and Welfare, 1975.

Mayeske, G. W., Okada, T., Cohen, W. M., Beaton, A. E. & Wisler, C. E. *A study of the achievement of our nation's students*. DHEW Publication No. (OE) 72-131. Washington, D. C.: U. S. Department of Health, Education, and Welfare, 1973.

Mayeske, G. W., Wisler, C. E., Beaton, A. E., Weinfeld, F. D., Cohen, W. M., Okada, T., Proshek, J. M., & Tabler, K. A. *A study of our nation's schools*. DHEW Publication No. (OE) 72-142. Washington, D. C.: U. S. Department of Health, Education, and Welfare, 1972.

Mays, J. B. *Education and the urban child*. Liverpool: University of Liverpool Press, 1962.

Medley, D. M. & Mitzel, H. E. Measuring classroom behavior by systematic observation. In N. L. Gage (Ed.), *Handbook of research on teaching*. Chicago: Rand McNally, 1963.

Meier, D. What's wrong with reading tests? *Note from City College Advisory Service to Open Corridors*, March 1972, 3-17.

Michelson, S. The association of teacher resourcefulness with children's characteristics. In *Do teachers make a difference?* Washington, D. C.: U. S. Department of Health, Education, and Welfare, 1970.

Mollenkopf, W. G. & Melville, D. S. A study of secondary school characteristics as related to test scores. *Research Bulletin 56-6*. Princeton, N. J.: Educational Testing Service, 1956.

Mood, A. M. Partitioning variance in multiple regression analyses as a tool for developing learning models. *American Educational Research Journal*, 1971, *8*, 191-202.

Morrison, P. The bell-shaped pitfall. *National Elementary Principal*, 1975, 54 (4), 34-37.

Mosteller, F. & Moynihan, D. P. A pathbreaking report. In F. Mosteller and D. P. Moynihan (Eds.) *On equality of educational opportunity*. New York: Vintage Books, 1972.

Moynihan, D. P. Sources of resistance to the Coleman report. *Harvard Educational Review;* 1968, *38*, 23-36.

Moynihan, D. P. *The politics of a guaranteed income*. New York: Random House, 1973.

Murphy, J. T. Title I of ESEA: The politics of implementing federal education reform. *Harvard Educational Review*, 1971, *41*, 35-63.

McCall, W. A. *How to measure in education*. New York: Macmillan, 1922.

McClelland, D. C. Testing for competence rather than for "intelligence". *American Psychologist*, 1973, *28*, 1-14.

McDermott, J. E. Introduction: Indeterminacy in education. In J. E. McDermott, (Ed.), *Indeterminancy in education*. Berkeley, Calif.: McCutchan, 1976.

McDill, E. L., McDill, M. S. & Sprehe, J. T. *Strategies for success in compensatory education: An appraisal of evaluation research.* Baltimore: Johns Hopkins Press, 1969.

McDill, E. L., McDill, M. S. & Sprehe, J. T. Evaluation in practice: Compensatory education. In P. H. Rossi & W. Williams (Eds.), *Evaluating social programs: Theory, practice and politics.* New York: Seminar Press, 1972.

McKeachie, W. J. Instructional Psychology. In M. R. Rosenzweig & L. W. Porter (Eds.) *Annual Review of Psychology,* Volume 25. Palo Alto, Calif.: Annual Reviews Inc., 1974.

Nay, J. N., Scanlon, J. W., Schmidt, R. E. and Wholly, J. S. If you don't care where you get to, then it doesn't matter which way you go. In C. Abt (Ed.), *The evaluation of social programs.* Beverly Hills, Calif.: Sage Publications, 1976.

Noonan, R. D. *School resources, social class, and student achievement.* International Association for the Evaluation of Educational Achievement Monograph Studies No. 5. Stockholm: Almquist & Wiksell, 1976.

Nozick, R. *Anarchy, state, and utopia.* New York: Basic Books, 1974.

Nunnally, J. C. Psychometric theory—25 years ago and now. *Educational Researcher,* 1975, 4(10), 7-21.

O'Donoghue, M. *Economic dimensions in education.* Dublin: Gill and Macmillan, 1971.

Orwell, G. New words. In S. Orwell & I. Angus (Eds.), *The collected essays, journalism and letters of George Orwell. My country right or left, 1940-1943.* New York: Harcourt, Brace & Jovanovich, 1968a.

Orwell, G. Politics and the English language. In S. Orwell and I. Angus (Eds.) *The collected essays, journalism and letters of George Orwell. In front of your nose, 1945-1950.* New York: Harcourt, Brace & Jovanovich, 1968b.

Owen, J. D. The distribution of educational resources in large American cities. *Journal of Human Resources,* 1972, 7, 26-38.

Palmer, I. *Tests and measurements.* New York: Barnes, 1932.

Passow, A. H. Urban education: The new challenge. *Educational Researcher,* 1977, 6(9), 5-10.

Peaker, G. F. The regression analyses of the National Survey. In Great Britain: Department of Education and Science. *Children and their primary schools. A report of the Central Advisory Council for Education (England). Volume 2: Research and surveys.* London: Her Majesty's Stationery Office, 1967.

Pedhazur, E. J. Analytic methods in studies of educational effects. In F. N. Kerlinger (Ed.), *Review of research in education 3.* Itasca, Ill.: Peacock, 1975.

Perkinson, H. J. *The imperfect panacea: American faith in education, 1865-1965.* New York: Random House, 1968.

Perrone, V. Alternatives to standardized testing. *National Elementary Principal,* 1975, 54(6), 96-101.

Philadelphia Board of Education, *A Report for 1926*. Philadelphia, Pa.: Board of Education, 1926.

Picariello, H. *Evaluation of Title I*. Washington, D. C.: American Institute for the Advancement of Science, 1968.

Pincus, J. Incentives for innnovation in the public schools. *Review of Educational Research*, 1974, 44(1), 113–144.

Porter, A. C. & McDaniels, G. L. A reassessment of the problems in estimating school effects. Paper read at the 140th Annual Meeting of the American Association for the Advancement of Science, March 1974.

Posner, J. Evaluation of "successful" projects in compensatory education. Washington, D. C.: U. S. Office of Education, Office of Planning and Evaluation. Occasional Paper No. 8, 1968.

Postlethwaite, T. N. The surveys of the International Association for the Evaluation of Educational Achievement (IEA). In A. C. Purves and D. U. Levine (Eds.), *Educational policy and international assessment. Implications of the IEA surveys of achievement*. Berkeley, California: McCutchan, 1975.

Purves, A. C. Evaluation of learning in literature. In B. S. Bloom, J. T. Hastings, & G. F. Madaus (Eds.), *Handbook on formative and summative evaluation of student learning*. New York: McGraw-Hill, 1971.

Purves, A. C. and Levine, D. U. (Eds.), *Educational policy and international assessment. Implications of the IEA surveys of achievement*. Berkeley, California: McCutchan, 1975.

Rakow, E. A., Airasian, P. W. & Madaus, G. F. Assessing school and program effectiveness: Estimating teacher level effects. *Journal of Educational Measurement*, 1978, 15, 15–22.

Rice, M. M. The futility of the spelling grind. *The Forum*, 1897, 23, 163–172.

Riecken, H. W. Social experimentation. In C. C. Abt (Ed.), *The evaluation of social programs*. Beverly Hills, Calif.: Sage Publication, 1976.

Riecken, H. W. & Boruch, R. F. *Social experimentation*, New York: Academic Press, 1974.

Rivlin, A. M. *Systematic thinking for social action*. Washington, D. C.: Brookings Institution, 1971.

Rivlin, A. M. Discussion: Payoffs of evaluation research. In C. Abt (Ed.), *The evaluation of social programs*. Beverly Hills, Calif.: Sage Publications, 1976.

Rivlin, A. M. & Timpane, P. M. Planned variation in education: An assessment. In A. M. Rivlin & P. M. Timpane (Eds.), *Planned variation in education: Should we give up or try harder?* Washington, D. C.: Brookings Institution, 1975.

Rosenshine, B. *Teaching behaviors and student achievement*. Slough: NFER Publishing Co., 1971.

Rosenshine, B. & Furst, N. Research on teacher performance criteria. In B. O. Smith (Ed.), *Research in teacher education*. Englewood Cliffs, N. J.: Prentice Hall, 1971.

Rosenthal, R. & Jacobson, L. *Pygmalion in the classroom: Teacher expectation and pupils' intellectual development*. New York: Holt, Rinehart & Winston, 1968.

Rossi, P. H. Testing for success and failure in social action. In P. H. Rossi and W. Williams (Eds.), *Evaluating social programs*. New York: Seminar Press, 1972.

Rotberg, I. C. & Wolf, A. *Compensatory education: Some research issues*. Policy Studies Program, Division of Research. Washington, D. C.: National Institute of Education, May 1974.

Samuels, S. J. & Edwall, G. E. Measuring reading achievement: A case for criterion referenced testing and accountability. *NCME Measurement in Education*, 1975, *6*(2), 1-7.

Schwartz, T. L. Math tests. *National Elementary Principal*, 1975, 54,(6), 67-70.

Schwartz, A. J. Social science evidence and the objectives of school desegregation. In J. E. McDermott (Ed.), *Indeterminacy in education*. Berkeley, Calif: McCutchan Publishing Co., 1976.

Shapiro, E. Educational evaluation: Rethinking the criteria of competence. *School Review*, 1973, *81*, 523-549.

Shaycroft, M. F. *The high school years: Growth in cognitive skills*. Pittsburgh, Pa.: American Institute for Research and School of Education, University of Pittsburgh, 1967.

Shea, B. M. Schooling and its antecedents: Substantive and methodological issues in the status attainment process. *Review of Educational Research*, 1976, *46*, 463-526.

Sheehan, J. *The economics of education*. London: Allen and Unwin, 1973.

Simmons, J. & Alexander L. The determinants of school achievement in developing countries: A review of research. Paper read at Annual Meeting of the American Educational Research Association, Washington, D. C., April 1975.

Smith, M. S. Equality of educational opportunity: The basic findings reconsidered. In F. Mosteller and D. P. Moynihan (Eds.), *On equality of educational opportunity*. New York: Vintage Books, 1972.

Smith, M. S. Commentary on the relation of school achievement to differences in the backgrounds of children. In A. C. Purves and D. U. Levine (Eds.) *Educational policy and international assessment. Implications of the IEA surveys of achievement*. Berkeley, California: McCutchan, 1975.

Smith, M. S. Discussion: Evaluation of educational programs. In C. C. Abt (Ed.), *The evaluation of social programs*. Beverly Hills, Calif.: Sage Publications, 1976.

Smith, M. S. & Bissell, J. S. Report analysis: The impact of Head Start. *Harvard Educational Review*, 1970, *40*, 51-104.

Smith, E. R. & Tyler, R. W. Appraising and recording student progress. *Adventures in American Education Series*, Vol. 3. New York: Harper, 1942.

Smith, H. L. & Judd, C. H. Plans for organizing school surveys. *Thirteenth Yearbook, NSSE, Part II*. Bloomington, Ill.: Public School Publishing Co., 1914.

Sohlman, A. Differences in school achievement and occupational opportunities: Explanatory factors. In Organisation for Economic Co-operation and Development. *Group disparities in educational participation and achievement.* Paris: Organisation for Economic Co-operation and Development, 1971.

Spady, W. G. The impact of school resources on students. In F. M. Kerlinger (Ed.), *Review of research in education 1.* Itasca, Ill.: Peacock, 1973.

Spaeth, J. L. Cognitive complexity: A dimension underlying the socioeconomic achievement press. In W. H. Sewell, R. M. Hauser and D. L. Featherman (Eds.), *Schooling and achievement in American society.* New York: Academic Press, 1976.

St. John, N. *School desegregation: Outcomes for children.* New York: Wiley, 1975.

Stanford Test of Academic Skills: Manual. New York: Harcourt, Brace & Jovanovich, 1973.

Stake, R. E. Measuring what learners learn (with a special look at performance contracting). Urbana, Ill.: Center for Instructional Research and Curriculum Evaluation, University of Illinois, 1972.

Stephens, J. M. *The influence of the school upon the individual.* Ann Arbor, Mich.: Edwards Brothers, 1933.

Stephens, J. M. *The process of schooling. A psychological examination.* New York: Holt, Rinehart & Winston, 1967.

Stodolsky, S. S. Defining treatment and outcome in early childhood education. In H. J. Walberg & A. T. Kopan (Eds.), *Rethinking urban education.* San Francisco, Calif.: Jossey Bass, 1972.

Tatsuoka, M. M. Multivariate analysis in educational research. In F. Kerlinger (Ed.), *Review of research in education 1.* Itasca, Ill.: Peacock, 1973.

Terman, L. M. & Merrill, M. A. *Stanford-Binet Intelligence Scale. Manual for the third revision Form L-M.* Boston: Houghton Mifflin, 1960.

Thorndike, E.L. & Woodworth, R. S. The influence of improvement in one mental function upon the efficiency of other functions. *Psychological Review,* 1901, *8,* 247–261; 384–395; 553–564.

Thorndike, R. L. *Reading comprehension education in fifteen countries: An empirical study.* New York: Wiley, 1973.

Timpane, P. M. Educational experimentation in national social policy. *Harvard Educational Review,* 1970, 40(4), 547–566.

Timpane, P. M. Evaluating Title I again? In C. C. Abt (Ed.), *The evaluation of social programs.* Beverly Hills, Calif.: Sage Publications, 1976.

Tinkleman, S. N. Planning the objective test. In R. L. Thorndike (Ed.) *Educational measurement* (2nd ed.). Washington, D. C.: American Council on Education, 1971.

Torrance, E. P. *Guiding creative talent.* Englewood Cliffs, N. J.: Prentice-Hall, 1962.

Tyler, L. E. The intelligence we test—An evolving concept. In L. B. Resnick (Ed.), *The nature of intelligence*. New York: Wiley, 1976.

Tyler, R. W. The relation between recall and higher mental processes. In C. H. Judd (Ed.), *The cultivation of high mental processes*. New York: Macmillan, 1936.

Tyler, R. W. *Basic principles of curriculum and instruction*. Chicago: University of Chicago Press, 1949.

Tyler, R. W. The use of tests in measuring the effectiveness of educational programs, methods and instructional materials. In R. W. Tyler & R. M. Wolf (Eds.), *Crucial issues in testing*. Berkeley, Calif.: McCutchan, 1974.

U. S. Comptroller General. *Assessment of reading activities funded under the Federal Program of Aid for Educationally Deprived Children. Report to the Congress*. Washington, D. C.: Office of Education, 1975.

U. S. National Center for Education Statistics. *The condition of education 1975*. Washington, D. C.: U. S. Government Printing Office, 1975.

U. S. Office of Education. *Education of the disadvantaged: An evaluation report on Title I, Elementary and Secondary Education Act of 1965, Fiscal Year 1968*. Washington, D. C.: Office of Education, 1970.

Walberg, H. J. Predicting class learning: An approach to the class as a social system. *American Educational Research Journal*, 1969, *6*, 529–542.

Walberg, H. J. Social environment and individual learning: A test of the Bloom model. *Journal of Educational Psychology*, 1972, *63*, 69–73.

Walberg, H. J. & Marjoribanks, K. Family environment and cognitive development: Twelve analytic models. *Review of Educational Research*, 1976, *46*, 527–551.

Walberg, H. J. & Rasher, S. P. Public school effectiveness and equality: New evidence and its implications. *Phi Delta Kappan*, 1974, *56*, 3–9.

Walker, G. A. *The IEA six subject survey: An empirical study of education in twenty-one countries. International studies in evaluation, Volume IX*. New York: Wiley, 1975.

Waller, W. *The sociology of teaching*. New York: Wiley, 1932.

Wargo, M. J. et al. *ESEA Title I: A reanalysis and synthesis of evaluation data from fiscal year 1965 through 1970*. Palo Alto, Calif.: American Institute for Research, May 1972.

Wargo, M. J., Campeau, P. L. & Tallmadge, G. K. *Further examination of exemplary programs for educating disadvantaged children*. Palo Alto, Calif.: American Institute for Research. 1971.

Weaver, W., & Bickley, A. C. Sources of information for response to reading test items. *Proceedings of the 75th Annual Convention of the American Psychological Association*, 1967, 293–294.

Wheeler, L. R. A comparative study of the intelligence of East Tennessee Mountain children. *Journal of Educational Psychology*, 1942, *33*, 321–334.

Wiley, D. E. Another hour, another day: Quantity of schooling, a potent path for policy. In W. H. Sewell, R. M. Hauser & D. L. Featherman (Eds.), *Schooling and achievement in American society*. New York: Academic Press, 1976.

Wiley, D. E. & Harnischfeger, A. Explosion of a myth: Quantity of schooling and exposure to instruction, major educational variables. *Educational Researcher*, 1974, *3*(4), 7-12.

Williams, W. & Evans, J. W. The politics of evaluation: The case of Head Start. In P. H. Rossi and W. Williams (Eds.), *Evaluating social programs*. New York: Seminar Press, 1972, 249-264.

Wilson, A. B. Social class and equal educational opportunity. *Harvard Educational Review*, 1968, *38*, 77-84.

Wiseman, S. The Manchester Survey. In Great Britain: Department of Education and Science. *Children and their primary schools. A report of the Central Advisory Council for Education (England). Volume 2: Research and surveys.* London: Her Majesty's Stationery Office, 1967.

Wisler, C. E. Partitioning the explained variance in a regression analysis. In G. W. Mayeske, A. E. Beaton, C. E. Wisler, T. Okada and W. M. Cohen, *Technical supplement to "A study of the achievement of our nations's students".* Washington, D. C.: U. S. Department of Health, Education, and Welfare, 1974.

Wolf, R. M. Identification and measurement of environmental process variables related to intelligence. Unpublished doctoral dissertation. University of Chicago, 1964.

Index

Name Index

Lindquist, E. F., 137, 143, 144
Linn, R. L., 58, 59
Linnan, R., 104, 112
Lohnes, P. R., 100, 119, 120, 126,
    127, 128, 156
Lourie, S., 132
Lowe, R., 11
Luecke, D. F., 87
Lukas, C. V., 84, 89

Macnamara, J., 165, 166
Madaus, G. F., 64, 95, 105, 112, 117,
    118, 127, 130, 138, 141, 146,
    147, 149, 150, 152, 153, 154,
    156, 163, 165, 166, 167, 168,
    184, 187, 188
Madow, W. G., 41
Mann, C. R., 143, 144
Mann, H., 5, 6
Marburger, C. L., 175
Marco, G. L., 57, 59
Marjoribanks, K., 88, 99, 104, 125
Marlard, S., 117
Marsden, D., 186
Martin, M., 64, 97, 187
May, P., 6
Mayeske, G. W., 33, 34, 35, 70, 82,
    90, 126, 127, 174, 177, 186
Mays, J. B., 186
Medley, D. M., 99
Meier, D., 157
Melville, D. S., 33, 97
Merrill, M. A., 130
Michelson, S., 32, 70, 90
Miller, N., 103
Mitzel, H. E., 99
Mollenkopf, W. G., 33, 96
Mood, A. M., 1, 67
Morgan, R. F., 46
Morrison, P., 138
Morse, R. J., 46
Mosteller, F., 10, 12, 32, 61, 173
Moynihan, D. P., 10, 12, 30, 31, 32,
    33, 52, 61, 173

Murphy, J. T., 37, 38, 82, 89
Murphy, R. T., 57, 59
McCall, W. A., 137
McClelland, D. C., 126, 164
McDaniels, G. L., 104, 145
McDermott, J. E., 103
McDill, E. L., 52, 53, 83, 107
McDill, M. S., 52, 53, 83, 107
McGinn, N. F., 87
McKeachie, W. J., 103, 109
McPartland, J., 1

Nay, J. N., 84, 88
New Jersey Department of
    Education, 149
Niles, B. E., 181
Nixon, President, R. M., 32
Noonan, R. D., 36
Nozick, R., 181
Nunnally, J. C., 148
Nuttall, R. L., 156

O'Donoghue, M., 23
Okado, T., 33, 34
Olver, R. R., 47
Orwell, G., 132, 166
Otis, A. S., 8
Owen, J. D., 87

Palmer, I., 137
Passow, A. H., 189
Patrick, C., 59
Patton, M. J., 58, 59
Peaker, G. F., 33, 81, 98
Pedhazur, E. J., 65, 67, 68, 71, 179
Perkinson, H. J., 187
Perrone, V., 112, 164
Philadelphia Board of Education, 8
Picariello, H., 32, 39, 83
Pincus, J., 23, 32
Pomfret, A., 89
Porter, A. C., 104, 145

Williams, W., 41
Wilson, A. B., 101, 127
Wisenbaker, J. M., 103
Wiseman, S., 81
Wisler, C. E., 33, 34, 65, 70
Wolf, A., 88
Wolf, R. M., 104

Wood, E. M., 156
Wood, R., 95
Woodworth, R. S., 6

York, R. L., 1

Subject Index

Absolute effects of schooling,
45–46, 48, 50, 72, 176, 188
Achievement gap, 40, 117–118
Adequacy of norms, 139
Aggregation of data, 90–94, 149,
152, 154, 168, 186
American schools, 178–181
"elitist," 180–181
"leveler," 180–181
as social equalizers, 178
as vehicles of social mobility, 178
Analytic procedures in estimating
school effectiveness, 45–74
analysis of covariance, use of, 55
assigning variables to blocks,
65–71, 92, 106, 127, 179
assumptions of additivity and
linearity in regression, 65, 69
assymetric variance
decomposition and problems
with, 70
commonalities, interpretation of,
68, 71–72, 169, 174, 186
delineation of input variables, 85
differences in scholastic
performance, 29, 33–34, 42,
94–95, 117
partitioning of variance, 68,
70–71, 186
random selection of unit, 50, 56

Analytic procedures in estimating
school effectiveness:
symmetric variance
decomposition method, 34,
36, 70–71, 94
"unit" of analysis, 90, 153
Assessing school effectiveness, 163,
167, 174–176, 179–180, 183
analytic procedures and problems
in, 45–74
characteristics, 95–101
components of variance as indices
of, 64
differential effectiveness of, 163,
168–171, 174, 184, 188
difficulties in interpretation,
96–101, 107–110, 132–133,
179
history of, 3–4, 6, 9, 165
inferences concerning, 157,
161–162, 164, 169, 174–175,
184
methodological problems, 72, 141
problems in evaluating input
measures, 75ff
problems in evaluating outcome
measures, 112–114, 149
production model of schooling,
75
role of economics, 10–11, 23

221

School input:
  resources present and pupil
    achievement, 28–31, 34–36,
    41–43, 46, 69–70, 80,
    90–112
  school facilities, 96
  school variables, 14–17, 21,
    28–30, 33–35, 69–70, 125,
    154, 158, 168, 176, 184
  selection and measurement of
    variables, problems in, 84–85
  teacher characteristics and quality
    of teaching, 98–100
  time devoted to school subjects, 97
  validity of measures, 91, 122–131,
    159–169
School outcomes, 111–131
  achievement gap, 40, 117–118
  choice of cognitive or affective
    outcomes, 112–113
  cognitive development, 46–47, 111
  collusive effect of home and
    school, 35, 104, 112, 174,
    177, 185
  congruence between test and
    school objectives, 136
  correlation between intelligence
    and test scores, 129
  covariance of expenditure and
    educational attainment, 81
  differences in scholastic
    performance, 19, 33–34, 42,
    94–95, 117
  educational disparities between
    races and classes, 117
  effective/ineffective schools, 95,
    111, 135
  evaluation of outcome measures,
    problems in, 112–114, 149
  language used, problem with,
    132–133
  occupational success, 78
  school achievement and economic
    success, relationship
    between, 11, 43–44, 46, 78

School outcomes:
  standardized tests as principal
    measures of school and
    program outcomes, 119ff
Standardized tests, 111–114, 156,
    160, 164–168, 170, 175, 180,
    184
  commercial feasibility, impact of,
    139–140, 183
  criterion measure of
    effectiveness, used as, 116,
    119–121, 123
  criterion-referenced, 152–153
  geared to specific syllabi, 64, 127
  to identify educationally
    disadvantaged pupils, 113
  implicit standard in evaluating
    school performance, 116,
    118, 127
  individual differences model of
    construction, 170, 181
  measures of school outcomes,
    used as, 114–122
  normality, assumption of, 137,
    183
  political validity of, 118
  public examinations to assess
    school effectiveness, 152,
    165–169, 171, 184
  sensitivity/insensitivity as measure
    of output, 136, 140, 145, 148,
    156, 158–159, 161, 168,
    183–184
Standardized tests of ability,
    119–131
  accountability, use of, 7, 11, 114
  adequacy of Coleman's measures
    of effectiveness, 124–126
  concept of intelligence, 7
  construct and content validity and
    problems with, 122,
    124–126, 131, 133
  differential effectiveness and,
    131–132, 157, 159, 169, 175,
    183

Teacher characteristics and quality
of teaching, 98–100
Traditional vs. progressive
education debate, 48–108

Validity of measures, 91, 122–133,
159–169
construct and content, validity of,
122, 124–126, 131, 133,
154–155, 159, 166–167

Variables related to school
achievement, 96–102,
154–155, 157–158, 161, 163,
168–169, 171, 174, 176–180,
184–186, 188, 190
Variance:
between and within, 61–65,
105–106, 108, 120, 127, 149,
152–154, 157–158, 161,
167–169, 171, 174–176,
178–179, 181–182, 186